an introduction to
exceptional children

an introduction to
exceptional children

WILLIAM R. VAN OSDOL • DON G. SHANE

Central Oklahoma State University
Edmond, Oklahoma

WM. C. BROWN COMPANY PUBLISHERS
Dubuque, Iowa

Contents

The purpose of this book is to present a comprehensive but somewhat nontechnical introduction to the field of exceptional children and Special Education. The authors have designed the book for use by undergraduate or graduate students in special education, general education, and psychology, as an introductory text to exceptional children. It may also serve the parents of exceptional children, school personnel, and lay persons, as a resource book for Special Education.

The introductory course in Special Education on a college or university level attracts many students who are not preparing for professional service in the field of Special Education, but wish to become more fully aware of exceptional children. Students may also take the introductory course to discover whether they wish to enter the field of Special Education; and, of course, the introductory course is required of majors in Special Education.

Each professor or student may ask why certain areas of information are not included. We have also asked ourselves many times about the relative importance of available material, realizing that an endless amount of material could be included. There must, though, be a cutoff point for a textbook; and we did not wish to write a 600-700 page text which would become a burden to the professors and students, causing them to skim quickly through the book in order to meet semester deadlines. Consequently, the authors' initial objective was to write a textbook that would introduce exceptional children and Special Education adequately, without overloading college students and professors with a gross amount of clinical information and a mammoth-size text.

A specific chapter on the severely multihandicapped child is not included inasmuch as that area constitutes so small a percentage of the exceptional population, and because the multihandicapped child can be introduced easily in the chapters on the sensorially impaired, or the physically and chronically disabled children. Moreover, hearing, speech, and visually impaired children are discussed in three separate sections within the chapter on sensorially impaired children. There is no need for a quantity of material and three different chapters to introduce these three areas which are appropriately and adequately covered within one chapter.

This book does not contain a quantity of tables, tables of statistics, anecdotal records, and case studies. Adequate statistics are generally offered in narrative form rather than by tables. A number of specific statistics are not included primarily because of rapid changes in the services for exceptional children. Consequently, specific details and conclusions regarding statistics would not generally serve a meaningful purpose. There also appears to be a certain aversion to statistical approaches; how many times, for example, have you heard a speaker or professor reflect negative attitudes by approaching his audience with a statement such as, "Now I shall bore you with some statistics"? The authors in no way mean to imply that statistics are useless; the point is, however, that in an introductory text, general statements regarding statistics relative to exceptional children can be presented as basic rather than as static detailed information.

Case studies and anecdotal records were not included because we do not believe that the reader can acquire realistic concepts of exceptional children unless the professor also teaches on the basis of his own experiential framework with exceptional children. We certainly emphasize that all exceptional children must be viewed as unique individuals, consequently sufficient information is provided to present problem-oriented discussions. Therefore, the uniqueness of individuals and problem-oriented discussions are included in the text without presenting case studies.

Including the introductory chapter, this book contains a total of eleven chapters. Seven chapters offer an introduction into the following areas of Special Education: Mental Retardation, Disadvantaged Children, Gifted Children, Physical Disabilities and Chronic Illnesses, Sensorially Impaired Children, Learning Disabilities, and the Emotionally and Behaviorally Maladjusted. In addition, there are four chapters devoted exclusively to History and Program Development (Introduction); Practicum; Special Education Teachers, Administration, and Parents; and Trends. Although some trends are not fully developed at this time, the reader should be aware of these trends in order to understand the current directions being taken in the field of Special Education, and to know something about the various ways in which school systems can and will be attempting to serve the needs of exceptional children. The chapter on Trends is recognized as a basic presentation regarding these particular areas. The authors do not attempt to be comprehensive with respect to trends because these are areas within the field of Special Education that may change quite rapidly. Information, however, has been prepared which may help school systems, university programs, or state departments of special education to consider the implementation of procedures which will result in improved and more comprehensive services for exceptional children.

The individual chapters are not to be confused with methods and materials courses nor are they to be considered for advanced study courses in the field of Special Education. The purpose of each chapter is to present basic concepts and material introductory to the various areas of exceptionalities, and to present the services which are or should be offered to exceptional children. Study sheets are included with several chapters; these sheets are intended to serve as materials for individual study, oral reports, outside readings, test exercises, and for general use at the discretion of the course instructors. Detailed study of a single exceptionality or of general Special Education programming may be accomplished by using the sources to which the authors have referred in this text, or by taking additional college courses in Special Education related to specific exceptionalities.

The authors express their thanks to the following Special Education teachers from Oklahoma, Kansas, Texas, Ohio, and South Carolina for their professional assistance: E.O."Buster" Meeks, Wesley Hodges, Diana Howe, Peggy Yeager, Jo Ann Hartwell, Karol McHugh, Barbara Wood, Pat Nation, and Diann Schwerdtfeger.

William R. Van Osdol, Ph.D.
Don G. Shane, Ph.D.

*'Everybody needs somebody.
Please help someone!'*

1

History and Program Development in Special Education

WHO ARE EXCEPTIONAL CHILDREN?

Exceptional children, within the context of this book, include those children who are mentally, and/or emotionally, and/or physically unable to manage or cope with the regular school program on a full or part-time basis. These areas of exceptionalities include children who are identified as mentally retarded, disadvantaged, gifted, physically disabled or chronically ill, emotionally or behaviorally disturbed, sensorially impaired; and children with learning disabilities.

Because of their limitations, whether of a permanent or temporary nature, exceptional children will require some type of special modification in their school programs if they are to succeed as individuals and become worthwhile, contributing members of society. Of course, many exceptional children will also require modifications in their living arrangements and in community services. Special modifications which are appropriate for these children will be discussed in this chapter and throughout the text.

Brief History of Special Education

Attitudes toward Exceptional Children

When one enters the broad field of providing educational services to exceptional children he often may have an experience which promotes or adds to negative attitudes toward the individuals who are having difficulties adjusting to the demands of their environments. Negative attitudes toward exceptionalities have no place in the field of Special Education; and the professional person, who is in contact with the exceptional child, must eliminate his negative attitudes toward these children.

The inappropriate use and misunderstanding of "labels" has caused the development of negative attitudes. Negative feelings prevent one from developing constructive, positive attitudes toward

1

helping exceptional children. For example, obtain a person's reactions to the child who has been assessed and "labeled" as mentally retarded and one will often encounter responses which reflect, "He is mentally retarded; therefore, he can't read; he can't spell; he can't adjust; he can't do anything." The authors maintain that if a child is diagnosed as mentally retarded, then it is imperative that one work with the whole child and not just his I.Q. score or his label.

A complete assessment of his strengths and weaknesses should be indicated. Attention must be given to his strengths. The professional should focus on the tasks which each individual child can do and make sure that the child is provided the educational environment in which the successful completion of these tasks is a possibility.

One who is teaching a class of exceptional children must also maintain that the class is not referred to as the "babysitting class," the "dummy class," or by any other derogatory term. Reduction of the use of these terms is difficult, but improvement can be established by providing an instructional program which is constructive, and appropriately planned for the intellectual, social, emotional, and physical needs of the children. The purpose of special education programs within the public schools must be viewed as an organized approach to complement and supplement the regular program, rather than programs which serve children who cannot be handled or controlled by the regular classroom teachers.

Negative attitudes call forth no active programs, but tend to discourage and even disillusion the professional person who is providing services for exceptional children. Personnel in the field of Special Education have the challenge and responsibility for promoting the development of positive attitudes toward all types of exceptionalities. Only through positive attitudes toward exceptional children can constructive programs provide meaningful objectives for exceptional children. The development of positive attitudes toward exceptional children is an additional reason why there must be promotion of comprehensive programs which will continuously strive to fulfill the needs of the total child.

Early Identification

The improvement of educational services for exceptional children includes the early identification of their problems in learning, adjustment, and health. Professional personnel have hesitated entirely too long in identifying exceptional children at an early age. Hesitation in identifying a child as exceptional in order to "wait and see" can only cause frustration on the part of the child, his parents, and his teachers. Waiting until the child has continuously failed in the regular school program in order to contribute information to the existing diagnostic assessment certainly cannot enhance the positive development of the child's self-concept; nor can it enhance the attitude the child will develop toward learning and adjustment.

Exceptional children must be provided adequate and functional educational services at an early age in order to prevent a significant loss of human potential. In this sense, special education services must be viewed as habilitative in that some exceptional children may be directly helped to overcome problems before the severity reaches a point of total debilitation. With appropriate supportive personnel and a prevailing attitude that special education is a positive approach, all professional personnel should strive to identify the child's problems and place him in an adequate learning environment as soon as possible.

Of course, the early identification of exceptional children means that professional persons must stop viewing special education placement as a social stigma. The special training of the teacher in the field of Special Education and the small number of children in the special class should enable the Special Education program to provide meaningful instructional outlets when the child is in his time of greatest need. Placement in a special education class should never mean that the child is destined to spend the remainder of his educational program within the special class setting. All exceptional children cannot and should not be moved in and out of special education classes, but a few children who exhibit severe problems during the early elementary school years, or even the preschool years, may be assisted to the extent that they will be able to move into the mainstream of education. These statements imply that the school principal, school superintendent, and any other person who may be responsible for teacher selection and assignment must strive to find and hire the best special education teachers to implement appropriate programs for exceptional children.

Program Development of Special Education

The education of exceptional children started in residential centers in the United States. This practice was partially in operation because the United States was a rural country at that time, and in order to meet the needs of many children, communities had to send their exceptional children to state and private residential centers. The lack of acceptance of individuals who were exceptional also influenced community leaders and schools to promote the development of residential facilities in lieu of the development of classes within the public school setting. Other factors which influenced the development of residential facilities for exceptional children included a lack of trained teachers and a lack of knowledge regarding the learning needs and characteristics of exceptional children. Of course, several of these factors, such as the lack of trained instructors and instructional methods, resulted in many residential centers becoming custodial facilities rather than rehabilitative or habilitative centers.

If one were to compare the residential centers which were in existence at the turn of the century to those centers which are currently in operation, one would find that many changes have taken place. Residential placement is now considered to be the last resource which should be contemplated for an individual exceptional child; however, a majority of our residential centers have improved their programs, their staffs, and their physical facilities. Of course, a majority of the residential facilities for exceptional children include a school program for those children who may benefit from a structured learning environment. Residential facility placement is frequently considered as temporary for an exceptional child; and one may find a single discipline residential facility such as a school for the blind, or one may find a multiple-discipline residential facility such as a school for the deaf-blind-mentally retarded child.

After starting in residential centers, the educational programs for exceptional children moved into the public schools. This movement into public schools was the result of parental influence on school boards, and came about with recognition of the fact that communities should provide school programs for children. In short, the right to be educated as close to one's home as possible was recognized and public school classes for exceptional children began around 1900. Although identification and diagnostic procedures which were available at that time were not very sophisticated; attempts were made to provide public school programs for children who were mentally retarded, blind, deaf, physically disabled, or emotionally disturbed.

Public school programs for exceptional children have increased steadily since 1900, with a few intervening periods of slackened interest. Classes or other special modifications for different groups of exceptional children may be found in the majority of large or medium sized communities. There have also been many awareness publications and considerable information relating to the characteristics of exceptional children, and school programs developed for them. However, the needs of a majority of exceptional children are still neglected in public and private schools, and in other community services, which should be obligated to maintain adequate facilities and personnel for mental, emotional, and physical health programs.

The fairly rapid change from residential facilities to provisions for exceptional children within the public schools has brought about many modifications. These changes include a tremendous increase for the need of special education teachers, an increase in the need for financing programs for exceptional children, and to some extent, an increase in the community acceptance of exceptional children.

Early program developments for exceptional children have also increased the need for well trained psychologists, counselors, and for better materials and approaches for appropriate education and training. Since the earliest program offerings for exceptional children, there have been continuous changes in diagnostic materials and techniques and in teaching and training techniques.

Estimates of Exceptional Children Receiving Services

Even though great strides have been made in establishing programs and preparing professional personnel to serve exceptional children, the authors estimate that adequate provisions are available for only about 30 to 40 percent of all exceptional children. This percentage may appear to be quite sufficient; however, when one conservatively estimates that approximately 15 to 18 percent of the school age population may be categorically identified within at least one exceptional group; then progress in meeting the needs of these children can be seen as very inadequate.

In 1971, Weintraub, Aberson, and Braddock reported on estimates of the numbers of exceptional children and compared the total estimated number of children to the number who were receiving some type of special education program. This recent report indicates that a large majority of exceptional children are still not receiving special services. For example, the estimated number of trainable and educable mentally retarded children was reported to be in excess of 1,330,000 and only 703,000 (approximately) were receiving special services. This means that nearly 53 percent of all moderately and mildly retarded children were receiving special services as of 1971. Approximately the same percentage of speech impaired children and only about 2 percent of the children with learning disabilities were being served. The reader should note that these figures are from 1971 data, and in all probability are already outdated for any current estimates. For further estimates pertaining to other exceptional children, the reader is referred to the original source of the information cited above. (See bibliography at the end of chapter.)

Because state and federal legislation has not closed the "gap" between the demand and supply of special services for exceptional children, educators are questioning the foundation in legislation, programs, teacher training, and certification on which special education policies and practices are based. The shift to self-analysis is a painful process which will help educators to reexamine the basic principles and structures that presently strengthen special education programs (Gallagher 1972).

A considerable amount of current discussion is centered around the issue of labeling and/or the effectiveness of etiological categories in developing programs for exceptional children. Although categorization of children according to their disabilities was once an effective method for public recognition and funding, it is presently being criticized. Lilly (1971) states:

> Substantial public support has been developed for special education programs, and as a result the frequency of outright exclusion of children from public education has been decreased. The accomplishments of special educators in the areas of public opinion and positive recognition of individual differences is commendable. These past activities have been both necessary and effective; however, in combination with a number of parallel forces, they may have changed the educational system to such an extent that as solutions, they are no longer appropriate. In solving the original problems facing special education, new problems have been created which demand new solutions. Thus come the present forces for change in the field of special education.

The Problem of Labels and Categories

Reynolds and Balow (1972) suggest that numerous problems may be created when labels and categories are assigned to groups of people. These problems are: (1) each label carries with it certain characteristics which do not necessarily fit each individual within the group; (2) stigmas attached to a group may result in "scapegoating," and serve as an excuse for inadequate educational procedures; (3) lower expectations by those working with handicapped children may be seen in their rapport with students and in curriculum development; and (4) categorical labels may be equated with specific educational techniques which disregard individual differences.

The authors recognize the need for changes in the field of special education and concur with many of the discussions which have been presented above. However, if the noncategorization goes too far and there is a tendency to eliminate all information which is directly related to the use of labels, then problems which existed in special education programs of the past may be rediscovered. If we hesitate to disseminate information with respect to the functioning level of some exceptional children, then a special educator may apply too much pressure for performance from a child who cannot meet these expectancies. Certainly, the authors would not want to promote a continuance of the use of labels and categories for the purpose of creating or continuing to create stigma. However, labels and categories, if used properly, can be productive for effectiveness in communication and need not present stigma and lowered expectations.

Regardless of views to the contrary, current trends in definitions assigned to the exceptional child are becoming more flexible and tend to reflect closer approximations of the functioning level of a child rather than reflecting the disabling condition. The trend is away from the precise clinical diagnosis to one which emphasizes behavioral and learning characteristics of handicapped children (Weintraub, Aberson, and Braddock).

Lilly (1971) describes a mildly handicapped child as one:

> ... whose problems can be seen as relatively mild, those children traditionally labeled as educable mentally retarded, emotionally disturbed, behaviorally disordered, educationally handicapped, learning disabled, or brain injured ... referred from regular education programs because of some sort of teacher perceived behavioral or learning problems.

With an awareness of a few of the current arguments and issues in the field of special education, the reader should recognize that constructive changes are being made. However, until there are indications that the majority of changes which are being implemented and proposed are effective; programs for many exceptional children which have been in existence for several years will remain ineffective.

Legislation for Exceptional Children

Direct involvement of the federal government in the education of exceptional children developed as a result of a serious shortage of qualified personnel in the field of special education. In 1959, Public Law 85-926 provided annual appropriations of one million dollars to colleges, universities, and state educational agencies, whereby graduate fellowships could be awarded to qualified individuals wishing to prepare for a career in the field of mental retardation (Tompkins 1969). Since special education programs at the graduate level were few, the appropriated funds were spent largely in developing leadership personnel (McCarthy and McCarthy 1969).

Appropriations of 1.5 million dollars were authorized in 1961 through Public Law 87-276 for the preparation of teachers of the deaf. These funds were made available over a three year period to colleges and universities, and were not restricted to graduate students (McCarthy and McCarthy).

In 1962, Public Law 85-926 (Title III, as amended), provided stipends and dependency allowances for persons preparing for careers as teachers, supervisors, speech correctionists, specialists, and administrators in the areas of mental retardation, emotional disturbance, speech and hearing impairment, deafness, visual impairments, crippling conditions, and other health impairments (McCarthy and McCarthy). This Public Law provided incentive to both institutions and students, and accounted for a rise in the number of personnel trained for careers in special education. Classes for the exceptional child were also either developed or expanded as a result of this legislation.

Legislative funding during the sixties expanded to include projects and programs for the exceptional child at various age levels. A new decade of legislation was initiated on April 13, 1970, when President Nixon signed Public Law 91-230, the Elementary and Secondary Education Act Amendments of 1969; Title VI, The Education of the Handicapped Act. The purpose of this law was to combine newly created and existing legislation into a single statue. This act has seven parts which includes provisions for general areas such as a Bureau for Education and Training of the Handicapped in the Office of Education; financial and consultant assistance to states; centers and services for the handicapped; training of personnel to serve handicapped children; research in education for the handicapped; instructional media; and special programs for children with learning disabilities. For a detailed description of the seven parts of this law, the reader is referred to Martin, LaVor, Bryan, and Scheflin (1970).

By combining newly created and existing legislation into a single statue, Congress has (1) established guidelines for identifying handicapped children as a major target population; (2) increased expenditure authorizations to prepare for a total response to the needs of the handicapped; (3) stimulated special education programs to continue an emphasis on humanity toward the handicapped individuals, and resisted rigid categorical classification; and (5) encouraged state agencies, local agencies, and university programs to implement cooperative endeavors in the field of special education (Martin, La-Vor, Bryan, and Scheflin).

Categorical versus General Aid

A controversy in legislation is rooted in the ultimate determination as to whether the form of federal aid granted to schools or agencies should be categorical or general. In categorical aid, unlike general aid, the use of funds is specified. General aid involves the distribution of federal funds on a formula basis and reserves the rights of the respective states to decide the educational purpose to which the funds would be used (McCarthy and McCarthy).

Special educators tend to favor categorical aid in which funds are earmarked. If funds are categorically specified for special education, then one is relatively assured that the funds will directly serve the needs of exceptional children. If federal financial assistance is in the form of generalized aid, then many special educators believe that the existing needs of regular education could siphon off these special funds. Earmarking of federal funds insures that these monies will be spent on the education of a particular category of exceptional children (McCarthy and McCarthy 1969).

Reynolds and Balow (1972) comment on categorical aid and reflect the current views of a number of professional educators:

> Special education should shift major attention to ways of inserting itself back into mainstream educational structures. The legislation, the "earmarks," and the special bureaucracies produced over the past decade have made their point in strong fashion; but, in the process, special educators have failed to win the leadership and concern of most progressive leaders in general education. Categorical aid should be used to build special education into broad programs rather than to build separate systems and to excuse general educators from concern with the handicapped.

Based upon these viewpoints, as given above, special educators are not advocating the elimination of categorical aid to the field of special education, but are emphasizing that the funds should be expended for purposes other than maintaining the present programs of rigid categorical classifications of children.

In the latter part of 1972 and the early part of 1973, federal revenue sharing began. This procedure of providing federal funds to state, county, and city governments was initially viewed as "soft" monies for which there may not be any direct accounting. When federal cutbacks were announced for such programs as the Elementary and Secondary Education Act Amendments of 1969, the Office of Economic Opportunity, and other programs, it was quickly realized that there should be a method of accounting with respect to federal revenue sharing. As of this writing, the full impact of federal revenue sharing and federal cutback in funding various programs is not evident; however, these procedures certainly seem to emphasize general federal aid as compared to categorical federal aid.

Direct Service Programs

The ultimate goal of education of children, both handicapped and nonhandicapped, " . . . is a productive, satisfying life as a member of society," (Martin 1972). Special educators have often failed to achieve this goal in existing programs for handicapped children. To emphasize this point, the authors quote from Martin (1972):

> From two-thirds to three-fourths of all special education programs are at the elementary school level, and in many, preparation for the world of work is only indirectly involved. Only twenty-one percent of handicapped children leaving school in the next four years will be fully employed or go on to college. Another forty percent will be underemployed, and twenty-six percent will be unemployed. An additional ten percent will require at least a partially "sheltered" setting and family, and three percent will probably be almost totally dependent."

The federal government, through legislation, is attempting to help reduce these figures by its direct-service programs. There are four direct-service programs administered or monitored in the Office of Education through which the federal government provides funds for educational aid to handicapped children. They are: (1) Part B of the Education of the Handicapped Act (Public Law 91-230); (2) Public Law 89-313, Amendment to Title I of ESEA; (3) 1968 Amendments to the Vocational Education Act of 1963 (Public Law 90-576); and (4) Title III of the ESEA (U.S. Department of HEW 1971).

These services are provided for handicapped children in both public and private schools who are under twenty-one years of age or from preschool age through high school age. The Vocational Education Act also extends services to handicapped adults. Children who have been identified by a state educational agency as mentally retarded, visually impaired, deaf, hard-of-hearing, speech impaired, orthopedically handicapped, seriously emotionally disturbed, learning disabled, or otherwise health impaired to the extent that they are unable to benefit from regular educational programs, are eligible for these services. Though services to the handicapped are provided by a variety of sources, these services are not adequately serving the educational needs of handicapped children. These services may range from comprehensive residential schools to limited contact with itinerant teaching programs.

Residential Schools

Residential schools continue to play an important role in the care and education of the handicapped child. Most states provide residential services by providing state facilities or paying for private schools located either in the home state or in neighboring states (Cruickshank and Johnson 1967).

In the early history of special education, the majority of handicapped children were placed in residential schools or kept at home. As local school districts assumed increasing responsibility for the education of handicapped children, the complexion of state schools changed. Children presently enrolled in residential schools are those who are so severely handicapped that they cannot participate in or profit from public school programs, or are children who reside in sparsely populated areas and do not have access to special classes (Calovini 1968).

The Wisconsin program has created an alternate solution for children residing in rural areas. This plan is designed for students who live too far to commute to special education programs. Instead of residential placement, these children live with boarding home parents during the week and attend special programs within the local schools (Melcher 1969).

Residential schools have received serious criticism in recent years. Essentially the criticism has revolved around three specific issues: (1) the handicapped child is isolated from both home and society; (2) there is a stigma attached to residential schools; and (3) generally the quality of the teaching staff and curriculum development is not equal to that of other types of education programs (Cruickshank and Johnson).

Community Special Schools

Special schools were developed as an alternative to residential placement and can generally be defined as one of two types. The first type serves children of a single etiological classification, for example, the physically handicapped, the mentally retarded, or any other specific group of handicapped children. The second type of special school is one in which children with many different types of handicaps are educated (Cruickshank and Johnson 1967). The purpose of special residential school facilities, is to meet the needs of seriously handicapped children who (1) are unable to cope with the normal school situation; (2) require a sheltered environment; or (3) need specialized equipment for treatment (Cruickshank and Johnson).

The authors' experiences have indicated that a special school may also be organized and established for the purposes of having a central location for providing the services of supplementary professional personnel such as a physical therapist, occupational therapist, speech therapist, and school psychologist. Rather than requiring such personnel to spend time traveling throughout the geographical area of a school district, they may be assigned to one special school; and, therefore, spend more of their time in serving the individual needs of handicapped children.

The special school in the local community has been subjected to the same criticism as that directed toward the residential schools. The primary objection is the lack of integration with the nonhandicapped members of society. Calovini suggests that a few children who have enrolled in special schools have difficulty in adjusting after they have returned to a regular school environment. Although the disadvantages of the special schools are numerous, these schools are preferred to residential schools, or to no placement at all in a special setting.

Special Classes

The special class provides for a group of handicapped children of a given classification and should be located in a regular elementary or secondary school. The number of special classes in a particular school building may vary, and often the number is increased to a point where programs may resemble a modified special school. This type of program is being utilized with all categories of handicapped children, both severely and mildly handicapped (Cruickshank and Johnson).

These classes may be varied in their operation. A few of these classes are completely set apart from the functioning of the rest of the school. The authors have seen a special class so segregated from the rest of the school that even the teacher could not share the same teachers' lounge with regular classroom teachers. This experience represented an extreme case; however, such cases do exist in many school systems. Contrary to this isolated program, special room programs allow for integration of the handicapped into the mainstream of school activities. The degree of integration is determined by the physical and academic abilities of the individual handicapped child (Calovini). If the handicapped child is capable of functioning with success in the mainstream of education, then he certainly should be permitted to do so.

Lilly suggests that the real focus of the present controversy in special education is on children who have been labeled mildly handicapped and have been placed in self-contained special classes. Studies concerning special class programs have produced conflicting evidence, and the majority of researchers have reported that special class programs show very little superiority over programs provided in regular classes (Lilly 1970).

In reviewing the literature, Lilly quotes several professional educators who question the effectiveness of special class programs. It is from this reference point that he suggests traditional special education services as represented by self-contained special classes be discontinued immediately for all mildly handicapped children.

This is, in all fairness, a commendable recommendation from Lilly; however, the authors question whether or not the majority of regular classroom teachers are ready to accept the mildly handicapped individuals back into their classrooms on a full-time basis. If the recommendation for discontinuing all self-contained special classes for the mildly handicapped were to be implemented in the near future; many of these children would be further alienated from school and learning, because administrators and regular classroom teachers are not prepared for quick and total mainstreaming. If mainstreaming is done slowly, and appropriate training is given to the regular classroom teachers; then such a plan might be an effective educational decision for the mildly handicapped.

Martin comments on special classes, stating:

> The predominant strategy today, in its most oversimplified sense, is to reduce the complexity of educating handicapped children by reducing the task to dealing with small, relatively homogeneous groups called special classes. We have discovered, however, that using etiological labels to establish homogeneity

is less efficient than we expected. And so we are exploring other categorization systems, the relevant behaviors of the child, the type process to be learned, etc. The ultimate reduction of this process is to move beyond small groupings to individualized instruction.

Resource Rooms and Itinerant Teaching

The resource room and itinerant programs are used in an effort to seek a solution to some of the criticisms of the special class approach to the education of the mildly handicapped child and to achieve more fully an integrated experience for handicapped children. The function of the two programs is very similar. The basic difference is that the itinerant teacher goes to the child in the regular schools; consequently the teacher may serve more than one school building.. The resource room teacher rarely serves more than one school building.

Although there is no stereotyped resource or itinerant program; the programs involve the presence of a special education teacher located in a regular school building, serving the needs of handicapped children who have been placed in regular class programs. Scheduling for these children depends on (1) the number of students involved in the programs, and (2) the type of instruction that is needed to allow the child to function adequately and remain in the regular program.

One variation of the resource room approach is operating in the school district of Buffalo, New York. The Board of Cooperative Education Services (BOCES) operations grew from eleven resource rooms in the 1969-70 school year to include twenty-three resource rooms in the 1970-71 school year. Two unique features of this program are its operation of a Child Evaluation Center; and teacher roles. The purpose of the Child Evaluation Center is to help the teachers to understand problem children in their rooms. There are several features of the evaluation center which are unique: (1) a "confidential" or "restricted" label is not applied to anything that happens within the center; (2) the entire evaluation process is done by the teacher; (3) parents are allowed to observe the entire evaluation process; and (4) children who are already enrolled in a BOCES special education class may not be referred to the center.

The necessity of close communications between the regular classroom teacher and the resource room teacher is common to all resource room programs. Usually the regular classroom teacher is the assistant in the learning program established for the child. In the BOCES program, the feeling is generated that the regular class teacher is the learning coordinator and the resource room teacher is an assistant who helps further the goals established primarily by the learning coordinator (Reger and Kappman 1971).

A very interesting adaptation and expansion of the resource room concept has been recently implemented in the State of Washington. According to Affleck, Lehning, and Brow (1973), this adaptation involves a resource school which has provided special services to a variety of exceptional children and eliminated the need for self-contained classrooms for the mildly handicapped child in this school.

There were 48 children who had been identified as mildly handicapped and in need of special services and an additional 51 children who needed special academic services. The program has provided many supportive services to regular classroom teachers; and, of course, to children with special needs. Training has also been provided for special education practicum students and master degree interns; therefore, the model has improved existing services for practical training of the future special educator who should be trained to provide services for any child who needs a modified program. Hopefully, this concept will expand its existing services and also be implemented by more states which are seeking different ways to serve the needs of exceptional children.

A Training Based Model

Lilly (1971) proposes in "A Training Based Model for Special Education," an alternative to the special services model presently utilized by special education. In this model plan, the focus is on children who are referred from the regular educational programs because of teacher-perceived behavioral or learning problems.

The goal of this model is very similar to the BOCES program. The objective is to equip regular classroom teachers with the skills necessary to cope with problem situations. The roles of the special educators would be to provide support and training for the classroom teachers, rather than to provide repositories for children from whom teachers need relief.

The implementation of this type of model will require more thorough training of special education teachers, and an acceptance of the special educator as a resource person. In addition, training programs for special education personnel will have to focus more attention on preparing teachers to become proficient in conducting informal evaluations of children and in demonstrating competency in the use of procedures, which may eliminate or alleviate the child's learning or behavioral problems. These types of adjustments are possible within a majority of special education training programs and should, if implemented properly, enhance the educational placements and environments provided for mildly handicapped children.

The Special Education Contract

Gallagher describes a contract that must be signed between both parents and educators before mildly handicapped children can be placed into a special education unit. This contract is designed for a specific time limit, a maximum of two years and is not renewable, and contains specific educational goals. With the termination of the contract period, the responsibility for education of the handicapped child is shifted back to the regular educational program.

Proficiency in stating and accomplishing specific instructional and behavioral objectives is relatively new to all fields of education. If contracts, as suggested by Gallagher, were to be required; then the special educator would be designating specific tasks which had to be accomplished by the handicapped child within specified periods of time. This procedure would require the special educator to develop and use skills in preparing tasks by specific steps and sequencing educational and behavioral acitivities. Several programs have started an emphasis in this area and would certainly enhance the feasibility of special education contracts.

A Comprehensive Plan for Programming

Programs and services to the handicapped are so diversified that in some instances services appear to overlap in some areas and are seriously deficient in other areas. A portion of these difficulties could be corrected or alleviated through the establishment of a voluntary organization within each state which would collect information relative to all services available to the handicapped. This type of organization could be developed through existing governmental agencies; and, therefore, would not necessitate the implementation of a new state organization (Cogan and Ohrtman 1971).

The entire system is based on a continuous and computerized record-keeping system, containing information on each handicapped person within a state from birth throughout the educational process. This system of record keeping makes possible longitudinal studies, evaluation of diagnostic procedures, and a method by which professional terminology may be standardized. The authors of this plan propose that the consolidation of activities currently existing and the proper utilization of agencies would not only be more effective in educating the handicapped, but also the proposed plan would result in less expenditures than that spent for existing programs (Cogan and Ohrtman 1971)

Teacher Training Programs

The traditional practice of organizing services for handicapped children on the basis of disability categories and the preparation of teachers in terms of specializations is presently used in most colleges and universities. These programs appear to reflect the legislation and program development of the 1960s. The United States Department of Education gives its supoort to the categorical system in both legislation and in programming. The most recent federal legislation, which reflects this support is Public Law 91-230 which specifically defines a new group of handicapped children—children with specific learning disabilities.

More flexibility in training programs has been suggested by the Office of Education and this trend will probably remain in existence for a number of years. This flexibility will aid universities and colleges in developing programs which will train teachers to provide instructional programs for children with learning and/or adjustment problems regardless of their disabilities. A new emphasis in teacher training programs will also bring about changes in special education services which have been described above.

Contemporary Approaches in Teacher Training

The National Education Association's National Commission on Teacher Education and Professional Standards identified three trends which may be significant in changing the standards for the preparation of teachers as educators of handicapped children. "These trends are (1) alternate routes into certification through the use of performance criteria, (2) student-teacher reforms, and (3) differentiated staffing," (Position Paper on Standards 1970).

Andrews (1970) proposes an almost entirely new and innovative program of teacher certification. The plan is program-centered and performance-centered. Certification as a teacher would be based on his competencies, that is, one's ability to teach.

Schwartz (1971) in "A Clinical Model for Interrelated Areas of Special Education" states:

> Clinical teaching, i.e., diagnostic, prescriptive, and individualized instruction, is not new or innovative, but rather is the renewed and continuing aspiration toward a fundamental goal of special education. The coupling of the heritage of the field

with the emerging sophistication in instructional systems and technology provides a conceptual framework for testing and building a data base for proposed changes in teacher education for the decade of the Seventies.

With this as his rationale, he describes a teacher preparation model for interrelated areas in special education. This model provides instructional objectives for training teachers as well as for educating handicapped children in the schools. The main emphasis in the model focuses upon: (1) using behavioral descriptions of desired competencies; (2) assessment procedures for measuring entry and proficiency levels of performance; and (3) a variety of instructional plans designed to accomplish the objectives of the program (Schwartz 1971).

Curriculum Development in Special Education

When implementing and planning materials for the special classes, the teacher must be very considerate of the child's particular level of growth and age range. The exceptional child will have a number of problems that differ from the "normal" child on the primary level through the high school level. As an exceptional child moves through the school program, he may have a mental or performance age that is significantly different from other children, and he is faced with many new needs and social expectations which may be extremely frustrating. The student who matures physically at a rate compatible with his chronological age range; but not emotionally or mentally, is unable to understand or possibly cope with additional demands which are placed upon him. If one is to be able to help constructively and meaningfully in what is perhaps the child's greatest hour of need, then one must meet the challenge of the individual exceptional child.

For example, a youngster may be faced with a newly developed sex interest and he may not be able to sustain the boy-girl interaction. The concept of self at this time would be most important if the students were expected to maintain a reasonable degree of logic and understanding of the social skills that are required in boyfriend-girlfriend communication. Consequently, there must be the right kind of curriculum planning in the special education or regular class to help these students understand themselves and society's demands.

If the exceptional child is ever to be a part of society, he must have help in learning how to function harmoniously in society. He needs to learn how to work with others, to play, and to communicate with others, and to be accepted by others. Therefore, if the student is to become efficient socially, economically, and personally, he must learn to develop adequate social relations as a student in a special class. To develop a more complete self-awareness of the here and now, the student must also be aided in transferring these learned skills into the realm of the total school program and the total functioning of the individual. The teacher's efforts of instruction must be coordinated to meet the three objectives of social, economic, and personal efficiency; consequently, learning how to function properly in society should be concretely a part of a curriculum that affords the student the opportunity to learn how to find a place in life that would be worthwhile to himself and to society.

In planning the curriculum for exceptional children, the school is faced with a number of developmental needs of these students and very little time to do the job. These students will enter school on an academic and social level significantly different from the regular school student; but the special class teachers have the responsibility of helping these students to become integrated, functional members of society in the same period of time that is granted to the regular student population. This task is a very difficult assignment for the special teacher, particularly if the exceptional child has been exposed to failure for long periods of time within the regular classroom program. However, in the majority of cases, the special class teacher should have more individual resources than a considerable number of other teachers; consequently, the special class teacher should be able to integrate his own resources with those of the community, vocational rehabilitation, his state department of education, and current literature, with a continuity that would enable the exceptional student to achieve social, economic, and personal efficiency. In some cases, these objectives may be realized in spite of the system to which the child is exposed.

A resourceful teacher will not be the teacher who permits a rigid enforcement of academic requirements for his students. The special class teacher must remember that he is working with students who usually have difficulty learning incidentally; and, therefore, must have concrete application in all or most areas of instruction (of course, this does not generally include the gifted child). Therefore, if a teacher were to enforce rigid academic standards upon these students, he would meet instant failure as a teacher. The academic program must be integrated with the objectives of social, economic, and personal efficiency if the special student is to achieve and receive an experiential framework that will be of value to him after he leaves high school. The special class teacher should constantly remind himself that he must afford opportunity to his students to do work that can be associated with life and society. These special students may have little ability to form true concepts; therefore, the teacher has to provide instruction that is meaningful to the student as a person and as a member of society, and this meaning cannot be transmitted through abstractions and theories. Instruction has to be practical for all areas of exceptional children.

It is understood that exceptional students will not be operating at a grade level that is consistent with other school students; therefore, the teacher should not expect an academic commitment from the special class students to compete with the rest of the student body. The special class student will not remain in his particular class for the entire school day. He will interact with other students at lunch, on the playground, at social functions, at athletic functions, and many other school activities. In some instances special class students have actively participated in athletic, musical, art, and driver's education programs, and in other classes which are chosen according to their appropriateness for the individual child. It should be noted that many of the activities in which exceptional children become involved in the total school program are not as functionally easy for the special student as they are for the regular class student. Some special class students may be physically larger than the other students and they may be chronologically older than the others. Even if the students are the same age, the exceptional student will not have, in many cases, mental and physical coordination that is consistent with the chronological age range of his peers.

These problems which exist in an exceptional student's world do not remain at school when he goes home in the evening. He will meet similar situations which remind him of his failures and deficiencies at home with his siblings, in the community with his peers, and many times with adults who do not have realistic insights into the exceptional student's characteristics. Therefore, it is very important that the teacher of a special class concern himself with the total environment—exceptional and normal—in which these students must live and learn, if the teacher is to be successful in helping these students become functional citizens. A teacher must constantly remain aware that the main difference between the special class and the regular class is not so much in the instructional, academic subject areas as it is in the matter of the emphasis which needs to be placed upon the application to daily life situations.

SUMMARY

Special education was conceived and nurtured as a separate field within the broad spectrum of education. Amid much controversy, this separatism of services is still the most common approach to special education. States, individuals, citizen groups, and their agencies are beginning to recognize the fallacies of methods currently used to educate the handicapped child and are proposing many approaches to change the existing programs (the reader is referred to the chapter on trends within this text for an overview of proposed and existing approaches for improved delivery systems in special education). The extent to which model programs, such as those described above, become a reality will depend upon the degree to which legislators, professional educators, and lay citizens of the respective states are willing to implement such procedures. Because of existing legislation in the various states, the establishment of new programs and new approaches for dealing with the problems of the handicapped child will not become a reality immediately. Changes proposed on each state level will have to consider many factors which are relevant to existing or future programs for the handicapped child.

The authors certainly agree with Blatt (1972) who indicates that existing programs are still not reaching the majority of handicapped children and that many handicapped children in need of specialized services are either not placed or are misplaced within our schools and institutional settings.

Most states provide education as a fundamental right which is guaranteed to both handicapped and nonhandicapped children. Yet statistics indicate that 60 percent of the approximately seven million handicapped children are denied needed help which is offered by special education programs and only 10 percent of those receiving special education services, in many metropolitan school systems, are returned to regular classroom situations (Gallagher).

> Today educators in local, state, and college systems cannot afford the luxury of separateness. We must show how college teachers of teachers, classroom teachers of normal and exceptional children, school administrators, and the other parties involved in the education of children can forget our own comforts and biases and cooperate for the benefit of the children we purport to serve. (Melcher 1972).

Categorization and/or separatism of the handicapped are only two of the many variables to be examined in maintaining or developing improved educational programs for exceptional children. In order to prevent the creation of new problems in addition to those which are already in existence with respect to educating and training the handicapped child, educators must test a variety of ways to improve existing services and, at the same time, continue to develop different approaches and programs to increase the level and appropriateness of services which are necessary for handicapped children.

Surely the development of new models and new or different approaches in attempting to meet the needs of handicapped children will result in the improvement of many services for the nonhandicapped. Caution must be exercised in the development of these programs so that the handicapped child is not "forgotten" in the process of developing new delivery systems. If we develop or return to an integrated educational system which is void of understanding of the needs of handicapped children, then we will be no better off than with our present form of segregation (Valletutti 1969).

In conclusion, the foremost consideration in the development of new or different models is whether or not these services will increase services and improve services which are available for handicapped children. If our new emphasis on reintegrating the handicapped child into the mainstream of education serves only to lessen the use of labels or categories and does not successfully reach more handicapped children and improve the quality of services for these children, then we have not served the purposes which are required for this group of children.

Bibliography

Affleck, James Q.; Lehning, Thomas W.; and Brow, Kateri D. "Expanding the Resource Concept: The Resource School." *Exceptional Children* 39, no. 6 (March 1973).

Andrews, Theodore E. "New Directions in Certification." *Improving State Leadership in Education.* Olympia, Washington: Department of Health, Education and Welfare, Office of Education, Institution of Washington State Board of Education, September, 1970.

Blatt, Burton. "Public Policy and the Education of Children with Special Needs." *Exceptional Children* 38, no. 7 (March 1972).

Calovini, Gloria. *The Principal Looks at Classes for the Physically Handicapped.* Springfield, Illinois: State Office of Superintendant of Public Instruction, November, 1968.

Cogan, Victor, and Ohrtman, William. "A Comprehensive Plan for Services for the Handicapped." *Journal of Special Education* 6, no. 1 (Winter-Spring 1971).

Cruickshank, William M., and Johnson, G. Orville, ed. *Education of Exceptional Children and Youth.* Englewood Cliffs, N.J.: Prentice-Hall, Inc, 1967.

Gallagher, James J. "The Special Education Contract for Mildly Handicapped Children." *Exceptional Children* 38, no. 7 (March 1972).

Lilly, Stephen. "A Training Based Model for Special Education." *Exceptional Children* 37 (Summer 1971).

———. "Special Education: A Teapot in a Tempest." *Exceptional Children* 37, no. 1 (September 1970).

Martin, Edwin W.; Bryan, Trudy; LaVor, Martin; and Scheflin, Rhonda. "Law Review." *Exceptional Children* 37, no. 1 (September 1970).

Martin, Edwin W., "Individualism and Behaviorism as Future Trends in Educating Handicapped Children." *Exceptional Children* 38, no. 7 (March 1972).

McCarthy, James J., and McCarthy, Joan F. *Learning Disabilities.* Boston: Allyn and Bacon, Inc., 1969.

Melcher, John, "A Boarding Home Program for Handicapped Children." *Eric.* Wisconsin State Department of Public Instruction, Division for Handicapped Children, October 1969.

———. "Some Questions from a School Administrator." *Exceptional Children* 38, no. 7 (March 1972).

"Position Paper on Standards for Professional Preparation of Special Education Personnel." Discussion Draft, Division of Special Education, Texas Education Agency, September 24, 1970.

Reger, Roger, and Kappman, Marion. "The Child Oriented Research Room." *Exceptional Children* 37, no. 6 (February 1971).

Reynolds, Maynard C., and Balow, Bruce. "Categories and Variables in Special Education." *Exceptional Children* 38, no. 5 (January 1971).

Schwartz, Louis. "A Clinical Teacher Model for Interrelated Areas of Special Education." *Exceptional Children* 37, no. 8 (April 1971).

Tompkins, James R. "An Analysis: Needs, Progress and Issues in the Education of Emotionally Disturbed Children." *Journal of Special Education* 3, no. 1 (Winter-Spring 1969).

U.S. Department of Health, Education, and Welfare, Office of Education. *Breakthrough in Early Education of Handicapped Children.* Reprint from *American Education,* January-February, 1970. Washington: Government Printing Office, 1970.

U.S. Department of Health, Education, and Welfare, Office of Education. *Four Programs for Educational Services to Handicapped Children.* Bureau of Education for the Handicapped. Washington: Government Printing Office, January, 1971.

Valletutti, P. "Integration vs. Segregation: A Useless Dialectic." *Journal of Special Education* 3 (1969).

Weintraub, Fredrick J.; Aberson, Albert R.; and Braddock, David L. *State Law and Education of Handicapped Children: Issues and Recommendations.* Arlington, Va: The Council for Exceptional Children, 1971.

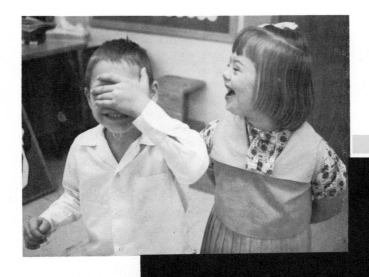

'All of us kids have fun, too.'

2

Mentally Retarded Children

DEFINITION

A discussion of mental retardation must begin with a definition which will functionally describe children who are mentally retarded. Many definitions are available which attempt to provide a meaningful understanding of mental retardation. Rather than to present a wide variety of definitions for this exceptionality, the authors chose to use the definition of mental retardation as formulated by Heber who was commissioned in 1959 by the American Association on Mental Deficiency for such a purpose. This definition appears to be the most comprehensive.

Mental retardation refers to subaverage general intellectual functioning which originates during the developmental period and is associated with impairment in adaptive behavior (Heber 1959).

Instead of presenting all of the descriptive material covered by this definition Heber prepared, the authors will summarize the main points. By subaverage intellectual functioning, Heber is referring to a child who scores one or more standard deviations from the mean on an individual intelligence test, such as The Revised Stanford-Binet Intelligence Scale or the Wechsler Intelligence Scale for Children. In more specific terms the I.Q. portion of the definition refers to individuals who score below 84 or 85 on an I.Q. instrument.

For many professionals this point makes Heber's definition somewhat unpalatable because it includes too many children. Many states do not go above an I.Q. range of 70 to 75 for identifying the educable mentally retarded individual. However, the reader should be aware that Heber was including in his definition children who were considered to be borderline mentally retarded, or more commonly referred to as slow learners.

By including the time in one's life during which subaverage general intellectual functioning occurs, Heber attempted to eliminate other learning problems which might be interpreted as mental retardation. He specified that the developmental period is the time during which mental retardation occurs, and set the age limits for the developmental period at approximately birth to sixteen. Perhaps a more realistic definitive period would be prior to and during the school age years.

Adaptation to one's environment may be assessed during several phases of life, and specific impairments in adaptive behavior would be a possible indication of mental retardation. Heber has divided the abilities of a person to adapt to his environment into three distinct and yet overlapping areas. The first area is that of maturation and would apply most appropriately to the preschool age child. If a child in this age group is slow in developmental skills, such as crawling, walking, talking, or developing self-help skills; then one might suspect that the child may be mentally retarded. However, upon further assessment, if the child did not obtain a low score on an individual intelligence test; then other problems should be considered.

During the school age years, academic and social learning is the primary task of the child. If a child is not learning at a level compatible with his age, then achievement tests should be administered to confirm or refute whether his learning lag is indicative of mental retardation. If a teacher observes that a child has fallen one, two, or more years behind his peers in academic subjects, mental retardation certainly becomes a possibliity.

Adapting to one's environment also includes adequate social adjustment, which is particularly important during the adult years. If a person has reached adulthood and is unable to maintain a job, maintain a home, or to establish meaningful adult relationships, then mental retardation may be indicated. Of course, the lack of adaptive behavior and social adjustment would hopefully be observed and corrected during the school age years.

An important aspect of Heber's definition is comprehensiveness. For example, if an individual has problems in the area of social adjustment, but does not score one or more standard deviations below the norm on an individual intelligence test; then other problems are suspected instead of mental retardation. In addition, if an individual's score on an intelligence test placed him within the range of mental retardation, but he continued to mature, learn, and socially adjust in accordance with levels expected of his age range; then possibly mental retardation should be excluded and other problems considered (Heber).

Consequently, educators, parents, and professionals should understand that failure in one test area does not necessarily mean that an individual is relegated to a category of mental retardation. Many factors of human development and functioning must be examined, and professionals must not be hasty in making decisions to place labels on children for singularly assumed reasons.

If professional educators were to examine closely Heber's definition of mental retardation, they would also learn that he never intended for mental retardation to be a rigid, lifelong type of classification. Heber specifically indicates that his definition should be one that focuses on the current functioning and behavior of the individual; because under a variety of circumstances, the child's functioning and behavior may change. The authors believe that Heber's emphasis on *current* functioning and behavior is most important, because this trend implies that the problem of mental retardation, particularly mild mental retardation, can change. If temporary placement in special programs implement a change in a young educable mentally retarded child's life, then his level of functioning can and often will change to a level above that of mental retardation. Changes in functioning will not be brought about as a result of miracles. Changes can be experienced, though, if teachers and other professionals who work with young mentally retarded children will maintain an attitude and philosophy that the child is a worthwhile individual, who can learn and can make progress in academics and daily living.

Through his definition, Heber has issued a challenge for comprehensive evaluations, thorough and well formulated education and training programs which will focus on the child's current needs; and periodic comprehensive reevaluations to keep in tune with the child's functioning, and possible to consider his removal from special class programs either on a full-time or part-time basis. Heber's definition reflects the current emphasis for appropriate evaluations, which tend to lessen the use of rigid labels and allow flexible programming for individual children. Additional definitions of mental retardation are reported by Tredgold (1963), Doll (1941), and Benoit (1959), as follows:

Tredgold defined mental retardation, "as a state of incomplete mental development of such a kind and degree that the individual is incapable of adapting himself to the normal environment of his fellows in such a way as to maintain existence independently of supervision, control or external support."

Doll indicates that "mental deficiency is a state of social incompetence obtained at maturity, resulting from developmental arrest of intelligence because of constitutional (hereditary or acquired) origin: the condition is essentially incurable through treatment and un-remediable through training except as treatment and training instill habits which superficially compensate for the limitations of the person so afflicted while under favorable circumstances and for more or less limited periods of time."

Benoit indicates that mental retardation is a deficit of intellectual function resulting from varied intrapersonal and/or extrapersonal determinants, but having as a common proximate cause a diminished efficiency of the nervous system thus entailing a lessened general capacity for growth in perceptual and conceptual interpretation and consequently in environmental adjustment.

Estimates of Prevalence

Estimates of the number of persons who fall within the classification of the mentally retarded population vary considerably. Many authors have formulated estimates from the normal curve using only school age children, or using the entire population, as a base. These factors may cause some misunderstanding of the estimates of the number of mentally retarded persons within the United States, because the reader may not understand the population base which was used in formulating the estimate. However, it seems that an estimate of about 3 percent of the general population prevails throughout the literature. With a general population in the United States of nearly 205 million in 1972, this would mean that one could estimate approximately 6,150,000 persons to be mentally retarded.

Of this total number the authors would estimate that approximately 85 percent of the mentally retarded population, or 2 to 2½ percent of the general population, would fall within the range of mild mental retardation. An estimate of the mildly or educable mentally retarded population (I.Q. range of 50 to 70 or 75) would be between 4½ million. The moderately or trainable mentally retarded population (I.Q. range of 30-35 to about 50) would number somewhere between 500,000 and 1 million; and the number of severely and profoundly mentally retarded population (I.Q. range 0 to 25-35) would range between 150,000 to 200,000. The estimates and percentages of the different levels of mental retardation are given in ranges, because no one knows with certainty how many individuals actually fall within each population group.

Estimates are valuable in that they help professionals predict how many children are in need of services as compared with the number of children who are receiving services. Thus, planning for comprehensive community services, such as special classrooms and sheltered workshops; and planning for the training of professional personnel, such as teachers, psychologists, and speech therapists, can be implemented. Estimates can also provide guidance in requesting and preparing legislative programs which will attempt to meet the individual needs of this portion of the handicapped population.

Caution should be exercised in applying estimates of the prevalence of mental retardation to all samples of the population, because many mentally retarded children are only mildly handicapped. Tremendous variations in population subgroups may be found when searching for the prevalence of mild mental retardation. For example, in a suburban population of high-middle socioeconomic to lower-upper socioeconomic groups, a very low percentage of the population may be educably mentally retarded. However, in a ghetto area or in an inner city area of lower socioeconomic groups, as high as 6 to 7 percent of the population may be functioning within the range of educable mental retardation.

Methods of Identification

Methods of identifying retarded individuals must be in relation to the symptoms exhibited. When attention is drawn to children because of learning and/or behavioral difficulties, tests are usually administered to determine the cause or extent of the problems. The type of test given is usually in relation to the behavior and adaptive symptoms observed, and the learning areas in which the child has difficulties. By symptoms, the authors are referring to behaviors such as low intellectual functioning, slow maturation, or a behavior problem which causes difficulties in social adjustment.

Mental retardation may be found to be the result of a child's culture, emotional problems, organic conditions, hereditary factors, or a combination of one or more of these factors (Robinson and Robinson 1965). Determining the possible cause of mental retardation is usually a very difficult, if not impossible, task. Mental retardation is generally considered to be multidetermined. However, if through appropriate assessment techniques a child was discovered to be functioning as a mentally retarded person because of an emotional disturbance rather than an organic or unknown condition, then the instruction procedures for this child with respect to techniques and content might take an entirely different direction. Perhaps the most important point that should be considered in discussing methods of identification is that the retarded individual should be reevaluated continuously. This reevaluation should help provide the most meaningful available program for the child.

Standardized testing instruments have been widely accepted as methods for the evaluation of the mentally retarded child. Although tests are only a part of the total evaluation system, they represent an important part and should never be regarded lightly. Professionals who are planning to work with mentally retarded individuals should familiarize themselves with some of the more commonly used test instruments in order to provide beneficial formal evaluations of the child. Test information has been used too long for the purpose of making administrative decisions; teachers especially should be focusing on the educational importance of formal evaluations. Otherwise, the evaluation and placement of mentally retarded children will not serve the child's needs, but will only serve to provide labels and classification systems for these children.

The following chart of educational tests (table 1) provides the reader with the name of the test, individual or group administration, the purpose of the measure, the age or grade level for which the instrument is appropriate, and the scoring information. Knowledge of these tests should provide a foundation on the basis of which a teacher can develop skills which will enable him to plan educationally for the child.

The reader should note that the tests, as summarized in table 1, are not all inclusive. There are many tests appropriate for administering to the mentally retarded child; the authors selected only a representative sample of those tests available. Perhaps the information presented in the table will clarify what is meant by a comprehensive evaluation and a battery of tests. None of the tests listed in table 1 should be used to the exclusion of all the others when one is attempting to evaluate a mentally retarded child. Single tests will provide labels, but generally will not provide information which is essential for improving the learning environment of a mentally retarded child.

The combined school achievement, mental, and language test scores are the most valid for the identification of school age children who are having learning difficulties. When a child is referred for testing because of possible mental retardation, he should be the subject of a comprehensive assessment. The primary objective of the testing should be to provide his teacher with the child's mental age, achievement test scores, and the child's current strengths and weaknesses in learning. The evaluation should also describe the child in terms of behavioral objectives and provide the teacher with information which is directly related to the teaching-learning process.

Table 1

SUMMARY OF EDUCATIONAL TESTS

Name	Type	Purpose	Age or Level	Score or Information
Stanford-Binet Intelligence Scale, 1960	Individual	Intellectual Assessment	2 years-Adult	I.Q., Basal Age, Mental Age
Wechsler Intelligence Scale for Children (WISC)	Individual	Intellectual Assessment	5-15 years	Verbal I.Q., Performance I.Q., Full-Scale I.Q.
Slosson Intelligence Test (SIT)	Individual	Screening test for Intellectual Assessment	Preschool-Adult	I.Q., Basal Age, Mental Age
California Test of Mental Maturity	Group	Mental Ability	Different test for K-Adults	I.Q.
Henmon-Nelson Tests of Mental Ability	Group	Mental Ability	3 sets—Grades: 3-6, 6-9, 0-12	I.Q.
Marianne Frostig Developmental Test of Visual Perception	Individual or Group	Visual Perception	3-9 years	Perceptual Age, Perceptual Quotient
Columbia Mental Maturity Scale	Individual	Intelligence	Mental ages: 3-12	I.Q., Mental Age
Gesell Developmental Schedules	Individual	Maturation, Motor development, adaptive behavior, etc.	4 weeks-6 years	Maturation age, Developmental age
Goodenough-Harris Draw-a-Man Test	Individual or Group	Intellectual Assessment	4-12 years	I.Q., Mental Age
Illinois Test of Psycholinguistic Abilities	Individual	Linguistic Ability	3-9 years	Language Age, Profile of Language strengths and weaknesses
Vineland Social Maturity Scale	Individual	Interview with parents to obtain social maturity	Birth-maturity	Social quotient
Durrell Analysis of Reading Difficulty	Individual	Diagnostic reading test	Grades 1.5-6.5	Reading skills

Table 1 (Continued)

Name	Type	Purpose	Age or Level	Score or Information
Gates McKillop Reading Diagnostic Test	Individual	Analysis of Reading Difficulties	Grades 1.6-8.5	Reading problems, Percentile Rank
Wide Range Achievement Test	Individual and Group	Reading, Spelling, Arithmetic Achievement	Preschool-College	Achievement scores, Standard scores
Wepman Test of Auditory Discrimination	Individual	Auditory discrimination deficits	5-8 years	Standard score
Hiskey-Nebraska Test of Learning Aptitude	Individual	Nonverbal test of intelligence	4-10 years	Learning age
Purdue Perceptual Motor Survey	Individual	Perceptual-motor development	6-10 years	Laterality, Directionality, Perceptual-Motor matching

Adapted from data in *Mental Retardation: Diagnosis and Treatment*, Charles M. Polser et al., Harper & Row, 1967.

Information as to how the teacher may provide an ongoing assessment of the child in the classroom should also be given. If the results of a test battery provide the teacher with nothing more than scores, then the time of the examiner, the child, and the teacher has been wasted.

After assessment, the evaluator should recommend the best educational placement for the child, based upon his current level of functioning. Recommendations for educational placement must take into account the various programs which are available within the community. All recommendations should be sound, and based upon a reasonable plan which is feasible for the child, the parents, and the professional personnel who will be working with the child.

Characteristics of the Mentally Retarded

In attempting to describe the characteristics of mentally retarded children there must be clarification of intent for presenting this type of information. The authors recognize that individual mentally retarded children vary considerably when they are compared within a group of mentally retarded children. However, certain characteristics are usually predominant in a large group of mentally retarded children. Therefore, characteristics can be descriptive enough to clarify the differences in the levels of mental retardation, and also to clarify the differences between mentally retarded children and the so-called normal child.

Perhaps the admonition for the use of caution when attempting to identify the type of problems which a child may have has been overstressed, but this point will be reiterated again with respect to a description of mentally retarded children. Educators should not assume that a list of characteristics will identify an individual child as having the problem of mental retardation. For example, the reader should not assume that a particular child is mentally retarded because he exhibits characteristics possessed by a group of mentally retarded children. As the authors have stressed previously, the determinism of mental retardation is multidimensional, and demands a comprehensive evaluation before reaching a decision.

A child may have the problem of mental retardation for various reasons, and his functioning may be effected to a degree ranging from mild to very severe. Children who are mildly mentally retarded generally have their most difficult problems in the area of learning abstract concepts. These children are referred to as educable mentally retarded within school populations, because education is meaningful and functional. Educable children are limited in learning academic skills; however, they can and do learn.

The moderately retarded children are referred to as trainable mentally retarded children in school systems. This term is used to denote that the children will have severe difficulties in learning academic skills, but they can be trained to care for themselves; and in many cases they can be trained to perform some types of vocational skills. Typically, the mongoloid child will be a trainable level child. In fact, the largest percentage of trainable children will probably be those who possess Down's Syndrome (mongolism).

The severely and profoundly mentally retarded children have no equivalent term within the school population, since children who fall within this level of mental retardation have extreme difficulties even in the area of developing self-help skills. Many children who are severely or profoundly mentally retarded have multiple handicaps to such an extent that they must be cared for within a residential facility. They will often require constant care and supervision because of their limited abilities in all areas of functioning, and they frequently have a variety of medical problems which further complicate their abilities to function.

Perhaps a presentation of the characteristics of the mentally retarded in chart form will convey this information simply and briefly. Table 2 presents the characteristics of mentally retarded children by area of functioning and the level of mental retardation.

One additional point will be made with respect to the characteristics of the mentally retarded as presented in table 2. Any individual who is working with a mentally retarded child should not accept these characteristics as a rigid blueprint for determining the present or future functioning level of an individual mentally retarded child. When working with these children, one must take the attitude that the child should be provided with conditions which will enable him to progress as far as he possibly can without any preset ideas as to the level at which he may be capable of performing. This type of flexibility must be incorporated in any endeavor which attempts to the needs of individual children. Certainly, one must recognize that programs are not presently in existence which can enable the more severely and profoundly retarded children to reach levels of functioning that are higher than those generally assumed for them.

The reader should also be aware that many severely and profoundly mentally retarded individuals are commonly referred to as the group of individuals with clinical syndromes. The terms which are applied to them are medical terms, since their problems of mental

Table 2

CHARACTERISTICS OF MENTALLY RETARDED CHILDREN

Area of Functioning	Mild or Educable	Moderate or Trainable	Severe and Profound
Self-help skills	Feeds and dresses self and cares for own toilet needs.	Has difficulties and requires training but can learn adequate self-help skills.	No skills to partial, but some can care for personal needs on a limited basis.
Speech and Communication	Receptive and expressive are adequate. Understands communication.	Receptive and expressive language is adequate. Has speech problems.	Receptive language is limited to good. Expressive language is limited to poor.
Academics	Optimal learning environment—3rd to 6th grade.	Very few academic skills. 1st or 2nd grade.	No academic skills.
Social skills	Has friends, can learn to adjust adequately.	Capable of friends but had difficulties in many social situations.	Not capable of having "real" friends. No social interaction.
Vocational Adjustment	Can hold a job. Competitive to semi-competitive. Primarily unskilled work.	Sheltered work environment. Usually needs constant supervision.	No employment for the most part. May be in an activity center. Usually needs constant care.
Adult Living	Usually marries, has children. Needs help during stress.	Usually doesn't marry or have children. Dependent.	Always dependent on others. No marriage or children.

The authors developed Table 2 from the narrative information by Hutt and Gibby (1965).

retardation are often the result of some type of organicity or hereditary disorder. Within the profoundly retarded population many different conditions exist, such as microcephaly, hydrocephaly, phenylketonuria, cretinism, galactosemia, Rubella, RH Blood factor, and kernicterus. These conditions involve the use of technical terms and in the majority of cases the educator in public schools does not meet children with these types of problems. However, any person who is working with the mentally retarded child should be aware of these conditions, and have some exposure to the more serious problems associated with these conditions. From the authors' viewpoints, this exposure is essential, because with proper medical treatment some of the more serious types of mental retardation can be prevented or controlled; and the professional working with this group of children should have an awareness of the controls which are relative to the various conditions. A detailed description of these terms may be found in the Merck Manual (1964) and Robinson and Robinson. The reader is referred to these excellent sources.

Knowledge of these conditions, and the ways in which they can be prevented, will help one to be more aware of the resources parents need when they have questions about possible causes of severe or profound retardation. Also, one should be knowledgeable with respect to programs which encourage the prevention of conditions such as German measles, PKU, cretinism, etc. Educators often serve as resource persons for parents; and the special education teacher in particular should be informed with respect to these more serious types of mental retardation, because of the services which he can perform in the total area of mental retardation.

To further elaborate, recent research indicates that many educable mentally retarded children may have some type of sensory deficit which could effect achievement in school. Chiappone and Libby (1972) conducted a study involving sixty normal children and sixty educable mentally retarded children in which they indicated that the retarded children were significantly more farsighted than the normal children. The primary emphasis of these authors pertains to specific differences among retarded children with regard to such areas as visual acuity rather than farsightedness as a single factor. In short, there may be many factors contributing to the educable mentally retarded child's lack of achievement, and educators may be routinely overlooking numerous child problems.

Public School Programs for Mentally Retarded Children

General objectives. One of the primary needs of mentally retarded children with respect to services is the provision of appropriate public school programs. Schools within the United States have made considerable progress in providing educational programs for the mentally retarded since the turn of the century; however, new classes and additional teachers are needed for these children to provide even more comprehensive and sequential programs. This may mean that two school systems will have to develop a cooperative agreement in order to provide programs from the preschool level through the high school level for these exceptional children. Cooperative agreements are being formed in various localities throughout the United States for this purpose. One should definitely question a policy of any school system which provides an early elementary school program for the mentally retarded, but does not provide junior and senior high programs.

In order for educational programs for the mentally retarded to be sequential, planning among the teachers of the various levels within the schools must be continuous. As pointed out by Shane (1967), teachers of mentally retarded children must focus upon organizing a system whereby they can and will communicate with one another regarding any one child. This communication should involve teachers at all levels, so that effective programs continue to be developed for a child. For example, if the primary special education teacher learns that an individual child is progressing in any area of development through the use of a particular approach, then, if still appropriate, the intermediate teacher could use the same or a similar approach. This does not mean that teachers should teach exactly the same way or use the same materials. The program should be varied; however, if a teacher in the primary class learns that a particular child is very capable of following directions and working semi-independently, then the intermediate teacher should have the benefit of being made aware of this information.

The authors have known several special education teachers of mentally retarded children who have had to spend a few weeks at the beginning of the school year to discover how an individual child approaches a learning situation. Granted the child may be with a new teacher, a new group of children, and in a new classroom; but his particular learning style will probably not change so drastically as to call for a completely different and perhaps inappropriate approach. The sequencing of a special education instructional program goes far beyond the single factor of a teacher presenting an appropriate curriculum. A sequential program must provide a means of insuring that teachers at all levels of training are building a program in unison and not in isolation, one from another.

Perhaps another example will serve to emphasize this point. How many primary special education teachers of educable mentally retarded children are knowledgeable about work-study programs which are so common in the high schools? How can a program be sequential if teachers don't know what happens within the instructional program at a level above or below that which he is teaching? The sequencing and continuity of a program must be an ongoing developmental process, and cannot be accomplished within one school year through conducting an inservice training program. Because of changes in teaching staff, the bringing of new children into the program, and the changing vocational picture within a community, the development of sequence and continuity in an instructional program for retarded children never ends.

School Programs for Trainable Mentally Retarded Children

Public school programs for moderately (trainable) mentally retarded children have been in existence for some time. Although at times there have been controversies regarding the role of the public schools in providing educational services for this group of children, the majority of schools which operate programs for them provide for several age levels. The names applied to the various levels of training usually denote the functional level of the children. For example, these levels are often referred to as preprimary (ages six to ten); primary (ages nine to twelve); intermediate level (ages eleven to fourteen); and teenage (ages thirteen to twenty or twenty-one). (See a Guide for Teachers of Trainable Mentally Retarded Children, 1971.) The names and ages for the various levels are not standardized across the country. In a rural area, for example, one may find only one unit for all trainable mentally retarded children; and in smaller communities, one may find two units consisting of an elementary school age group and a secondary school age group. Children who are trainable mentally retarded do not constitute a large group. Therefore, modifications in the way in which they are grouped for education and training must be implemented.

The instructional program for trainable mentally retarded children should be planned to focus on the development of practical skills. These children will need training in self-help skills such as learning to dress and feed themselves and learning to care for their bodily needs. Language development should also be included in the program, so these children can learn to communicate with one another and with others. Many of these children will have speech impediments; and services should be provided to correct or minimize these problems. Trainable mentally retarded children should also be trained in the area of developing social skills. They will need to learn how to play with others and how to cooperate in a social situation. The development of appropriate and functional social skills will be a very important part of the total curriculum.

In order to help this group of children become as independent as possible, the teacher should also emphasize the development of work skills. One objective in training the trainable retarded child is to help him become as independent as he possibly can during his adult years. As the children progress and mature, some of them may be able to develop minimal basic reading and number skills. These skills can be presented in a practical manner (one should not expect a traditional academic level of functioning) for the purpose of improving the children's safety habits, their abilities to travel in the community, their abilities to read high interest and low reading level books, and their abilities to handle money concepts. The children should also be provided a motor development and physical education program that will enable them to improve their functioning in this area. As a group, the majority of trainable mentally retarded children will require some type of sheltered employment during their adult years; so much of the prospective teacher's school preparation should consist of exploring the possibilities of preparing the children for this type of employment (A Guide for Teachers of Trainable Mentally Retarded Children, 1971).

Recognizing the vocational potential of the majority of trainable mentally retarded children should direct the teacher toward helping these children develop an ability to follow directions, an ability to travel in the community, an ability to communicate regarding their needs, an ability to use fine and gross motor skills, and an ability to endure physical work from four to eight hours per day. This emphasis should be provided throughout the children's school age years with tasks which are in accord with their ages and levels of development.

One should recognize that some trainable mentally retarded children will not be able to work in a sheltered workshop, and that there will be a few who will develop the ability to work in a semi-competitive work environment. Therefore, when working with these children in a school setting, one must be flexible and understand that all of the children will not enter a single type of adult employment. Keeping these possibilities in mind should enable a teacher to realize that a few trainable mentally retarded children will require more intensive training in order to help them reach their potentials. For those children who, for any reason, are unable to hold employment in a sheltered environment, the instructional training program should focus on helping them to become useful in accomplishing meaningful tasks around the home. An important point for the parent, teacher, and other professional persons to keep in mind, is that the child should not be considered employable or unemployable based solely upon his I.Q. score. Therefore it becomes essential to provide a comprehensive training program for trainable mentally retarded children in such areas as self-help skills, language skills, social skills, and work habits.

School Programs for Educable Mentally Retarded Children

The school program for mildly (educable) mentally retarded children is structured somewhat differently from that for trainable mentally retarded children. The levels are usually described as follows: primary class (age range six to ten); intermediate class (age range ten to thirteen); junior high class (age range thirteen or fourteen to fifteen); and senior high class (age range fifteen or sixteen to twenty or twenty-one). (See A Guide for Teachers of Educable Mentally Handicapped Children, 1970.) The levels and age ranges will differ for grouping educable mentally retarded children when one is in a rural area or a small community. There may be smaller groups of children within one school building, and the children may have to be grouped into an elementary class with the age ranges from approximately eight to fourteen.

The authors believe that the philosophy and training of teachers of educable mentally retarded children should differ from that provided teachers of trainable mentally retarded children. As pointed out earlier in this chapter, the majority of mentally retarded children fall within the educable or mild range of retardation. Therefore, classes for these children will be more common in the public schools than classes for trainable mentally retarded children. Educable mentally retarded children are capable of reaching higher levels of performance in all levels of functioning; and the teacher should be prepared to work with these children to help them achieve whatever functioning capacity they may have. Children who are educable will also be more capable of finding and holding jobs in competitive employment fields; and should, therefore, be prepared for the higher levels of responsibility which will be demanded of them.

If training for this group of children is provided early and is appropriate to their needs, several of these children may be candidates for the regular classroom program on a part-time or full-time basis. In brief, working with these children in the classroom presents a challenge to the teacher, because he must provide a program that will benefit the children to such an extent that they will be prepared for regular classroom functioning if they happen to possess this level of functioning. In essence, this means the instructional program provided by a special education teacher must focus on specific objectives, and involve the children in learning. The role of a special education teacher of educable mentally retarded children should never be considered an easy one within the field of teaching, or a position in which all the teacher has to do is "to take care of" the children.

The training of educable mentally retarded children within the classroom must focus on the same skills as those applicable for the trainable mentally retarded. In other words, it is important to develop alike skills in these children; however the potential development is greater, will be more progressive and will reach much higher levels with the educable mentally retarded. According to Telford and

Sawrey (1967), this group will need training with a teacher who will have objectives that focus on the following areas of development: perceptual-motor, language, social skills, academics, work habits, prevocational skills, practical living skills, and vocational skills. The primary objectives in providing educational programs for educable mentally retarded children is to help them become functional adult citizens in the areas of family living, employment, homemaking, good citizenship, and self-understanding (A Program of Education for Exceptional Children in Oklahoma, 1971).

Work-Study Programs

Because employment is one of the main objectives in the education of mildly retarded children, a large number of school systems have established work-study programs. Work-study programs are relatively new program developments within the field of special education, and these classes have grown tremendously since the early 1960s. There are many variations in work-study programs throughout the United States. Some programs operate essentially with the services of one teacher, who may be referred to as a teacher-coordinator or a vocational teacher. In other programs, the personnel involved are numerous and include such positions as a vocational rehabilitation counselor, a job evaluator, a job placement specialist, a psychologist, a speech therapist, and a teacher. A large majority of these programs are established with the cooperation of the state vocational rehabilitation agency either through a formal contract agreement or by means of a system of using vocational rehabilitation as an appropriate referral agency.

Work-study programs are primarily concerned with the employability of the students. The students will generally receive an academic program for half a school day and a work program for the other portion of the day. The morning session may consist of the academic subjects and the afternoon session may be work-oriented. It is the teacher's responsibility to coordinate the vocational rehabilitation services, to help find job placements for his students, and to teach the academic subjects. For a brief historical review of work-study programs for the educable mentally retarded, the reader is referred to Kokaska (1968).

School programs which are provided for educable mentally retarded children are viewed as terminal programs, because the children will generally not pursue further formal education. Therefore, it is imperative that these children be educated and trained to the greatest extent possible during their school years. There has even been an emphasis on including aspects of the work-study program in an elementary school program for the mildly retarded. This emphasis has focused on the development of positive attitudes toward work and learning the concept of being a worker, as well as other types of skill and attitude development (Allen and Cross 1967). Any elementary teacher of educable mentally retarded children should seriously consider adapting these concepts into his training program.

In addition, all teachers of retarded children should be prepared to develop programs which will enhance the vocational potential of these children, and assist the children to prepare for adult life. Cohen (1972) has suggested that teacher education programs should involve the placement of future teachers of the retarded in the communities where the children live. This type of placement would be for the purpose of gaining first-hand experience and information relative to the children's current life styles, what his community resources are, what his children's parents do for a livelihood, and to learn ways in which the team concept can be used to combat the problems of mental retardation. Through a separate and distinct field station the teacher could be prepared to learn how to function within the child's existing community and how to aid in the total rehabilitation program for the mentally retarded.

Work study programs have also recently taught mentally retarded students how to implement simple behavior modification approaches to improve their acceptance in school and on the job. Retarded children were taught techniques such as how to make positive statements to regular classroom teachers and how to avoid students who responded to them in a negative manner (Rosenberg 1973). This training was provided in one-to-one and group settings and gave the junior high-age youngsters ample opportunities to "test" their new skills before applying them in regular classrooms and on the job. The results of the project have indicated that retarded youngsters can learn to change attitudes and learn how to react toward their environments in a positive manner.

Residential Facilities for the Mentally Retarded

Residential facilities for the mentally retarded are probably the oldest types of programs offered within the United States for this group of children. At the turn of the century the program within this type of facility placed primary emphasis on providing care for the mentally retarded. Admission criteria were extremely lax and there was not much chance for children to be returned to the community with appropriate types of training for community living. Of course, in recent years the criteria for admission and the training programs have become more appropriate to the needs of the children (Jordan 1966).

For a brief but excellent review of basic facts regarding residential facilities for the mentally retarded, the reader is referred to Butterfield (1969). This source discusses the need for residential facilities, the cost involved in operating the programs, the population of the retarded who are served in facilities, and the training of the staff of the residential facility.

Programs offered within residential facilities have changed drastically since the mid 1960s. In a majority of residential facilities, vocational training and evaluation centers have been incorporated as an essential feature of the total training program. The provision of a vocational training and evaluation center within a residential facility should have several objectives. One of the objectives is to evaluate and train those children who are capable of returning to the community and to return them, as soon as it is feasible, with saleable skills. Another objective of the vocational training and evaluation center is to improve the skills of the resident so that he may perform higher levels of work within the residential setting.

One of the authors has visited many residential facilities throughout the southeastern United States having vocational training and evaluation centers that have successfully trained retarded individuals, returning to the community those who could feasibly be sent back. Several of these institutions have established the use of a quarterway house on the campus of the residential facility. The quarterway house is a cottage which has been set aside for those residents who are preparing to return to the community. When the residents are selected for vocational training and evaluation, they are moved into the quarterway house and must gradually assume more and more responsibility for themselves. With supervision, they learn the skills which are necessary for keeping themselves clean, keeping their quarters clean, washing and ironing their own clothes, and even in some instances, preparing their own meals. This training is for the purpose of helping the individual become capable of caring for himself in the community. If he can perform successfully in a quarterway house, then the indication is that he can also do the same in the community. The use of a quarterway house is an efficient method of determining the extent to which an individual will be able to develop and maintain a degree of independence.

Residential facilities are also developing short-term training for the more capable trainable mentally retarded individuals, so that they may remain at home during the major portion of a calendar year. The short-term training involves admitting the individual to the residential facility for a period of approximately three months, and providing him with specific types of training in areas such as self-help skills, grooming, controlling his own behavior, learning appropriate social skills, and learning to be more effective in his communication. At the same time the child is being trained, his parents are also being trained to help the family with certain management problems in the home. This trend in residential facilities will provide services to many children, who are currently on a waiting list to be admitted to the institution, but do not need full time placement. These services will also enable parents to improve their skills in working with their own child, develop a better understanding of their child; and as a result the child should also increase his level of functioning.

As more professionals view the residential facility as a program which can offer training for retarded children instead of providing merely custodial care, residential facilities will continue to improve in the comprehensiveness and appropriateness of training and evaluation. The institutional setting will then become recognized as an important community service for children who need a program of short-term intensive training and boarding.

Community Services

In association with residential facilities two services are becoming more widely offered within several communities for retarded children. These services are the halfway house or boarding home and the sheltered workshop.

The Halfway House. The halfway house is an extension of the quarterway house which is becoming popular within the residential facility. The halfway house is a facility in the community which offers closely supervised community living for the retarded individual. The authors' experiences with halfway houses indicate that a majority of these services are offered in cooperation with the state division of vocational rehabilitation. The halfway house is a home which has been renovated to serve the function of a boarding home. Several young adults who have been returned to the community from a residential facility live within the halfway house; and usually a married couple live in the home to serve as parents for the young people. The individuals who have returned to the community have been placed on jobs and gradually assume responsibility for themselves. They generally pay partial room and board upon first entering the halfway house and after a period of approximately six to eight months they are paying full room and board. As they gain self-confidence and maintain their jobs, they are released from the halfway house to find their private living quarters and manage for themselves within the community. The halfway house program has been successful and has been appropriate for many young people who are mentally retarded and cannot, for one or more reasons, return to their own communities.

The Boarding Home. The boarding home is much the same as the halfway house with one exception: it may, in several communities, be an extension of or one step beyond the halfway house. In other words, after a young adult has indicated that he can maintain a job and be responsible for himself in the community, he may move from the halfway house to a boarding home. The boarding home requires that he pay his own way. However, the boarding home may be subsidized by vocational rehabilitation; and, thus, require less cost for room and board from the individual than he would be required to pay in a private facility.

Sheltered Workshops. Sheltered workshops have also been established within the community as an extension of the services of a residential facility. One may also find sheltered workshops on the campus of a residential facility for those individuals who are capable of performing work, but need a sheltered living environment. According to *Sheltered Workshops—a Handbook* (1966), prepared by the National Association of Sheltered Workshops and Homebound Programs, a sheltered workshop may be defined as:

> A work-oriented rehabilitation facility with a controlled working environment and individual vocational goals which utilize work experience and related services for assisting the handicapped person to progress toward normal living and a productive vocational status.

This handbook is an excellent resource for any individual or group who may be contemplating the establishment of a sheltered workshop within a community. It is most comprehensive with respect to planning, programs, operations, staffing, labor laws, and workshop standards.

As the reader will note from the definition given above, sheltered workshops are usually for handicapped persons in general rather than for handicapped persons of any one type. Upon visiting a sheltered workshop, a person may find many different types of handicapped individuals receiving an opportunity to work and be a contributing member of society. There are several hundred sheltered workshops in the United States today, and these facilities are providing a work and training station for many young people who are unable to compete in the larger labor market. The establishment of sheltered workshops has provided a means for many young retarded individuals to return to community living, having found a place of employment to which they could go and be successful.

Leisure Time

Programs for leisure time activities which are within the individual and the economical capabilities of retarded persons are a necessity. All children, including the mentally retarded, need opportunities to participate in programs of leisure. With the advent of shorter working hours for many workers, participation in leisure time activities will become more of a necessity in the future. Of course, this particular area is partially the responsibility of the special education teacher, because he must provide an instructional program which will enhance the development of appropriate leisure time activities for mentally retarded children. As the mentally retarded individuals approach secondary school age, they should receive specific information regarding leisure time activities in which they can participate during their young adulthood and later adult years. The younger mentally retarded individuals should also receive training within the instructional program which will help them to develop interests in leisure time activities and skills which they can use in participating in these types of activities. During school-age years, the retarded youngsters should be directed to community agencies that will include them in leisure time activities. Several communities have formed boy and girl scout troops which are specifically for mentally retarded children. Other recreational activities which are sponsored during the summer months by the city, by a school recreational department, or by a voluntary agency should be encouraged to include or provide specific programs for mentally retarded children.

Parents of Mentally Retarded Children

Parent Awareness

Parents who have mentally retarded children will have difficulties in coming to grips with the fact that they have a retarded child. Generally, the more severe the child's retardation, the greater the difficulties the parents will have in facing the fact of mental retardation. Some parents may easily recognize that their child's severe

retardation is obvious, because it may be manifested by hydrocepha-
lus, mongolism, etc. Therefore, they realize quickly that the situation
is severe and that they cannot cling to hopes for drastic changes. It is
somewhat like the obvious difference between a broken leg and a
muscle strain. Parents do not want to have a defective child and if
the ability of the child is severely affected, the parents may need
continuous support and guidance in helping them to accept their
child.

Of course, acceptance of the retarded child by his parents and
his family will depend, to some extent, on the socioeconomic status
of the parents. If the parents are within the lower socioeconomic
group of the population; and they have a child who is educably
mentally retarded; they may not recognize that he is functioning at a
level which is lower than the rest of the siblings in the family. Therefore, being told that the child is mentally retarded may have very
little, if any, effect. In the higher socioeconomic group of the population, the fact that a child is mentally retarded will have a greater
impact, because the parents will readily understand that their child
will not be able to achieve their aspirations for him because of his
retardation. The reactions on the part of parents who are within
different levels of socioeconomic structures have nothing to do with
the love of the parents for the child. The differences in reactions is
due primarily to the variance in the expectations of parents. Parents
within the higher socioeconomic groups have higher expectations for
their children, because of the level of functioning which they have
been able to reach for themselves. Probably the main point which
must be remembered when attempting to help parents function with
their retarded child is that constructive efforts will not begin until
the parents accept the fact that the child is mentally retarded.

Farber (1968) refers to this process as a redefinition of the
child. In other words, once the parents have been told that they have
a child who is mentally retarded, they must redefine all of their
child's characteristics and functioning before the process of acceptance begins. Prior to this time, parents may continuously go from
one resource to another attempting to find a person or an agency
who will tell them that their child is not mentally retarded, and that
certain activities or procedures may be undertaken which will cause
the child to function in a normal way. The process of going from one
agency to another, and avoiding the fact that their child is mentally
retarded, may be a result of the manner in which the parents were
first told of the retardation. The acceptance of their retarded child is
referred to as a process for the parents, for as the child continues to

grow and mature, new problems will develop and new redefinitions will have to be formulated. For example, it may become very difficult for parents to accept their teenage child as a retarded child when he continues to grow physically and matures physically in a way that strongly resembles the growth and development of a normal child. Therefore, acceptance of their retarded child will not be a one-time event for the parents. Functioning with their retarded child will be a continuous process and as the parents continue to redefine their child, they will also have to redefine continuously their own roles as parents.

Many reactions on the part of parents may be exhibited when they are first told that their child is mentally retarded. They may immediately reject the definition which has been given to them, and attempt to ignore the fact that their child is having difficulties in maturational or adjustment processes. This stage will usually not last long if their child is severely handicapped, because the problems of the child will not go away through parents' ignoring the obvious. As soon as the parents *begin* to realize the retardation of their child, parent growth may continue if they receive periodic support as the child continues to grow and mature.

Of course, the majority of problems in the acceptance of a mentally retarded child takes place when the child is severely, profoundly, or moderately mentally retarded. As Farber explains, the fact of having a mentally retarded child in a family in the upper middle class is viewed as a crisis which is tragic, and in a family in the lower socioeconomic class this fact would be viewed as a role or organization crisis. Thus, the impact of a mentally retarded child on parents and the total family will depend upon the socioeconomic status of the family, the severity of the child's retardation, the child's sex, the child's age at the time his condition is identified, the family's orientation with respect to organization, and the time in the parents' lives when the retarded child is born (Farber).

Parental acceptance of their retarded child is a factor which school personnel must consider, because school programs must provide for the moderately retarded. In several communities, school programs for trainable retarded children are established as special schools, because a school building may be designated as the building in which the majority or all of the moderately mentally retarded children will receive their education. This procedure means that many parents of trainable mentally retarded children will go directly for help to the school program, the school principal, or the classroom teacher. Through parental contacts of this nature, school personnel will begin to realize the impact of mental retardation on the various parents; and should recognize their roles as professional persons in helping these parents to develop acceptance and understanding of their children.

Parent Counseling

Contact with parents of mentally retarded children in the school setting will require teachers, principals, and school counselors to develop skills which will enable them to conduct parent counseling. In fact, each time a teacher meets with a mother, a father, or both parents to discuss their child's school progress, the teacher will be conducting parent counseling. Educators must learn to work with parents effectively to help them to understand their child's school work. Parents also will often seek assistance from school personnel in order to be better able to cope with their child at home. If asked for this type of assistance, school personnel must remember that the child is the responsibility of the parents, and that the child will be in the home for much longer periods of time than he will be in school. Teachers should be careful to provide realistic assistance that will help parents work through their adjustment problems, and not to give them rigid child-care guidelines to follow. In brief, don't talk to the parents as if the child were not their child, and don't indicate to the parents that the school intends to assume major responsibility for their child. The parents may want you to be frank with them about their child's learning problems, but in other domestic areas they may be seeking guidelines and assistance rather than the advice of an "expert" from the school.

A few programs have been established which have as their main objective the training of parents of mentally retarded children. These programs have concentrated on developing better communication with the child and helping the child to develop his language, social, and physical skills. These types of programs may be beyond the role of the public school. However, if such a program does exist in the community, school personnel should be aware of it, and if necessary refer the parents to this source.

If at all possible, parent counseling should include both parents. This procedure would help to avoid any misinterpretations in the relaying of information from one parent to the other; and help the parents to work together to develop an improved home environment for their child. Both parents may not be able to come to the school during school hours, but this should not prevent the teacher, principal, or counselor from making one or two home visits during the school year. Home visits should be accepted as an integral part of the special education program in the area of mental retardation. By making home visits the classroom teacher will have an opportunity to meet both parents, visit in the child's home to learn about family relationships, and to learn about the emphasis which is placed on educational activities in the home. A new teacher should probably contact his school principal about home visits prior to making any visits. Teachers and parents should understand that a teacher making home visits is doing so for the purposes of improving the child's instructional program by developing a more thorough understanding of the child. A home visit should never be made to satisfy a teacher's curiosity about the child's living conditions. If parent understanding and communication, or improvement of the child's instructional program is not the purpose of a home visit; then home visits should not be made.

An inexperienced person in the field of counseling should not undertake an intensive counseling program with parents of retarded children, because of the background of skill and training which is necessary in order for one to be successful in this type of endeavor. Again, one of the main roles of the classroom teacher, school principal, or school counselor in this particular function is to know of possible community resources and to be able to refer parents who may be in need of these services. For further information in the area of providing counseling for parents of mentally retarded children, the reader is referred to Farber or Jordan.

Parent Groups

The formation of a parent group for parents of the mentally retarded has taken place in the majority of the larger communities within the United States. These groups usually become a part of the National Association for Retarded Children (NARC), and therefore, become known as the local association for retarded children (ARC).

In many cases, the local ARC will form a school program for preschool trainable mentally retarded children and will promote appropriate types of activities for these children within the community. The parents and professionals who become members of the local ARC will also serve as a group to promote needed legislation within a state for all retarded children. These groups have been most effective in helping to establish programs, better community awareness of retarded children, and comprehensive legislative programs.

Becoming a member of a local ARC will be an additional means through which parents may receive support and understanding about their retarded child. Parent counseling may take place during some of the meetings and this is an additional community resource for parents of mentally retarded children.

Published Materials for Use With the Mentally Retarded

In recent years many publishing companies have printed materials which are suitable for use with mentally retarded children. A teacher may find resources through publishing companies which were not in existence as recently as the early 1960s. The authors' experiences in teaching mentally retarded children took place during the years when teaching materials were scarce. Teachers today have many materials available to them, but they need to be very concerned with the suitability of these materials.

An excellent guideline source for teaching materials for mentally retarded children is *Instructional Resources for Teachers of the Culturally Disadvantaged and Exceptional* (1969). Teachers may also use their Regional Instructional Materials Centers as a resource for materials. A list of the location of these centers may be obtained from the national office of the Council for Exceptional Children in Arlington, Virginia. The use of these centers is restricted to special education teachers who are employed in school programs.

The authors have included a sample of published materials below for a teacher's use. This list includes the author, name of the material, publishing company, year and price (although the price may not be current).

List of Resources

American Association for Health, Physical Education and Recreation. *A Resource Guide in Sex Education for the Mentally Retarded.* Washington, D.C.: AAHPER (or New York: Sex Information and Education Council of the United States, 1855 Broadway and 61st Street), 1969. Single copy free upon request to publisher.

Arena, John L., ed. *Teaching Educationally Handicapped Children.* San Rafael, Calif.: Academic Therapy Publications, 1967. $2.95.

Brickman, William W., and Lehrer, Stanley, eds. *Education and the Many Faces of the Disadvantaged.* New York: John Wiley and Sons, Inc., 1972. Price unknown.

Cratty, Bryant J. *Development Sequences of Perceptual-Motor Tasks.* Freeport, Long Island, N.Y.: Educational Activities, Inc., 1967. $2.95 (020135).

Egg, Dr. Maria. *Educating the Child Who is Different.* New York: John Day Co., 1968. $4.50.

Karnes, Merle B. *Helping Young Children Develop Language Skills: A Book of Activities.* Washington, D.C.: Council for Exceptional Children, 1968. Price unknown.

Kirk, Samuel A. *Diagnosis and Remediation of Psycholinguistic Disabilities.* Urbana, Ill.: University of Illinois Press, 1966. Price unknown. (020036)

Kirk, Samuel A., and Kirk, Winifred D. *Psycholinguistic Learning Disabilities: Diagnosis and Remediation.* Urbana, Ill.: University of Illinois Press, 1971. $2.45, ppbk.

Programming for the Mentally Retarded. Washington, D. C.: American Association for Health, Physical Education, and Recreation, 1968. $2.00.

Smith, Robert M., ed. *Teacher Diagnosis of Educational Difficulties.* Columbus, Ohio: Charles E. Merrill, 1969. $5.95.

Thomas, Janet K. *Teaching Arithmetic to Mentally Retarded Children.* Minneapolis, Minn.: T.S. Denison and Co., Inc., 1968. Price unknown.

–––. *Teaching Language Arts to Mentally Retarded Children.* Minneapolis, Minn.: T.S. Denison and Co., Inc., 1968. Price unknown.

–––. *Teaching Reading to Mentally Retarded Children.* Minneapolis, Minn.: T.S. Denison and Co., Inc., 1968. $3.98.

Wagner, Guy, and Dorlan Mork. *Free Learning Materials for Classroom Use.* Cedar Falls, Iowa: Extension Service, State College of Iowa, 1967. $1.50.

Witty, Paul A., ed. *Educationally Retarded and Disadvantaged.* Chicago: National Society for the Study of Education, distributed by University of Chicago Press, 1967. Price unknown.

Bibliography

A Guide for Teachers of Educable Mentally Handicapped Children, vols. 1 and 2. Oklahoma State Department of Education and Oklahoma Curriculum Improvement Commission, 1970.

A Guide for Teachers of Trainable Mentally Retarded Children. Oklahoma State Department of Education and Oklahoma Curriculum Improvement Commission,1971.

A Program of Education for Exceptional Children in Oklahoma. Oklahoma State Department of Education, Special Education and Oklahoma Curriculum Improvement Commission, 1971.

Allen, Amy A., and Cross, Jacque L. "Work-Study for the Retarded–The Elementary School Years." *Education and Training of the Mentally Retarded* 2, no.1 (February 1967).

Anderson, Robert M., Hemenway, Robert E.; and Anderson, Janet W. *Instructional Resources for Teachers of the Culturally Disadvantaged and Exceptional.* Springfield, Ill.: Charles C. Thomas, Publisher, 1969.

Benoit, E. "Toward a New Definition of Mental Retardation." *American Journal of Mental Deficiency* 63 (1959).

Butterfield, Earl C. "Basic Facts About Public Residential Facilities for the Mentally Retarded," from *Changing Patterns in Residential Services for the Mentally Retarded.* Edited by R.B. Kugel and W. Wolfensberger. President's Committee on Mental Retardation Monograph, Washington, D.C. 1969. Also published in *Mental Retardation: Readings and Resources,* 2d ed., Jerome H. Rothstein, ed. New York: Holt, Rinehart and Winston, Inc., 1971.

Chiappone, Anthony D., and Libby, Bruce P. "Visual Problems of the Educable Mentally Retarded." *Education and Training of the Mentally Retarded* 7, no. 4 (December 1972).

Cohen, Julius S. "Vocational Rehabilitation Concepts in the Education of Teachers of the Retarded." *Education and Training of the Mentally Retarded* 7, no.4 (December 1972).

Doll, E.A., "Definition of Mental Retardation." *Training School Bulletin* 37, (1941).

Farber, Bernard. *Mental Retardation: Its Social Context and Social Consequences.* Boston: Houghton Mifflin Co., 1968.

Heber, Rick. "A Manual on Terminology and Classification in Mental Retardation." *Monograph Supplement to the American Journal of Mental Deficiency,* 64, 1959.

Hutt, Max, and Gibby, Robert. *The Mentally Retarded Child: Development, Education, and Treatment,* 2d ed. Boston: Allyn and Bacon, 1965.

Jordan, Thomas E. *The Mentally Retarded,* 2d ed. Columbus, Ohio: Charles E. Merrill Publishing Co., 1966.

Kokaska, Charles J. "Secondary Education for the Retarded: A Brief Historical Review," *Education and Training of the Mentally Retarded* 3, no. 1 (February 1968).

Polser, Charles M., et al., *Mental Retardation: Diagnosis and Treatment.* New York: Harper & Row, Publisher, Inc., 1967.

Robinson, Halbert B., and Robinson, Nancy M. *The Mentally Retarded Child: Psychological Approach.* New York: McGraw-Hill, Inc., 1965.

Rosenberg, Harry E., "On Teaching the Modification of Employer and Employee Behavior." *Teaching Exceptional Children* 5, no. 3 (Spring 1973).

Shane, Don G. "The Role of Special Education in the Habilitation of the Mentally Retarded." *Education and Training of the Mentally Retarded* 2, no. 1 (February 1967).

Sheltered Workshops–A Handbook. Washington, D.C.: National Association of Sheltered Workshops and Homebound Programs, Inc., 2d ed., 1966.

Telford, Charles W., and Sawrey, James M. *The Exceptional Individual.* Englewood Cliffs, N.J.: Prentice-Hall, Inc., 1967.

Tredgold, A. F. *A Textbook of Mental Deficiency,* 10th ed. Baltimore: The Williams & Wilkins Co., 1963.

MENTALLY RETARDED CHILDREN
Study Sheet #1

1. Use one of the references listed in the chapter or another source and write a description of a trainable mentally retarded child who is a mongoloid.

   a. Physical characteristics

   b. Types of mongolism

   c. Learning characteristics

MENTALLY RETARDED CHILDREN
Study Sheet #2

1. Provide the following information with respect to a child who has Phenylketonuria (PKU).

   a. The cause of PKU

   b. Prevention and diagnosis of PKU

   c. Symptoms or characteristics of PKU

   d. Legislation, if any, relative to PKU in your state

MENTALLY RETARDED CHILDREN
Study Sheet #3

1. Write a brief summary of the factors relative to the diagnosis, classification, and prognosis of children who are educable mentally retarded.

   a. Diagnosis

   b. Classification

   c. Prognosis

MENTALLY RETARDED CHILDREN
Study Sheet #4

1. Write a brief summary of the factors relative to the child who is trainable mentally retarded.

   a. Diagnosis

   b. Classification

   c. Prognosis

'There must be some way
out of this place!'

3

Disadvantaged Children from Lower Socioeconomic Areas

INTRODUCTION

To find or formulate a single definition which would adequately describe all disadvantaged children would be an impossible task. Moreover, any attempt to do so could prove futile because many children would be examples of exceptions to the definition. Therefore, this discussion focuses on children who have experienced serious deprivations of one or more types during fetal development or early childhood—deprivations which caused severe limitations in their ability to learn or gain meaningful information from the environment. In essence, these children are born to mothers who have had little, poor, or no medical care during pregnancy, and/or mothers who have experienced severe dietary deficiencies during their pregnancies. Also included in the discussion are children who, born into families of lower socioeconomic status have not had appropriate maternal or paternal care, appropriate diets during early childhood, and/or adequate types of stimulation to prepare them for school experiences.

The particular group of children who may be described as disadvantaged are disadvantaged in that they cannot participate fully or meaningfully in the normal school environment, nor can these children be expected to learn in the manner which is typical of most children—the usual way. This does not mean that these children cannot learn. They most definitely can learn—and profit from educational services. It is the task of educators, psychologists, sociologists, and other professionals to learn more about these children and to implement programs and techniques which will enhance this learning. The positive characteristics of the environments and culture of these children must be learned and accentuated.

Educators should never pity or "look down on" disadvantaged children. If one assumes that these children are inferior and have a lower status position; then one's approach is negative and in many instances the child's reactions will unwittingly become negative. To view these children as the "cannots" of society will perpetuate cultural disparity and discrimination, and the children who are disadvantaged will continue to exhibit severe learning deficiencies and social difficulties.

Children who are disadvantaged come primarily from families who live in poverty. These statistics may be difficult to accept but there are approximately 11 million children in the United States who live in poverty. What criterion should be used to determine poverty? With 1974 wages and prices, the criterion may be difficult to pinpoint, but certainly the situation is becoming worse rather than improving. Can a family of four live adequately on a minimum income of $5,000.00 a year? Obviously not. The barest needs of a family of four would undoubtedly exceed the provisions of a $5,000.00 a year minimum. Budget management will help with these families but will by no means totally alleviate their financial difficulties.

A tremendous impact to improve the multiple problems of the disadvantaged is the objective, which cannot be met without a concentrated effort in energy, time, and money as well as innovations which have not yet been tried to any great extent. If educators and other professional personnel are truly concerned about the plight of the disadvantaged, then educational programs will be devised which will improve children's opportunities to learn and function in society.

In 1970 approximately 3 percent (6.4 million) of the population was classified as mentally retarded. Of the nation's mentally retarded, approximately three-fourths are found in low socioeconomic areas. Estimated incidence of mental retardation in the inner-city neighborhood is 7 percent or higher (the national average is 2 to 3 percent). Deprivation of adequate opportunities to learn and other environmental factors may adversely influence the intellectual development of the children in these lower socioeconomic areas.

The following information is concerned with the areas of prematurity, nutrition, and education in low socioeconomic areas as they relate to mental retardation and learning problems. It is difficult to separate the etiological effects relative to genetic and environmental factors because of the constant interaction between heredity and environment. Therefore, the authors' investigation is limited to a descriptive research of environmental causes and means of prevention of mental retardation and learning problems in low socioeconomic areas. The following definitions reflect a brief description of the areas of concern.

1. Mental Retardation: refers to specific intellectual deficits which originate during the developmental and postnatal periods, and are associated with impairment in the child's adaptive behavior.
2. Learning Problems: those manifestations of academic, social, and behavioral inabilities to perform functionally in a "normal" environment, because of one's disadvantaged environment and lack of experiential involvement with proper diet and material care.
3. Intelligence: cognitive behaviors which reflect an individual's capacity to solve problems with insight, to adapt himself to new situations, to think abstractly, and to profit from his experience.
4. Socioeconomic: a combination of social and economic factors (income and social position considered as a single factor).
5. Environment: all the conditions, circumstances, and influences surrounding and affecting the development of an organism or group of organisms (often contrasted with heredity).
6. Heredity: the transmission from parents to offspring of certain characteristics.

ASSUMPTIONS

1. There is a high incidence of mental retardation and learning problems in lower socioeconomic areas.
2. I.Q., as measured by a given test, is subject to change if the life or environment of the individual is changed.
3. There is a constant interaction between heredity and environment.

Prematurity and Mental Retardation

Premature birth appears to be one of the major causes of mental retardation. Koch (1966) indicates that approximately 15 to 20 percent of all cases of mental retardation are associated with prematurity. Cooke (1964) reports that in the United States, prematurity occurs in 7 percent of all births, but runs as high as 12 percent in some communities. Robinson and Robinson (1965) cite Pasamanick (1959) who found, when he compared Negro and Caucasian groups in Baltimore, that the incidence of prematurity was twice as great in the Negro group as in the upper portion of the Caucasian group (11 percent as compared to 5 percent), while Caucasian infants born to mothers in lower socioeconomic groups suffered an intermediate risk of prematurity of 8 percent. Hardy (1965) indicates that social factors, such as socioeconomic status have been found to play a role in the incidence of premature births and there appears to be an inverse relationship between socioeconomic level and the incidence of premature delivery.

The term prematurity is a misnomer. Many children are born fully developed before the normal nine-month period of gestation. On the other hand, some babies fail to grow properly and are poorly developed even when delivered after a full-term pregnancy. For this reason, pediatricians now base the diagnosis of prematurity on the baby's weight, regardless of when he is born. The baby under 5½ pounds is considered to be premature or a "low-birth-weight infant" (Thompson, "Protecting the Preemie," 1968).

Maternal Factors Related to Prematurity

Many maternal factors are related to prematurity, such as alcoholism, heavy smoking, tuberculosis, diabetes, and kidney disease. The age of the mother is one factor in determining the likelihood of premature delivery. Hardy reports that Battaglia, Frazier, and Hellegevers (1963) published results of a study on approximately seven hundred fifty juvenile patients followed in the Women's Clinic of the Johns Hopkins Hospital. Approximately 25 percent of the girls who were fourteen years of age or less at the time they became pregnant had a premature delivery compared to approximately 16 percent prematured births for girls fifteen to nineteen. It has also been found that the more children a mother has had, the greater are the chances of her next child being premature. "If there is too rapid a succession of pregnancies, the mother does not have adequate time to replenish her depleted nutritional and emotional needs" (Thompson 1968). In addition to all these factors, the economic circumstances of the mother are important, inasmuch as poverty and prematurity apparently go together.

Developmental Picture of Premature Infants

A developmental picture can be drawn for most premature infants. Jordan (1966) relates that in the first two years, the picture will be one of delayed development, a condition proportional to the degree of prematurity and lower social-class standing. Walking and talking are less likely to be present at the usual point in the first twenty-four months of life; and at three years, evidence of cognitive impairment as well as perceptual motor limitations may be present. Harper, Fischer, and Rider are cited as saying that between ages three and five, depressed intellectual and neurological signs can often be found, and by the age of six, perceptual-motor dysfunction, immaturity of speech, as well as comprehension and reasoning difficulties are often present (Hardy).

Correlation Between Prematurity and I. Q.

The possibility of a correlation between low birth weight and low I.Q. has been investigated. Hardy reports that intelligence tests administered at the ages of three and five years by Harper, Fischer, and Rider (1959) to approximately one thousand premature infants and a like number of normal controls, revealed that in the group weighing 1,500 gms. or less at birth, there was a higher incidence of defective and dull children and fewer above-average children, than in the group of larger premature infants or in the group of controls who weighed 2,501 gms. or above at birth. Also, the larger premature infants were intermediate in performance. The Negro children in all weight groups performed significantly lower than the Caucasian children in comparable weight groups. Waisman (1966) reports that in premature infants weighing 1,500 gms. or less, Lubchenco et al. (1963) showed that I.Q. was inversely related to birth weight and they felt that poor performance in school can be related to prematurity. Dr. Heinz Berendes of the National Institute of Neurological Diseases and Blindness (Thompson 1968) reported that the I.Q.'s of four-year-old Caucasian youngsters who weighed less than three pounds at birth averaged 94 as compared with I.Q.'s of 105 for the four-year-olds born at normal weight. Waisman (1966) reports, however, that McDonald (1964) showed that children weighing not more than four pounds were mentally inferior to the general population. Whereas it was true that some premature females weighing less than three pounds had lower I.Q. scores than those weighing between three and four pounds, this same finding could not be confirmed for the males.

Long Term Effects of Prematurity

The long-term effects of prematurity can be illustrated in the presence of school problems. Jordan cites several studies which revealed a significant relationship between prematurity and enrollment in special education classes. Other symptoms found in classroom investigations were pervasive disorders such as reading problems, poor concentration, motor disabilities, shyness and immaturity. Hardy reports that the result of Douglas' Study (1960) on some six hundred Caucasian children in England revealed that, based on behavior ratings by teachers, children in the premature group presented more difficulties in school and generated more complaints than those in the mature group; and that less than half of the premature children, as compared with the controls, passed the qualifying examination for admission to secondary school.

Koch (1966) expresses concern that the women most likely to bear damaged children—the economically and culturally disadvantaged in our population—must be reached if prematurity is to be reduced. Many of these women depend entirely on public medical and health services for prenatal and postnatal care. "Protecting the Preemie" (1968) reports that in 1964 a $30 million dollar program to start pilot clinics to find and treat economically disadvantaged mothers was initiated in the United States. Operating in some eighty hospitals throughout the country, these clinics concentrated on expectant mothers suffering from anemia, chronic illnesses, and other factors linked to prematurity. So far the program has reached only a fraction of the mothers who need it. Of the estimated 1 million babies delivered to "poverty" mothers in 1970, only 83,000 were cared for in these clinics.

Social class should be recognized as one of the great concomitants of prematurity. If positive preventive measures are not taken, we can expect to see lower social classes continue to produce a disproportionate number of premature infants; and consequently, contribute a greater number of mentally retarded and learning disabled children to our society.

Malnutrition and Poverty

Malnutrition and undernutrition are also major causes of mental retardation. One of the most important causes of malnutrition is poverty. Upwards of 25 million Americans live on incomes of less than $3,300 a year for a family of four, and half of these Americans—including some five million children—live in households having annual income of $2,200 or less. To maintain an adequate diet such families would have to spend over one-half of their income for food. A preliminary report of the National Nutrition Survey, in which the United States Public Health Service collected nutrition data on 70,000 persons, found evidence of malnutrition in an unexpectedly large percentage of low income families, with up to a third of the children studied showing malnutrition-associated characteristics similar to those of undernourished populations in some of the world's poorest nations (The Decisive Decade MR70, 1970).

Nutrition and Neurointegrative Development

The time at which malnutrition occurs is crucial to the further development of the child. The earlier the malnutrition the more severe the effects and the more likely that they cannot be reversed. It is now known that the prenatal period and first six months of life are the most important in terms of proper nutrition (The Decisive Decade MR70). According to Bakan (1970) undernutrition from birth to twenty-one days produces a persistent and permanent reduction in brain weight. The earlier the malnutrition the more severe its effects, and the less likely the recovery. Undernutrition also results in specific degeneration within brain cells; again, the earlier the restriction, the more severe the damage. Bakan (1970) indicates that Winick (1969) felt that malnutrition curtails the normal rate of increase in head circumference. He believed that this reduced head circumference of the malnourished children, especially during the first six months of life, accurately reflected the reduced number of cells present in their brains.

Bakan also reported animal studies which have shown that during the preweaning period in the rat an enormous amount of chemical change takes place within the brain and that the preweaning is the time when the brain is most sensitive to the detrimental effects of undernutrition. She discovered that the brain of the mature rat which was malnourished during this period was not only physically smaller but showed degenerative cell changes. It was found that when the deprivation occurred early in infancy, these changes were irreversible, while the effects of later deprivation were reversible through proper feeding. Other animal studies reported by the Decisive Decade MR70 have proven that malnutrition or undernutrition of the mother and offspring at certain critical prebirth and postbirth periods of rapid growth can impair both physical and mental development; can cause permanent and irreversible retardation, regardless of the quality of later nutrition; and, are most harmful when they consist of a lack of specific nutrients such as certain essential vitamins, amino acids, or proteins. An examination of the brains of infants who had died of Maramus (a starvation-related condition marked by progressive emaciation) revealed that their brains' structure and characteristics were significantly altered and abnormal in the same ways as the brains of young animals which suffer from starvation.

Bakan reports that a series of studies by Cravioto and his associates (1966) in Mexico and Guatemala showed that the performance of children on psychological tests was related to nutritional factors, not to differences in personal hygiene, housing, income, or other social and economic variables. Those children who were exposed to severe early malnutrition exhibited perceptual defects as well as smaller body size; and the earlier the malnutrition, the more profound the psychological retardation. The most severe retardation seemed to occur in children under six months of age who were admitted to the hospital; and these children failed to improve even after 220 days of treatment. Children who were admitted later with the same socioeconomic background and the same severe malnutrition, but a different time of onset, did recover after prolonged rehabilitation. Cravioto et al. concluded that nutritional inadequacy may interfere with both the staging and the timing of development of the brain and of behavior.

Studies of animals have indicated that growth in all organs occurs in three phases: (1) hyperplasia, during which the number of cells increases; (2) hyperplasis and hypertrophy, during which the number of cells continues to increase and the size of the individual cells also increases; and (3) hypertrophy, where growth occurs only by increase in cell size (Cravioto et al.).

These studies suggest that during the phase of hyperplasia, malnutrition can interfere with cell division, resulting in fewer cells in the brain, which seems to have a permanent effect. Malnutrition during hypertrophy, however, results in smaller than normal cell size, which can be corrected by providing adequate nutrition. In humans, the brain grows most during the fetal period and by the end of the first year has assumed 70 percent of its adult weight. By the end of two years it is nearly complete in growth.

Relatively free from unfactored environmental contamination, are some studies made by Dr. Fernando Monckeberg of the University of Chile who reported the progress of fourteen children with severe marasmus. Those subjects were diagnosed at ages one month to five months, were treated for long periods, discharged and observed during visits to the out-patient department. As each child was discharged from the hospital, the mother was given twenty liters of free milk per month for each preschool child in her family. Three to six years later the children were clinically normal. Their height, head circumference, and intelligence quotients, however, were significantly lower than in Chilian children of the same age having no history of clinical malnutrition (Cravioto et al. 1966).

Retardation in physical growth and development is generally found to depend upon family dietary practices and on the occurence of infectious disease. As previously mentioned, it is not related to differences in housing facilities, personal hygiene, proportion of total income spent on food, or other indicators of social and economic status.

It is clear that under circumstances common to developing countries, malnutrition can interact with infection, heredity, and social factors to bring about physical and mental impairment. The social factors responsible are multiple and difficult to correct, but the elimination of malnutrition and infection among underprivileged populations is a feasible goal.

In industrialized countries a child's inadequate intellectual or social performance is the result of a complex interaction over a period of time, of genetic variables, and primarily nonnutritional factors in the social or cultural environment. But in developing countries, variations in educational and economic status and in beliefs and customs from family to family may be relatively small, and together with genetic differences, may actually be insignificant as determinants of intellectual performance, because the children are so greatly affected by problems of nutrition, and by infection (Profiles of Children 1970).

According to White (1971) the problem of malnutrition or undernourishment is responsible for poor health, high fatigue level, and insufficient learning. An additional factor related by White pertains to the high absenteeism of these children which also leads to insufficient or faulty learning. If corrective measures are not employed then many children who are disadvantaged will function as mentally retarded children all of their lives. There is no justification for allowing this gross waste of human potential.

Malnutrition and Pregnancy

"The relationship between diet in pregnancy and a healthy offspring has been widely studied. It was formerly believed that the baby was a parasite and could derive any nutrients it needed from the mother's body, but evidence now shows that if the mother has a deficient diet the fetus will suffer" (Inzer 1970). Furst (1970) feels that many children suffer malnutrition before birth because their mothers are poorly fed and poorly developed physically, receive inadequate medical care, or have had children too often.

One of the most intriguing findings reported by Bakan in this area of concern was that poor nutrition of the infant female may effect the development of her offspring many years later. Robinson and Robinson (1965) cite that Masland (1958) reported that Wolf and Drillien (1958) found a higher correlation between prematurity and the class of the mother's father than between prematurity and the economic class of the child's own father. Masland interpreted these results as indicating the possible influence of nutrition during the mother's childhood. He also pointed out that the mother's early nutritional habits would probably carry over into her marriage.

Naeye, Diener, Dellinger and Blane's (1969) study reported by Bakan (1970) identified undernutrition of poor urban mothers as the cause of the low birth-weight of their offspring (prematurity). They felt that since evidence has shown that both low birth-weight and a high infant mortality rate are more common in poor families, the finding that undernutrition appears to be the cause of prenatal growth retardation is an important one. In addition to being 15 percent smaller in body weight, the infants from poor families had irrelevant weights of such organs as the thymus, spleen, and liver. Inzer (1970) reports a study in rural Iowa which evaluated the dietary practices of 404 indigent pregnant women and the incidence of prematurity. Forty-four percent of the mothers were poorly nourished. The study concluded that the increase in prematurity was in direct proportion to the decrease in nutritional status. The lowest birth weight and the highest death rate in the neonatal period occurred among the infants of the most poorly nourished mothers.

Malnutrition, Growth of the Brain, and I.Q.

The nutrition of a mother is an important variable related to the intellectual performance of her children. Erickson (1967) as reported by Bakan found that when a vitamin supplement was given to pregnant and lactating women with poor nutritional environments the offspring at four years of age appeared to have an average I.Q. score eight points greater than the average score of the children whose mothers were given placeboes over the same period. Bakan reports that Kugelmass et al., as far back as 1944, demonstrated an increase in the I.Q. of both retarded and mentally normal children as a result of prolonged nutritional rehabilitation. The children, ranging in age from two to ten were divided into two groups: those who were malnourished, and those who were well-nourished. The malnourished retarded children gained ten I.Q. points and the normal children gained eighteen I.Q. points after a period of dietary improvement. In contrast, there was relatively little change in the score of the already well-nourished retarded and normal children.

Undernutrition of pigs and rats from birth to twenty-one days produces persistent and permanent reduction in brain weight. The earlier the malnutrition the more severe its effects and the less likely the recovery. Undernutrition also results in specific degeneration with brain cells; again, the earlier the restriction, the more severe the damage (Bakan 1970).

The effects of postnatal malnutrition on animals which have already suffered prenatal malnutrition are more marked than effects of either prenatal or postnatal deprivation separately. It seems the prenatal malnutrition made these animals more susceptible to post-natal undernutrition. If the deprivation occurs early in infancy, these changes are irreversible, while the effects of later deprivation may be reversed through proper feeding (Bakan).

Available evidence from human studies reinforces the findings of experiments with animals and suggests that early infancy is a critical period for the development of the brain. This is also the time when the brain is extremely vulnerable to the effects of malnutrition. Indirect measurements of the brain growth in humans show that malnutrition will curtail the normal rate of increase in head circum-ference, which accurately reflects the reduced number of cells present in the brain. When a fluid, similar to spinal fluid is used to fill the cavity between the brain and the skull, and a diffused light is used to make the fluid glow, a very small area is shown with normal children. But the malnutritioned child's entire brain case glows, from the forehead to the back of the head.

Follow-up tests of children restored to health showed that they achieved lower scores than children who had not suffered from malnutrition. Similarly, the malnourished children who exhibited reduced head circumference had lower I.Q.'s even after long-term follow-up (Bakan).

In addition to the negative impact of malnutrition on the growth rates and intersensory development of children Cravioto found a relationship between these aspects of development and infection. It has also been shown that certain infections in malnourished children may produce severe and prolonged hypoglycemia, a condition which can by itself cause brain damage. In addition, various biochemical defects of children with malnutrition are accentuated by infection. Infection and malnutrition thus act synergistically to produce a chronically and recurrently sick child less likely to react to sensory stimuli from his already inadequate social environment.

Malnutrition and Education

How can malnutrition and its counterpart, mental retardation, be arrested or prevented in poverty areas? What can be done to insure that every child in America has the same chance of being "created equal" or the opportunity to live his life outside of poverty and hunger? Inzer indicates that a high priority must be set for greater accessibility to prenatal clinics and positive teaching of all mothers and mothers-to-be in the areas of nutrition and child care. She tells us that efforts must be made to help every prospective mother learn the principles of good nutrition and how to budget her food dollar by using less expensive foods to provide the necessary nutrients. Also that more emphasis must be laid constantly on the importance of a proper diet, and, that emphasis reinforced to each school child beginning at the elementary grade level. Perhaps in this way the health status of future generations can be improved.

Malnourished children will quite likely have problems in school. They are often apathetic, irritable, and inattentive children. They lack a sense of curiosity or a desire for exploration. Dr. Birch, research professor of pediatrics at the Albert Einstein College of Medicine says:

> A society genuinely concerned with educating socially disadvantaged children cannot restrict itself merely to improving and expanding educational facilities. . . it must concern itself with the full range of factors contributing to educational failure. . . . We hope for an awareness of the size and scope of the danger confronting children born *of* and *into* poverty. We hope for a changed system of providing for those who cannot provide for themselves (Furst).

Furst also reports that the problem of decreased educational performance among the children of the lower socioeconomic levels cannot be solved merely through school breakfast or school lunch programs. Evidently, the proportion of effort put into such programs should be determined by the severity and scope of malnutrition and by the influence of other factors such as the home life of these children.

The most noxious of poverty's effects is malnutrition. Until the cycle of poverty is broken the success of all efforts at compensatory education or remedial education will be limited if not doomed to failure. As Margaret Mead has said:

> Human beings have maintained their dignity in incredibly bad conditions of housing and clothing, emerged triumphant from huts and log cabins, gone from ill-shod childhood to Wall Street or the Kremlin. . . but food affects not only man's dignity but the capacity of children to reach their full potential, and the capacity of adults to act from day to day. . . . It is true that the

starving adult, his efficiency enormously impaired by lack of food, may usually be brought back again to his previous state of efficiency. But this is not true of children. What they lose is lost for good. . . deprivation during prenatal and postnatal growth can never be made up (Bakan).

Education and Mental Retardation

Many children from low socioeconomic areas are placed in special education classes and the possible benefits of preschool for these children have been somewhat investigated. According to the President's Task Force on the Mentally Handicapped (1970), the greater part of those described as mentally retarded have suffered from developmental difficulties associated with social and environmental deprivation.

Mercer (1971) studied the "labeling process" of mental retardation in the public schools in California. She found that ethnic surveys conducted annually since 1966 by the California State Department of Education have consistently shown rates of placement for Mexican-Americans and Negro children in special education classes that were two to three times higher per 1,000 than rates for children from English-speaking, Caucasian homes (Anglos). The "labeling process" study in the public schools was investigated by reviewing and identifying the characteristics of all 1,234 children referred for any reason in a single school year to the Pupil Personnel Department of the Riverside Unified School District. Approximately 80 percent of the children in the school district were Anglos, 11 percent Mexican-American, and 8 percent Negro. Low status and/or minority children were not referred at a higher rate than their percentage in the population or were they tested by the psychologist at a higher rate. Of the 865 children tested by the psychologist, 82.9 percent were Anglo, 7.6 percent Mexican-American and 9.5 percent Negro. Among the children tested there were 134 children who received an I.Q. of 79 or below. Based on their test performance they were eligible for placement in a special education class. There were approximately four times more Mexican-American children among those who failed the test than would be expected compared to their percentage in the tested population. There were twice as many Negro children and only about half as many Anglo children. There were 71 children who were actually placed in a status as a mental retardate in this school district. Six times more Mexican-American children (45.3 percent) and two and a half times more Negro children (22.6 percent) were placed than would be expected from their proportion in the school district population. Mercer also found that children from ethnic minority groups were not only failing I.Q. tests at a higher rate, but selective factors operating in the "labeling process" resulted in disproportionately more minority children being recommended and placed in the status as mental retardates from among all the children who were eligible for placement. She concluded that the analysis of the"labeling process" in the public schools indicated that children from minority groups were more likely to be recommended for placement and placed in the status of mental retardate than Anglo children, after they failed an I.Q. test.

Sabatino, Kelling, and Hayden (1973) specifically refer to linguistically different children such as Mexican-American and American Indian children who have been placed in special education classes because they obtained low scores on standardized test instruments. The children who are discussed by Sabatino et al. seem to fit the authors' suggestions regarding disadvantaged children.

Specific recommendations are given by Sabatino and his coauthors to stress the child's native language in his early education programs and prepare him linguistically to live and be educated in the dominant culture. Thus it is not the child alone *per se* with whom one must deal; the school curriculum must be modified to accept the child's present linguistic functioning, and adequately prepare him to function away from his home. This does not mean that the child's linguistic and cultural background should be eliminated, but that these strengths should be used to prepare the child to enter his school culture and function bilingually.

Classroom Characteristics

Many times we receive in the classroom a child who exhibits some symptoms of learning disabilities, among which are: hyperactivity, disorders of attention, disorders of speech and hearing, specific learning disabilities in reading, arithmetic, writing, and spelling; impulsivity, and the test results find low scores in the areas of verbal and/or performance scores. A look at his environment leads us to believe that he is culturally deprived.

As a result of extreme poverty, a child may be far removed from reaching the potential of his maturational ceiling. This may explain, in part, why the child from deprived areas shows poor performance on standardized tests of intelligence. These factors need to be taken into consideration in any appraisal of the ability levels of children. The range of stimuli offered the child in many areas is very limited. He has little play space or few interesting things in the home. He may have a few pictures on the wall, but attractive objects are not the order of the day for him.

There is little doubt that the deprived child typically works on academic problems in a slower manner. This is shown in many different ways; he requires more examples before seeing a point, arriving at a conclusion, for forming a concept. He is unwilling to jump to conclusions or to generalize quickly (exceptions to the rule bother him). He is a slower reader, slower problem solver, slower getting to work, and slower in taking tests. It is, on the other hand, important to note that in many areas of life the underprivileged individual is not at all slow; quite to the contrary, he is frequently remarkably quick in athletic activities and in many games he functions rapidly and seems to think quickly.

Often the culturally deprived child lives on the level of his basic psychological responses of love, anger, and sensual behavior. He expresses these directly as he grows up in the culture of deprived areas. He follows the characteristic patterns of pleasures and ambitions of those about him. Not only is he allowed to fight when angry, but he is expected to do so. However, he is permitted to laugh when he meets with success. He has learned that he must be able to protect himself rather than rely on authorities to do it for him. Hence physical aggression is often regarded as the normal way of life.

Language in the lower class is not as flexible a means of communication as in the middle class. It is not as readily adapted to the subtleties of the particular situation, but consists more of a loosely patterned repertoire of the same phrases and expressions which are used without much effort to achieve a subtle correspondence between perception and verbal expression. Much of lower-class language consists of a kind of incidental "emotional" accompaniment to action here and now.

The child from a disadvantaged environment may have missed some of the experiences necessary for developing verbal, conceptual, attentional, and learning skills requisite to school success. These skills play a vital role for the child in his understanding of the language of the school and the teacher, in his adapting to school routines, and in his mastery of such a fundamental tool subject as reading. In this absence of the development of these skills by the child, there is a progressive alienation of teacher from child and child from teacher. In the school, the child may suffer from feelings of inferiority because he is failing. He may withdraw or become hostile and find gratifications elsewhere, such as in his peer group.

One reason for the difficulties in the education of disadvantaged children is that many of them are relatively slow in performing intellectual tasks. In our society, speed is rewarded. In many intelligence tests, speed of reaction is an important factor in determining the level of mental ability of individuals. Slowness of response needs to be given attention in terms of the final learning outcome. Speed of reaction, although important, may have received more attention than it rightly deserves. Perhaps it is incorrect to associate speed of reaction with gifted children and slowness of response with dull children. There are values that can accrue from slowness of response if the individual has sufficient persistence.

Motor, Visual Perception Difficulties. The culturally deprived child, is more adequately described as a disadvantaged child. He has a culture, but an inferior one, as compared to the middle class culture, and since it is the middle class structure upon which the school's expectations are built, the disadvantaged is often handicapped in school learnings.

It is estimated that the disadvantaged child is functioning one to two years below the middle class child in many areas of learning when he enters first grade. And this gap may widen through the school years.

Typically, his gross motor skills are well developed, often superior in early life. It is probable he receives positive reinforcement for motor development. Parents may feel this shows superiority. They may feel the child will be less dependent on them, and so they encourage gross motor development. Less emphasis is placed on fine muscle coordination skills, and few stimuli are provided to encourage these skills.

Perceptual development, which emerges as a product of experience with an environment and with the maturation of the individual, is a development with a widespread dysfunction among disadvantaged children. They are usually exposed to a minimal amount of stimuli to enhance normal perceptual development, bare beds and rooms, and few objects in their environment for exploration. The disadvantaged may also have overstimulation with noises, TV, radio, shouting, and fighting which may cause withdrawal, and less exploration of their surroundings. Thus their limited environment, limited motivation, and lack of systematic interpretations cause developmental retardation and limited generalizations.

Even though gross motor is usually well developed, the disadvantaged usually have not learned to deal with their bodies in space, nor do they have a positive body image. They usually have poorly developed laterality, directionality, time sequencing, and chronological ordering abilities.

Regardless of whether learning disabilities derive from organic impairment, developmental lag, or genetic inheritance—remediation is largely the same. Areas of weakness must be determined and activities developed to provide the learning experiences needed for building the necessary concepts.

It has been suggested that enrichment, for the sake of enrichment, may fail for the disadvantaged; that they do not need additional or more varied stimulation, but experiences to give stimuli a pattern of sequential meaning. The disadvantaged are often slower learners (not poorer or stupid learners), needing programming to insure readiness and success experiences. They seem to profit from having the abstract associated with the immediate, the sensory, and the motor. They seem to succeed more easily in a structured environment, with rules, order, and organization; but they also need to learn by doing—by active participation. Because they tend to be physical learners; movement and action play important roles in their remediation.

Space concepts can be taught through motor activities. Body awareness, impluse control, serial memory, and identification of forms can be remediated through motor activities. Some visual perception activities are possible without motor, and some may be artificially paired with movement to aid the educational process. Many gross motor learnings can, by teaching the application, be transferred to fine motor activities. And both motor abilities and perception need to be trained until they are automatic.

Motor learnings are the earliest learnings. Kinesthetic experiences provide feedback about movement and the body parts. Motor information provides the base for organizing information from the senses. From reflex movements, the child differentiates body parts and the movement, recombines movements, integrates them and learns generalized movement patterns. A generalized pattern allows a child to focus on the goal of his movements, not the movement itself.

Laterality is the inner awareness that the body has two sides. Without this inner awareness, there is no left, right, up, and down. Laterality develops as it is associated with posture and the balance of the body. After learning about objects within arm's reach, the child begins to structure objects that fill space. As space is organized, information from it is matched to his motor base. Without this match, stimuli remain just stimulation.

To function adequately in school, a child must be able to learn to perceive form, organize information gained through vision, and perceive relationships of objects in space. He must be able to structure space and time. Without a time structure, involving synchrony, rhythm, and sequence, he cannot follow directions.

After motor development, a motor perceptual level is reached, whereby the eye follows the movement, in turn followed by a perceptual motor level where the eye leads the hand, ultimately leading to the ability to learn perceptually—to organize incoming data without reference to motor. If a lack in these structures is creating a learning problem, then activities to promote balance, posture, laterality, body image, eye-hand coordination, figure ground, and form concepts must begin. Such perceptual-motor training is to help the child structure himself, and the space-time-world in which he functions.

Behavior of the Culturally Deprived. Children who fall into the category "culturally deprived" are typically ill at ease and uncertain in the classroom. These traits too frequently manifest themselves in aggressive, even hostile behavior.

The lack of self-esteem accounts for much of their hostility, their negative outlook on life, and their apparent lack of enthusiasm for learning. Because most of the parents of these children are so occupied with earning a living or so harassed by unemployment and financial pressures, they pay little, if any, attention to these children. By the time the child is six or seven, he gravitates to the street where he achieves a feeling of belonging. The gang code becomes his moral code, gang values become his values. He is unwilling and often afraid to upset his status in the gang hierarchy. If going to school, learning, and reading are considered a waste of time by and for the gang; he, too, adopts that attitude. The gang follows the leader. If the leader sleeps in class, the gang follows. If he provokes the teacher, the others do, too. The student's violently defensive reactions, developed as survival measures in the streets, are difficult to overcome.

In his environment, physical strength and cunning are admired as desirable traits. A boy grows up fighting for his place among his peers. At home breaches of rules set up by the head of the house result in physical, punitive action. Authority seems to be designed more to keep the child "in line" than to help and protect him. Thus the teacher's task is made more difficult since he, too, represents authority.

Immediate reinforcement of sought-for behavior is particularly suited to the disadvantaged child. The learning style of the deprived child requires that considerable ego-enforcement be given him, and encouragement or discouragement be given right away, for this is how his society operates. In the street corner curriculum, if the child displays undesired behavior, the reprimands are immediate and forceful; if he displays what is deemed by his peers the "right" behavior, the rewards, too, are immediate.

An example of one teacher's utilization of the principle of immediate reinforcement is as follows: the name of each child was printed on the chalkboard; immediately following any demonstration of good manners by any child, a star was drawn with colored chalk next to his name. Soon there was "catching on" by the children and a deliberate attempt was made to perform in that manner which would beget a reward. Consistent use of this method resulted in a sharp increase in demonstration of good manners patterns in these children.

Another example is the technique of giving many spot quizzes from which the feedback follows immediately. This should be done not so much to evaluate in terms of a grade as to allow the child to see his problem immediately. In the case of testing, it has been found that instead of a letter grade, a reward of commercial trading stamps which can be cashed in for material goods seem to have more tangible meaning to "object oriented" deprived children.

An individual photograph can be a very striking reward—especially a photo showing the child in a positive learning situation. In addition to the child's own work being displayed on a bulletin board, photographs of him with his name clearly visible below them may be put next to his work. This not only fosters the image of the positive learning situation—the behavior one wants to encourage—it also gives the deprived child, who typically suffers from lack of a positive self-image, a great degree of ego-reinforcement.

Role playing is extremely successful with this "action-oriented" child. If a child walks in front of the teacher without saying "excuse me," the teacher immediately engages him in role playing in order to dramatically drive home this breach of manners. The peer group itself might be asked to evaluate a role playing situation. By inviting the classes' immediate analysis, there would be on-the-spot reinforcement by peers. Feelings of self-worth and hopefulness increase as a result of continuous daily exposure to challenging situations in an atmosphere of mutual acceptance.

Preschool Education

Kirk (1965) reports an experiment in preschool education based on the hypothesis that if education were started with very young children (excluding extreme clinical types) training and experience could very possible accelerate the rate of mental development and prevent some cases of mental retardation. The study involved groups of mentally retarded children below the age of six. Some children were offered preschool education while others were left without training. In follow-up studies after three or four years, it was found that preschool education had some effect on social and mental development.

Goldstein (1966) felt that the real test of preschool education was the ability of the preschool program to increase the child's rate of social and intellectual development beyond that which would ordinarily occur with the first exposure to formal school, and to teach children skills and abilities that are meaningful so that long-term retention takes place. Goldstein cites Jones (1954) who stated that one could expect gains in intelligence among children whose environment is changed from static, unstimulating routines to an environment that is fresh and dynamic.

Strickland (1971) relates information about the Milwaukee Project which was launched in 1964 when a multidisciplinary team from the University of Wisconsin under the direction of Dr. Rick Heber, Professor of Education and Child Psychology, began a series of surveys which were designed to learn more about the relationship of poverty to mental retardation. Surveys were taken in the residential section of Milwaukee which, according to census data, had the lowest median family income, the greatest population density per housing unit, and the most dilapidated housing in the city. This section of town, also had a much higher rate of mental retardation among school children than was present in any other area of the city. The first survey in 1964 revealed that maternal intelligence was the most reliable single indicator of the level and character of intellectual development of the children. Even though, mothers who had I.Q.'s below 80 consisted of less than half of the total group of mothers in the study, they accounted for about four-fifths of the children with I.Q.'s below 80. The survey data also indicated that the lower the mother's I.Q. the greater the possibliity that their children would score low on intelligence tests. The team observed in their repeated visits with hundreds of families that the mentally retarded mother created a social environment for her offspring that was distinctly different from the environment that was created by her neighbor of normal intelligence. From this data, the team established an Infant Education Center in 1966 in the area where their surveys had been conducted. Their goal was to see if intellectual deficiency might be prevented—as opposed to cured or remediated later—by introducing an array of positive factors in the children's early lives, and displacing factors that appeared to be negative or adverse.

Forty mothers with I.Q.'s of 70 or less, and their newborn children, participated in the Infant Education Center Project. The newborn babies of these mothers were divided into two groups. One group consisting of two-thirds of the population was placed in the experimental program and the remaining one-third was placed in a control group. Shortly after the mother had given birth and returned from the hospital, the teachers began visiting the home for several hours each day where they focused most of their attention on the baby. Some weeks later, the mother and the child were admitted to programs at the Infant Education Center. The infant child, at approximately three to four months of age, was exposed to mental stimulation of a wide variety for many hours each day. Meanwhile, the mother was encouraged, but not required to participate in a center program which was designed to teach her improved homemaking and baby-care techniques and in some cases to provide basic occupational training. At 42 months of age, the children in the active stimulation program measured an average of 33 I.Q. points higher than the children in the control group. Some of the children measured I.Q.'s as high as 135. Equally of interest was the fact that the children in the experimental program were learning at a rate that exceeded the norm for their age group.

The trend of the data developed in the Milwaukee Project gives real hope that mental retardation occuring in children whose parents are poor and of poor ability can be prevented. Longitudinal studies may eventually provide absolute conclusions relative to the effects of the environment on the attainment of learning and developmental skills. The approximately 85 percent of mental retardation which has unknown etiology may then be considerably reduced.

OVERVIEW

Evidence seems to indicate that nutritional factors at a number of different levels contribute significantly to depressed intellectual level and to learning failure. These effects may be produced directly as the consequence of irreparable alterations of the nervous system or indirectly as a result of ways in which the learning experiences of the developing organism may be significantly interfered with at critical points in the developmental course.

It is argued that a primary requirement for normal intellectual development and formal learning is the ability to process sensory information, and to integrate such information across sense systems. However, evidence indicates that both severe acute malnutrition in infancy as well as chronic subnutrition from birth into the school years results in defective information processing. Therefore, by inhibiting the development of a primary process essential for certain aspects of cognitive growth, malnutrition may interfere with the orderly development of experience and contribute to a suboptimal level of intellectual functioning.

Moreover, the adequate state of nutrition is essential for good attention and for appropriate and sensitive responsiveness to the environment. One of the most obvious clinical manifestations of serious malnutrition in infancy is a dramatic combination of apathy and irritability. The infant is grossly unresponsive to his surroundings. This unresponsiveness characterizes his relation to people as well as objects. Behavioral regression is profound, and the organization of his functions is markedly infantilized.

Children who are subnourished also indicate a reduction in responsiveness and attentiveness. In addition, the subnourished child is easily fatigued and unable to sustain either prolonged physical or mental efforts. Improvement in nutritional status is accompanied by improvements in these behaviors as well as in physical state.

It should not be forgotten that nutritional inadequacy may influence the child's learning opportunities by yet another route, namely, illness. Nutritional inadequacy increases the risk of infection, interferes with immune mechanisms, and results in illnesses which are both more generalized and more severe. The combination of subnutrition and illness reduces time available for instruction; and, therefore, by interfering with the opportunities for gaining experience, disrupts the orderly acquisition of knowledge and the course of intellectual growth.

Also pointed out in this discussion was intergenerational affects of nutrition upon mental development. The association between the mother's growth achievements and the risk to her infant is very strong. Poor nutrition and poor health in the mother when she was a girl results in a woman, at maturity, who has a significantly elevated level of reproductive risk. Her pregnancy is more frequently disturbed and her child more often of low birth weight. Such a child has an increased risk of neurointegrative abnormality and of deficient I.Q. and school achievement.

Malnutrition never occurs alone. It occurs in conjunction with low income, poor housing, familial disorganization, a climate of apathy, ignorance, and despair. The simple act of improving the nutritional status of children and their families will not and cannot of itself fully solve the problem of intellectual deficit and school failure. No single improvement in conditions will have this result. What must be recognized is that within an overall effort to improve the condition of disadvantaged children; nutritional considerations must occupy a prominent place, and together with improvements in all other facets of life (including relevant and directed education) contribute much to the improved intellectual growth and school achievement of disadvantaged children.

This writing has been concerned with the three-fourths of the mentally retarded and learning problem children in the United States that live in low socioeconomic areas. Their lives are plagued by prematurity, malnutrition, and inadequate educational experiences.

Maternal factors such as age, number of pregnancies, and economic circumstances are all related to the high incidence of premature births to poverty mothers. Low birth weight has been correlated with low I.Q. and the long-term effects of premature births are seen as these children enter school. Prenatal and postnatal care should be available to all mothers in these areas as a positive preventive measure against premature birth and possible mental retardation.

As previously indicated, the first six months of life are the most crucial in terms of proper nutrition. The nutrition of the mother is an important variable related to the intellectual performance of her children. Positive steps must be taken to educate mothers and mothers-to-be in the areas of nutrition and child care. School breakfast and lunch programs do not reach the children who need it most. Again, free prenatal and postnatal clinics could partially provide the needed care and education in these low socioeconomic areas.

The "labeling process" of mental retardates in our educational system needs to be questioned. If a child is to be "labeled" mental retardate, adequate care and attention should be given to the process employed in labeling. Discrimination against minority groups on tests of intelligence and subsequent placement in classes for the mentally retarded should be investigated further. Dr. Heber and his Milwaukee Project gives definite hope that through preschool and infant care centers, these children from low socioeconomic areas can be helped and the high incidence of mental retardation in these areas can be reduced.

Bibliography

"Action Against Mental Disabilities." *The Report of the President's Task Force on the Mentally Handicapped.* (September 1970).

Bakan, Rita. "Malnutrition and Learning." *Phi Delta Kappan* 51 (June 1970): 529.

Cooke, Robert E., M.D. "Freedom from Handicap." *The Special Child in Century 21.* Edited by Jerome Hellmuth (Special Child Publications of the Seguin School, Inc.), 1964.

Cravioto, Janquin; De Lacardie, Elsa; and Birch, Herbert. "Nutrition, Growth, and Neurointegrative Development: An Experimental and Eologic Study." *Pediatrics* 38, no. 2, Pt. 12 (Aug. 1966).

"The Decisive Decade MR70," The President's Committee on Mental Retardation, Department of Health, Education, and Welfare, 1970.

Furst, Caryn M. "Nutrition's Effect on Mental Development." *Forecast* 16:F-160. (Sept. 1970).

Goldstein, Herbert. "Preschool Programs for the Retarded." In *Prevention and Treatment of Mental Retardation.* Edited by Irving Philips. New York: Basic Books, Inc., 1966.

Hardy, Janet B. "Perinatal Factors and Intelligence." In *The Biosocial Basis of Mental Retardation.* Edited by Sonia F. Osler and Robert E. Cooke. Baltimore: Johns Hopkins Press, 1965.

Inzer, Lenore C., R.N. "A Study of Nutrition in Pregnancy." *The Journal of School Health* (Oct. 1970).

Jordan, Thomas E. "Patterns of Development." *The Mentally Retarded.* 2d ed. Columbus, Ohio: Charles E. Merrill Publishing Co. 1966.

Kirk, Samuel A. "Diagnostic, Cultural and Remedial Factors in Mental Retardation." In *The Biosocial Basis of Mental Retardation.* Edited by Sonia F. Osler and Robert E. Cooke. Baltimore: Johns Hopkins Press, 1965.

Koch, Richard A. "Diagnosis in Infancy and Early Childhood." In *Prevention and Treatment of Mental Retardation.* Edited by Irving Philips. New York: Basic Books, Inc., 1966.

Maternal Nutrition and the Course of Pregnancy. Committee on Maternal Nutrition. Food and Nutrition Board. Washington, D.C.: National Research Council, National Academy of Sciences, 1970 p.25.

Mercer, Jane R. "Sociocultural Factors in Labeling Mental Retardates," *Peabody Journal of Education.* (April 1971).

Pasamanick, Benjamin, M.D. "A Child is Being Beaten—The Effects of Hunger," *Vital Speeches.* (May 15, 1971).

Profiles of Children. White House Conference on Children, 1970 Washington, D.C.: U.S. Government Printing Office, 1970.

Robinson, H.B., and Robinson, N.M. *The Mentally Retarded Child, A Psychological Approach.* New York: McGraw-Hill Book Co., 1965. Citing B. Passamanick, "Influence of Sociocultural Variables Upon Organic Factors in Mental Retardation," *American Journal of Mental Deficiency.* Vol. 64. (1959).

Sabatino, David A.; Kelling, Kent; and Hayden, David L. "Special Education and the Culturally Different Child: Implications for Assessment and Intervention," *Exceptional Children* 39, no. 7 (April 1973).

Strickland, Stephen P. "Can Slum Children Learn?" *American Education* (July 1971).

Thompson, John D. "Protecting the Preemie," *Newsweek.* 71 (Jan. 29, 1968).

Waisman, Harry A. "Recent Advances in Mental Retardation." In *Prevention and Treatment of Mental Retardation.* Edited by Irving Philips. New York: Basic Books, Inc., 1966. Citing Lula O. Lubchenco et al., "Sequelae of Premature Birth. Evaluation of Premature Infants of Low Birth Weights at Ten Years of Age," *American Journal of Diseases of Children.* (1963).

White, William F. *Tactics for Teaching the Disadvantaged.* New York: McGraw-Hill Book Company, 1971.

DISADVANTAGED CHILDREN
Study Sheet #1

1. Report and reference recent studies relative to nutrition and its effect on learning.

   Author:

   Title:

   Source:

   Population and Setting:

   Study Conducted:

   Procedures:

   Results (effects on learning):

DISADVANTAGED CHILDREN
Study Sheet #2

1. What behaviors would distinguish the culturally disadvantaged child from the socioeconomically disadvantaged child?

Personal
Counseling

Enrichment

Seminars

Special
Grouping

Resource
Person

'I need special
modifications, too!'

Acceleration

Educational Counseling

Individual Projects

Gifted Children

DEFINITION AND ESTIMATES OF PREVALENCE

Giftedness is becoming a popular topic for discussion, research, and action in the field of education, and particularly in special education within recent years. "Despite divergent opinions about what constitutes 'giftedness' or 'creativity' or 'talent', workable criteria must be established to provide for the young people we know are there" (U.S. Commissioner of Education 1971). The same office also indicates that generally speaking, the following evidence would indicate special intellectual gifts or talent:

1. Consistently very superior scores on many appropriate standardized tests.
2. Judgment of teachers, pupil personnel specialists, administrators and supervisors familiar with the abilities and potentials of the individual.
3. Demonstration of advance skills, imaginative insight, and intense interest and involvement.
4. Judgment of specialized teachers, pupil personnel specialists and experts in the arts who are qualified to evaluate the pupil's demonstrated and/or potential talent.

Gowan (1971) reports that giftedness has variously been defined as a cutoff point on the Stanford-Binet Individual Intelligence Test. Terman used the cutoff point of 140 I.Q. and above. Recent researchers have used 130 I.Q. The problem existent with many definitions appears to be that there is no real rationale for what constitutes a gifted child. If a definition doesn't have functional or operational implications it becomes a useless description. Gowan (1971) says, "A gifted child is one who has the potential to develop creativity. Giftedness, after all is potentiality, since it is an I.Q." Creativity logically should be a product of intelligence, but evidence seems to support the fact that gifted children are no more creative than normal range children. Therefore, if giftedness is creativity, then normal range children may also be gifted. There is observation which seems to show that there is a correlation between 120 I.Q. as a cutoff for creativity. Gowan also expresses the idea that mental health helps a child's creativity, because mental health obviously increases the child's rate of mental development. Therefore, an increase in the child's rate of mental development should possibly be an increase in the child's I.Q. Consequently, a person in the 110-120 I.Q. range with a high degree of mental health should be able to push his measured I.Q. into the range where he may be defined as potentially creative.

For the purpose of federal funding for educational projects, these definitions must be more specific. The federal government of the United States has defined "gifted and talented" for purposes of federal education programs by Public Law 91-230, Section 806, as follows:

> Gifted and talented children are those identified by profession-ally qualified persons who by virtue of outstanding abilities, are capable of high performance. These are children who require differentiated educational programs and/or services beyond those normally provided by the regular school program in order to realize their contribution to self and society. Children cap-able of high performance include those with demonstrated achievement and/or potential ability in any of the following areas, singly or in combination:
>
> 1. general intellectual ability
> 2. specific academic aptitude
> 3. creative or productive thinking
> 4. leadership ability
> 5. visual and performing arts
> 6. psychomotor ability (U.S. Commissioner of Education 1971)

This definition is primarily applicable for federal program fund-ing. Each state has the opportunity through state legislation to devise a definition for its own educational needs. However, in the late 1960s, there were approximately only seventeen states which had legislative acknowledgment of these children and their educational needs.

In order to make funds available, an operating definition is required. There are, however, some pitfalls in describing giftedness too specifically. Gensley (1970) cited the Special Study Project for Gifted Children in Illinois as a case in point. From the beginning of the program in 1959, planners avoided a definition for "gifted children" in the legislation for two reasons: First, specification and description of human abilities were, they thought, a problem for behavioral scientists rather than legislators. Therefore, they reasoned that definitions at the operational level in schools should respond to new scientific findings and not be delayed by legal restrictions. Secondly, they recognized that allocation of funds usually requires a description of the special category; but they felt that description for giftedness should be made through administrative regulations, not by law. The Illinois definition does appear to be educationally functional: "Gifted children are those children whose mental development is accelerated beyond the average to the extent that they need and can profit from specially planned educational services" (U.S. Commissioner of Education 1971).

Another example is in the state of Oklahoma where no laws or specific programs for the gifted existed until 1969. At that time the legislature recognized that many gifted children and youth do not receive the kinds of educational programs necessary for development of their potentials. The Oklahoma definition designates gifted children as those who test above 135 on an individual test of intelligence, indicate high academic potential, and are not adequately provided for in the general program (Special Education No. 8, Oklahoma 1971).

Considering the difficulty in defining this group, it is not easy to sort out the number of gifted young people in our society. Many gifted children go unnoticed by teachers and administrators. Many children cover their abilities in order to fit into the group. Many children, moreover, do not find adequate systems for the application of their talent in the public schools.

There is no absolute procedure for finding the exact number of children in the schools who are gifted, although, the socioeconomic level of the community does seem to be an important aspect when trying to discover the percentage of gifted children. Telford and Sawrey (1967) indicate that in an average community, 16-20 percent of the elementary school population can be expected to have an I.Q. above 115, but in a superior community 45-60 percent may be found above 115 I.Q. They also point out that between three and five times as many children in the elementary schools in a superior community will have I.Q.'s above 115-140, than will children in a school in an average area.

Thomas (1966) has shown that gifted and talented pupils may constitute 20-30 percent of the school population on a nationwide basis. He continues by indicating that these children are the ones who should be making the "A's" in the average classroom, but this is not always the case because they are undiscovered genius and talent. The number of children presumed to be gifted has varied considerably in recent estimates. Before the 1960s, many research workers agreed that the gifted included those within the upper 2 to 3 percent of intellectual ability. However, recently more variables have been introduced such as social, mechanical, and other aptitudes which are intrinsically important in an estimate of prevalence. The total census projection for the 1970 United States elementary-secondary school population was approximately 51,600,000. A reasonable estimate indicates that the gifted population is a minimum of 3 to 5 percent of that school population.

Methods of Identification

The way in which intelligence is defined is a partial determinant of the way in which the intellectually gifted will be identified. Uniformity of definition will not be found. A commonly used method of defining and identifying the gifted is in terms of scores on an intelligence test. The use of the I.Q. in identifying the gifted has the advantage of objectivity. It can also be applied relatively early in life (Telford and Sawrey).

The I.Q. method of identification has been patterned after Terman's studies. Terman laid the basic groundwork for research on the gifted child as early as the 1920s. Jacobs (1970) indicates that Terman relied on teachers to nominate those children who might possibly be gifted, then those children were screened for their actual levels of mental ability. He indicates, though, that before the children nominated by the teachers were individually tested, they first had to survive the screening of a group intelligence test. The I.Q. method is still being used but in most cases there are variable inclusions and this method of identification is being changed gradually. Issacs (1970) also reports that Peganto and Birch (1959) and Cornish (1968) concluded that when teachers nominate children as being gifted, they miss half the gifted children; and Hughes and Converse (1962) and Cornish conclude that the gifted are not the high scorers on group intelligence tests.

The factors involved in identifying the gifted child are much more intricate than the score of one group intelligence test. The U.S. Commissioner of Education's Office expressed that the factors of importance are as follows: (1) age of identification (research reveals early identification does not fight concealed giftedness for the purpose of peer group relations); (2) screening procedures and test accuracy; (3) the identification of children from a variety of ethnic groups and cultures; and (4) tests of creativity. The Commissioner of Education's Office also reports that Bloom, after an analysis of major longitudinal studies, concluded that general intelligence develops lawfully; that the greatest impact on I.Q. from environmental factors would probably take place between ages one and five, with relatively little impact after age eight. This observation is very similar to Hollingsworth's observation that methods of measuring intelligence had low predictive value when applied before seven or eight years of age.

A number of other studies cited by The Commissioner of Education's Office have shown that individual tests identify gifted children much more accurately than do group measures. There is possibly evidence that group test ratings tend to be higher for the below average individual, while for the above average, group test scores are lower than those obtained on the individually administered I.Q. scales. Data seem to show that the discrepancies between group scores and individual scores increased as the intelligence level increased. The most highly gifted children were penalized most by group test scores; that is, the higher the ability the greater the probability that the group test would overlook such ability.

It is unsafe to assume that teachers will consistently identify even the highly gifted. Plowman (1969) reports that identification of the gifted must be acquired by multiple means, including measures of intelligence, achievement, talent, and creativity. Practice seems to indicate to the authors of this text that one of the best methods, the individual intelligence test, is presently not being used in many states because of the cost involved. Plowman also feels that school personnel are important in identifying these children. The personnel valued as most critical are school psychologists, talent specialists, guidance counselors, teachers, and school administrators, (last because they lack direct contact with the children).

Identification of gifted children should be a continual process. The screening and search for these children must be a conclusive search involving a battery of methods including individual tests, school staff observations, case studies, and class evaluations. It is important that after identification has been made, at least an annual reevaluation should be employed to be certain placement and educational planning are appropriate.

An interesting new type of identification worthy of notation is a supportive device called "A Diary of Learning" by Juliana Townsend Gensley (1969). It is a teacher, pupil, and parent approach to identification through communication and evaluation of learning by keeping a diary of daily achievements. It is a mutual evaluative technique which may prove especially good for the gifted underachiever.

A number of methods of identification are being used, but one must remember that in order to meet the needs of these individuals, they must first be identified. Identification is not merely referring a child to another class or program. Identification should encompass all identifying procedures that are functional for attaining the educational goals for the gifted children.

Characteristics of the Gifted

Krippner (1967) indicates that the gifted person is regarded as one who demonstrates consistently remarkable performance in any worthwhile line of endeavor. First of all, though, he reports that gifted children are children, and that they have the same developmental needs of love, security, companionship, acceptance, challenge, self-determination, guidance, respect and other support which offers optimum development in children. Generally, these needs are satisfied until the child enters school. When the child does enter school it probably becomes obvious to him that his interests, abilities, and values may be at a different pace from his classmates.

Torrance (1970) relates that gifted children need a rich and varied challenging program because they have broad and numerous interests, high level of abilities, curiosity, and an insatiable desire to learn. He indicates that from their earliest years bright children delight in examining details of their surroundings and in constantly asking adults questions. Generally, these children will express inquisitive and curious behavior as they grow older, unless they are inhibited by schools, adults, or other children.

Issacs (1970) reports that superior intellectually gifted children in the classroom are usually capable of abstract reasoning with little teacher help as long as they are guided properly, and that they have the capacity to perform numerous processes mentally that are considered laborious for average pupils. Issacs, also agrees with Torrance that one of the attributes of the gifted is the ability to do several things at once. She indicates that these boys and girls are able to think in terms of symbols or group situations instead of specific data or concrete objects.

Krippner referring to Project Talent concluded after studies on the high school level that nonintellectual characteristics such as sex and emotional control are related to academic success. He related that the National Merit Scholarship program revealed that exceptional students are marked with continued academic success, are first born children, from small families, and are personally more independently oriented. Krippner reports a series of studies by M.J. Stern (1957) which indicate that the creative person is less authoritarian and less anxiety ridden than the noncreative person.

Professional school personnel cannot assume that the gifted and talented children live only in privileged environments. Gifted children have been found in many different environments and cultures. The number of gifted children, though, appears to be concentrated in particular ethnic, religious, socioeconomic, and occupational groups. This concentration is probably because of problems in identification rather than true prevalence.

Characteristically the gifted children are curious and explore different situations earlier than do their peers. They enjoy social association as other children do, but they seem to relate earlier to older companions and games which require higher degrees of individual skill and intellectual involvement. The U.S. Commissioner of Education reports that biographical data from studies of large populations reveal that gifted individuals excel in widely varied organizations and that the total impression is of people who perform superbly in many fields and do so with ease.

The U.S. Office continues by reporting that the composite impression from studies of gifted people ranging from childhood to adulthood shows a population which values independence, which prizes integrity and independent judgment in decision making, which rejects conformity for its own sake, and which possesses unusually high social ideals and values. Apparently, of all human groups, the gifted and talented are least likely to form stereotypes.

Groth's (1969) studies have somewhat characterized gifted children as separate entities, boys and girls. The results on a study of the hierarchial needs of gifted boys and girls concluded that girls seemed to have a narrower spectrum of needs than boys. The two highest categories of needs for gifted girls were love and belongingness with self-actualization third. Gifted boys appeared less mature and more oriented toward a multiplicity of goals than girls. Their three most important needs were safety and security, love and belongingness, and self-esteem. This study supports Maslow (1954) and Gowan (1967 and 1968). Groth concluded that development in the cognitive domain is interdependent upon development in the affective domain. The present authors wish to note that even though gifted children appear to be functioning at a higher level than average children, the former still are not free from emotional or affective problems.

Some of the creative positives indicated by Torrance (1970) which may be characteristic of gifted children are as follows:

1. Ability to express feelings.
2. Ability to improvise with commonplace materials.
3. Articulate in role playing, creative activities.
4. Enjoyment and ability in art.
5. Enjoyment and ability in creative dramatics.
6. Enjoyment and ability in music.
7. Expressiveness in speech.
8. Fluency and flexibility in nonverbal media.
9. Enjoyment and skills in group learning.
10. Responsiveness to the concrete.
11. Responsiveness to the kinesthetic.
12. Expressiveness of gestures.
13. Humor.
14. Richness of imagery in informal language.
15. Originality of ideas in problem-solving.
16. Problem centeredness.
17. Emotional responsiveness.
18. Quickness of warm up.

These creative positives do not necessarily fit a stereotyped homogenous group. Any teacher can observe data which may be characteristic of and correlated with the gifted child's performances.

Services Needed for the Gifted

The use of Federal funds has markedly strengthened federal, state, and local programs for the handicapped, through improved preparation of specialized personnel, quality of research, and understanding and support of the education profession and the public. These programs vividly demonstrate the social benefits from a federal investment in the education of specific target populations with needs which cannot be met by general education (U.S. Commissioner of Education 1971).

Too often in past years the gifted have been overlooked as a group in need of support. One of the most powerful ways to aid this group is through federal, state, and local programs which can aid and support. The U.S. Office relates that the need for funding for the gifted and talented is critical; therefore, if funds can be devoted to program improvement, personnel preparation, improved and extended research, and general support and understanding; the educational opportunities and life possibilities for gifted children also will improve.

The U.S. Commissioner's Office reports from a federal survey that the gifted children were losing to the competition of other problems. The survey (1970) revealed that 295 persons from diverse backgrounds gave oral testimony to the Regional Assistant Commissioners of Education on the perceived needs of the gifted child. The testimony analysis was divided into statements of specific needs and recommendations. One major theme mentioned was the need for curriculum flexibility to allow talented students to move forward on their own. A second strong need was for better prepared teachers. There was a consensus that teachers are currently not prepared and cannot handle the special educational issues presented by gifted youngsters. Under organizational needs, testimony stressed the need for partial separation of the educational program to allow gifted students to work with one another and to allow for necessary freedom to explore. There was a general rejection of a complete separation for the entire day in either special schools or special classes. There are many ways to provide for gifted children and some of these procedures will be discussed later.

The recommendations from the testimonial report to the U.S. Commissioner of Education generally supported the following suggestions:

1. A strong need was expressed for additional funds and higher priority for gifted programs.
2. Funds should be specifically earmarked for spending on the gifted.
3. Request for more teacher training help in both in-service and preservice programs, which could be made possible through fellowships and scholarships.

Issacs (1970) shows that the needs for the gifted are more specific than stated above because these children's needs are specific to their educational differences. She states,

> The learning styles and rates vary from those of the average child. Smaller teacher-pupil ratio are needed. Individualized and flexible programs are desirable. More freedom for self-initiated learning is required. There is a need for all boys and girls to learn to value and treasure the gifted. The emotional needs of

the gifted must be met in order to insure mastery of academic and communicative skills.

Plowman states that programming starts with an assessment of a child and proceeds to placement in environments and experiences. Characteristic rating sheets, screening and nomination forms, case study records, and child study programs may suggest that a given gifted child needs access to intellectual peers, exemplary individuals, empathetic mentors, or special resource persons. He indicates further that programming is a continual process, and as such must be based upon continual appraisal of development of interests, knowledge, intellectual skills, traits of creativity, attitudes, aspirations and values.

Program Differences

Plowman has expressed that enrichment in regular classes is often advocated for gifted children who may not be physically or socially mature enough for special classes or grade acceleration. In general, enrichment programs in regular classes should provide greater breadth and depth of learning, more opportunities for developing creative behaviors, increased emphasis on rich social experiences, and ample freedom to pursue independent study.

Plowman has also included private study as a method of instruction for gifted children. Private study includes correspondence courses and certain tutorial and independent study programs which are pursued most satisfactorily by children who require a minimum amount of direction from the teacher.

Acceleration is another program that has been used and is still being used. Plowman indicates that the acceleration program appears to work well with high achieving gifted children who are emotionally and physically mature and who seek opportunity to associate with older children and adults.

Torrance (1970) reports on a recently developed program for the gifted which is called the open ended program. The open ended program simply means that it is a nongraded arrangement. School work is done inside and outside the school building. This type of program has been criticized because of a lack of structure. It is felt that these children need structure as much as the average child.

Gensley has given information on another service for gifted children which is called programmed learning. It consists of the use of machinery to stimulate and teach subject matter. The machine, though, cannot be asked questions, which presents a disadvantage. However, programmed learning used as a tool can help provide for creativity.

Many model programs have been introduced in recent research. One such program was a special project by the Boston School System (1970) in which a trailer was used as a facility for twenty gifted children. These children attended on a half day basis. The program was focused on language arts and all materials and equipment were selected to offer instruction in a particular field. When the program originated, ESEA Title III money funded it, but it is now existing out of local financing. The project personnel felt that an important facet of the program was the focus on individual responsibility, which caused each child to be accountable for his own work. The gifted students in this program manifested improvement in self-concept, behavior, and attendance; and their attitudes made them better students in their regular classes.

Torrance (1969) has reported on another new program, which was started by George Witt of New Haven. This program was called the Life Enrichment Activity Program; the objective was to discover unrecognized potential in low socioeconomic areas. This program was established because research revealed astounding numbers of unrecognized gifted and talented children. Joseph H. Douglass (1969) estimated 80,000 of the youth who drop out of school each year have I.Q.'s within the top 25 percent of the population.

There are other programs being initiated presently, but the need for gifted classes exceeds the availability of classes. Programs are a necessity in order to meet the ever-present needs of these children. Not only are services needed for the school child, but community services should be made available to parents of these children. Programs may include seminars, work-study programs, remedial instruction, personal counselling, and cooperative programs with colleges.

Whatever type of program is developed, Bruch (1969) indicates that the following suggestions should be considered:

1. Provisions for the gifted should be available at every grade level for every gifted student.
2. Programs should be designed for the high achieving, the low achieving and the gifted with special needs in mind.
3. The students should be selected for the programs which best meet their educational needs.
4. Factors such as staff appraisal, achievement, interests, aptitudes and individual intelligence test scores should be used in the selection process.

Recognition of Abilities in Early Childhood

The ever-increasing complexity of society and expanding horizons of scientific investigation have served to emphasize the necessity for early identification. It is theorized that early identification and training will help to bring about more complete utilization of the potential of these people (Telford and Sawrey). Obviously giftedness does not manifest itself at a set time, and even though difficult to recognize, potential giftedness is present at birth. Therefore, evaluation of the preschool children should receive serious consideration. Torrance (1969) reports that individuality is established largely in the early years of a child's life and therefore these years are critically important in the emergence of a healthy strong identity and realization of potentialities.

In view of what is speculated on the importance of early learning processes, adequate identification must be available. The U.S. Commissioner of Education reports that attempts to identify gifted children through tests at the preschool and kindergarten level have been successful when careful preliminary search and screening have been utilized. Data have shown and it is interesting to remember that young gifted children can be individually tested and accurately identified more easily than can young mentally retarded children, who are similarly deviant from the norm.

A good example of early identification of gifted children as reported by Rellas (1969) is the method used by the Pasadena City Schools in California. They use the Weise Predictability Scale to screen children and these children are labeled Potentially Academically Talented (P.A.T.). Later these children are tested by an individual intelligence test such as the Binet or Wechsler. By this method all of the children are included in the appraisal and given the opportunity of being described as gifted.

One cannot deny that early identification of these children would be an asset to educational planning. Also, one should not ignore the obvious fact that these children have specific needs that must be met before they become older and their potential becomes correspondingly more difficult to identify.

Resources Available for the Gifted Child

Bruch feels that there seems to be a particular gap in basic research on how gifted children develop and learn. The present authors believe that because of this inconsistency, resource material which is especially designed for the gifted child is limited. However, there have been in recent years, many new books written about gifted children, and some of these books are specifically for teachers of gifted children. The books and periodicals which are listed below may be of value for those people who are involved with gifted children:

Rosner, Stanley and Abt, L.E. *The Creative Experience.* New York: Grossman Pub., 1970.

Gowan, J.C. and Torrance, E.P. *Educating the Ablest.* Itasca, Ill.: F.E. Peacock Publishers, Inc. 1971.

Gowan, J.C. and Bruch, C.B. *The Academically Talented Student and Guidance.* Boston: Houghton Mifflin Company, 1971.

Purkey, W.A. *Self Concept and School Achievement.* Englewood Cliffs, N.J.: Prentice-Hall, 1970.

Torrance, E.P. and Myers, R.E. *Creative Learning and Teaching.* New York: Dodd, Mead & Company, 1970.

Rice, J.P. *The Gifted: Developing Total Talent.* Springfield, Ill.: Charles C. Thomas, Publisher, 1970.

Gowan, J.C. *The Development of the Creative Individual.* San Diego, Calif.: Robert Knapp Publishing Co., 1971.

Provisions for Talented Students: An Annotated Bibliography. Washington, D.C.: U.S. Dept of HEW, Bureau of Research, 1966, Document Catalog No. FS5235:35069

The Gifted Child Quarterly. Editor: Ann F. Issacs. National Association for Gifted Children. Cincinnati, Ohio 45236.

The Exceptional Parent. Edited by Klebanoff, Klien and Schleifer. 264 Beacon Street, Boston, Mass.

OVERVIEW

Concannon (1969) believes that the gifted child poses one of our greatest present day problems beginning in the home and ultimately becoming a concern in the school. School staffs bear the responsibility for recognizing and planning for the needs of the gifted. The authors of this text agree with Concannon and also feel that programs for gifted children should obviously result in improvement for the total public school system.

Issacs (1970) indicates that the question whether enrichment, acceleration, or some other administrative form of organization best cares for the needs of the gifted, has not yet been answered. The present authors favor the enrichment program. The acceleration plan would have definite social and maturity limitations. The young student who is accelerated to a higher class will eventually reach a level at which he is not compatible even though he may possess the academic abilities. The grouping plan appears to place gifted children into a disadvantaged culture, because they would not be integrated totally and functionally with the balance of the school program. The enrichment program enables the child to embellish upon his present grade level of study, but allows him to remain with his peers. Therefore, the enrichment program should provide the teacher with the opportunity to make provision for the gifted child within that child's own classroom.

Whatever a gifted child may be, he is still a child and must be able to enjoy and profit from the activities that are common to a youngster's world. He needs a lot of play activity and he needs to be with other children his own age. The gifted child should not be a difficult child to discover. He generally will possess a rich vocabulary. He will be curious. He will be searching for materials on a higher grade level. He will appear somewhat mature in his conversation. He should be a delight to have in a classroom.

Gifted children do not fit the stereotyped picture of a physically deficient child with eye-glasses at the back of the room with his head in a book. Gifted children are usually physically well children, and they manifest activities in all parts of the school program.

Bibliography

Boston Public Schools Learning Laboratories. American Institutes for Research, "Model Programs: Childhood Education." Palo Alto, California, 1970.

Bruch, Catherine. "Problems and Intentions in the Education of Gifted Students." *Gifted Child Quarterly.* (Summer 1969).

Concannon, S. Josephina. "The Gifted: A Major Concern." *Peabody Journal of Education* 46, no. 5 (March 1969).

Gensley, Julian "Programmed Learning for Gifted Children." *Gifted Child Quarterly.* (Summer 1970).

Gensley, Juliana Townsend. "A New Method of Evaluation for Gifted Students." *Gifted Child Quarterly.* (Summer 1969).

Gowan, J.C. "The Relationship Between Creativity and Giftedness." *Gifted Child Quarterly.* (Winter 1971).

Groth, Norman Jean. "Hierarchial Needs of Gifted Boys and Girls in the Affective Domain." *Gifted Child Quarterly.* (Summer 1969).

Issacs, Anne F. "Additional Observations and Recommendations Given During the Congressional Hearings of the Gifted." *Gifted Child Quarterly.* (Winter 1970).

———. "Listen Young Gifted Ones." *Gifted Child Quarterly.* (Summer 1970).

Jacobs, John C. "Are We Being Misled by Fifty Years of Research on Our Gifted Children?" *Gifted Child Quarterly.* (Summer 1970).

Krippner, Stanley. "Characteristics of Gifted and Talented Youth." *Marmodes Medical Center.* (January 1967).

Plowman, Paul B. "Programming for the Gifted Child." *Exceptional Children* 35. (March 1969).

Rellas, A. "The Use of the Wechsler Preschool and Primary Scale WPPSI in Early Identification of Gifted Students." *California Journal of Educational Research* 20, no. 3 (May 1969).

Special Education System, Oklahoma State Department of Education. "Program of Education for Exceptional Children in Oklahoma." *Bulletin S.E.* no. 8 (1971).

Telford, Charles W., and Sawrey, James M. *The Exceptional Individual.* Englewood Cliffs, N.J.: Prentice-Hall, Inc., 1967.

Texas University Research and Development Center for Teacher Education. "Dimensions and Criteria of Talented Behavior: Final Report." (July 1968).

Thomas, George I. "Gifted Child." *Guiding the Gifted Child.* Candam Hse., N.Y.: Joseph Crecimbeni, 1966.

Torrance, E. Paul. "Broadening Concepts of Giftedness in the 70's. *Gifted Child Quarterly.* (Winter 1970).

———. "Creative Positives of Disadvantaged Children and Youth." *Gifted Child Quarterly.* (Summer 1969).

U.S. Commissioner of Education. *Education of the Gifted and Talented.* Vol. 1 and 2, Report to the Congress of the United States. (August 1971).

GIFTED CHILDREN
Study Sheet #1

1. In what ways will a gifted child differ from other children in learning?

2. Discuss and defend your choice of either grouping, acceleration, or an enrichment plan for the gifted child.

GIFTED CHILDREN
Study Sheet #2

1. Discuss the appropriate procedures and methods which should be used in identifying gifted children.

GIFTED CHILDREN
Study Sheet #3

1. Select a recent *journal* article pertaining to gifted children and write an abstract using the following format:

Author:

Title:

Source:

Population and Setting:

Study Conducted:

Procedure:

Results:

'I can get up by myself!'

5

Physically Disabled and Chronically Ill Children

INTRODUCTION

Physically disabled and chronically ill children are included in one chapter primarily because there has been less emphasis in recent years on providing special classroom programs for these children. A large number of physically disabled children are now provided an instructional program in the regular classroom, and if a chronically ill child needs special provisions for his educational program these provisions may be offered through homebound teaching, hospital teaching, or home-school telephone teaching, rather than some type of special provisions within the public schools.

The trend towards not providing special program modifications *within the public schools* for the physically disabled or chronically ill child does not mean that the regular or special class teacher should not be informed about these children. Information about the characteristics and needs of physically disabled and chronically ill children is very essential if adequate provisions are available for their educational, emotional, physical, and adjustment needs.

There are many conditions which can cause a child to be physically disabled or chronically ill. This chapter will not be a comprehensive presentation of the various conditions which cause physical disabilities or chronical illnesses, but will attempt to provide a basic understanding of the conditions of physical disabilities and chronic illnesses, and present the more common types of problems encountered by these children. The common problems to be discussed will include the psychological and emotional overlay, as well as the physical problems.

Program Changes

The physically disabled child is probably included within the regular class program to a greater extent than he was in the past, because the design of a majority of elementary and secondary school buildings of today has eliminated a large portion of the architectural barriers. Older elementary and secondary schools are usually multi-story buildings without elevators or ramps into the buildings. The disabled children could not, in the majority of cases, attend these schools because they could not climb the stairs, doors were not wide enough for a wheel chair, or the building had many steps to be climbed prior to the child's entering the building; consequently, these children could not even reach the main door. As a result, these children were either placed in special self-contained classrooms which were on the first floor of the building, placed in groups in a special school which was modified for their use, or they were not provided a school program within the public schools. The modern architecture of schools usually places the building on one floor and eliminates the need for elevators. Federal legislation, which was followed by legislation in all fifty states, requires that all new public buildings be built so that they are accessible for the physically disabled or the chronically ill. This means that ramps must be built; wider doors or openings into buildings, classrooms, and restrooms must be provided. Special facilities in the restroom must be installed, and, when necessary, elevators must be provided for any person who is physically disabled or chronically ill to the extent that he or she could not otherwise use the facilities within the building. These provisions pertain for the chronically ill, if the person has a condition such as rheumatic fever or severe asthma.

Consideration for the problems of the physically disabled child and the chronically ill child have usually not included consideration for the problems brought about by a mental disability in addition. There are exceptions to this combination of handicaps when one considers the multiply disabled child, such as the mentally retarded child who has cerebral palsy. However, many physically disabled and chronically ill children have intellectual abilities well within the normal range of intelligence; their primary difficulties have often come about as a result of their being excluded from attending school because of architectural barriers. Thus, by the time a school program was provided they were one or more years behind their peer groups in academic achievement as well as general social adjustment. With the construction of public schools which are accessible to physically disabled and chronically ill children, many of their learning problems should be minimized.

Definitions

Physically disabled children and chronically ill children are those children who are so disabled physically or so ill physically that they cannot profit from school without some types of special provisions or modications. The category of children with a physical disability who would require special provisions or modifications in school programs includes those children who have such conditions as cerebral palsy, muscular dystrophy, multiple sclerosis, wry neck, congenital club foot, and poliomyelitis. A chronically ill child has an illness which is so severe as to cause him to need frequent intensive care services in a hospital setting, or he is so ill that he must receive his instructional program within his own home. Therefore, he is prevented from attending classes in the public schools on a consistent day-to-day basis. A chronically ill child is one who has such conditions as epilepsy, chronic and severe asthma, ulcers, cystic fibrosis, and rheumatic fever. The more common problems of cerebral palsy, muscular dystrophy, multiple sclerosis, epilepsy, and chronic asthma are presented in this chapter. For conditions such as bone imperfections, postural conditions, conditions because of infections, and other conditions, excellent reviews are provided in Cruickshank and Johnson (1967) and Kirk.

An Interdisciplinary Approach

It is usually necessary to use an interdisciplinary approach if the needs of the crippled or chronically ill child are to be properly met. To determine whether psychology, physical therapy, education, and/or rehabilitation would play the leading role depends upon such factors as the age at onset of the condition, the severity of the problem, and the prognosis. Each profession must play a part in the interdisciplinary approach. To appreciate the part each profession must play, members of the cooperating disciplines must have, therefore, an understanding of the various orthopedic impairments and the problems that are often associated with them.

Various agencies such as schools, clinics, and rehabilitation centers are well aware of the need for united efforts; and when properly staffed, can do much to help crippled and chronically ill children become well-adjusted adult citizens.

Almost every disabled person can be helped. The whole process of helping the disabled to make the most of his possibilities is called rehabilitation. The first step in rehabilitation is medical and surgical treatment. Transplanting bone from another part of the body causes a short, twisted leg to be straightened and even lengthened. The pain and swelling of arthritis may be relieved by the use of certain drugs. The doctor in physical medicine takes over after the other specialists have done all they can. A program is then designed to include exercise and training for the patient, and the doctor may prescribe aids such as a brace or an artificial limb.

The nurse, physical therapist, speech therapist, occupational therapist, vocational counselor, social worker, and psychologist work with the specialist in physical medicine and rehabilitation. In the rehabilitation process, the social workers and psychologists are very important. Their work is especially important because the patient's feelings about his disability and his family's attitude can make the difference between success and failure.

Often clinics and rehabilitation centers are not available, and schools may lack the needed specialized personnel. It then becomes the responsibility of the school to devise some means for adequately serving crippled or chronically ill children.

Distinction of Disability versus Handicap

Children with physical disabilities or chronic illnesses may be considered together in a discussion of a disability as opposed to a handicap. These conditions, in the opinion of the authors and others, are disabling conditions and should be recognized by the classroom teacher as disabilities rather than handicaps. Hamilton (1950) has made this distinction by describing a disability as a condition which may be either physical or mental and can be defined and described medically; whereas a handicap refers to the way in which a person's disability interferes with his ability to function in accordance with his capability. This means that a person who is disabled is not necessarily handicapped in that the disability of the individual will depend upon the situation in which he finds himself and the demands of the particular environmental situation. Many people could find, if they have not already done so, a situation in which they would be handicapped according to a definition of handicapping conditions; however, a disability does not automatically limit all areas of one's functioning. Therefore, the important point seems to be that provisions should be made for the child who is physically disabled or chronically ill to have an environment in which he can function at his best. This will mean a structuring of the environment, psychologically as well as physically, in order to insure that these children are able to function according to their abilities. In other words, without modifications in the environment, the physically disabled or the chronically ill child may not be able to perform adequately and he may become grossly handicapped (Wright 1960).

Special Considerations

Although the physical environment, may be modified, nevertheless, teachers and other school personnel who are working with physically disabled or chronically ill children must modify the attitudes and the approaches they use with these children besides. If, because of a child's physical disability or chronic illness, one assumes that the child, cannot perform certain tasks, and therefore provides him with nothing to do, then one may cause that disability to become a handicap. In other words, the teacher and parents should not approach the disabled child with physical or medical problems as a child who, because of his disability, cannot perform. Developing a positive attitude toward the physically disabled and the chronically ill child is not an easy task. Doing so will entail the use of one's ingenuity in order to modify the learning environment and the psychological environment so that the child can progress in his learning. Learning to accept frequent absences and frequent interruptions because the child needs the services of a physical or occupational therapist, or because the child may need hospitalization for short periods of time in order to receive appropriate medication and treatment, will not be an easy adjustment for the classroom teacher. Factors such as those mentioned above will require the classroom teacher to be flexible—to plan an individualized instructional program for the child. Adjustments in attitudes and preparing instructional programs will be necessary if the physically disabled or chronically ill child is going to remain within the mainstream of regular education.

When a teacher has one or more children who are physically disabled or chronically ill, he may be inclined to do too much for those children. For example, the teacher may want to pick up the child when the child is capable of walking; or to get something for the child when the child can get it for himself. Several of these children may take lengthy periods of time in order to accomplish a task such as moving from one part of a room to another, but the teacher must permit the child to complete the task by himself. A primary objective in working with children who have physical or medical problems is to help them build and maintain as much independence as possible. Fostering or encouraging dependency on the part of the child should be avoided at all times.

The authors have experienced several demonstrations of training programs which have enabled physically disabled children to promote their independence and physical activity. In one situation the children involved in the training program were in wheel chairs and all of the youngsters were multiply disabled. During the training demonstration, these children were required to remove themselves from their wheelchairs without assistance, move across a padded floor for a distance of approximately five to ten feet, return to their wheelchairs, and lift themselves into their wheelchairs. The objectives of these exercises were not for the purpose of mere demonstrations, but were part of a program which focused on developing physical movement which was within the capabilities of the children.

It is not recommended that teachers of physically disabled or chronically ill children follow these procedures, as presented above, without being certain that the activity is within the child's capability. Determining the child's capabilities for physical activity must be accomplished through consultation with the child's medical doctor, and never arbitrarily decided by the classroom teacher or other school personnel.

The ways in which a teacher can promote independence and safety habits on the part of the physically disabled or chronically ill child are quite varied. The teacher should become a part of the total program provided for the child in order to promote independence and safety habits. He should also consistently check any special equipment the child has to insure that it is safely operating. This safety awareness includes such things as checking crutches for breaks, for missing crutch tips or missing screws, for defective wheelchairs which won't lock, for broken chin straps on helmets, and for safety features throughout the school area (Swack 1969). The teacher may also assist in reminding children to take their medication, aiding in the acceptance of the children in the classroom and in the total school, and insuring that the children are provided adequate rest periods.

School personnel who are working with children who have physical disabilities or chronic illnesses must consistently be aware of the child's current functioning. For example, the teacher, principal, school nurse, and school counselor will need to request and carefully read periodic reports from the child's medical doctor. These reports should provide answers or guidelines to such questions as:

1. Is the child presently taking medication?
2. Has the child's medication been increased or decreased recently, and if so, in what ways might this affect the child's behavior?
3. Is the child's physical or health problem improving or worsening?
4. Does the child's condition warrant any specific physical restrictions?
5. Does the child's present condition require any specific approaches or cautions on the part of school officials?
6. Can the child safely be removed from his wheelchair; or, can his braces be moved once or twice daily?
7. May certain pieces of equipment, such as standing tables, be provided to give the child a change from his wheelchair?
8. In what ways might the child's physical or health problem affect his ability to perform tasks such as reading and writing?
9. If the child is to be confined temporarily at home or in a hospital setting, may he have visitors?
10. Can and should the child, if confined at home or in a hospital for a temporary period of time, continue to perform his school work?
11. What is the child's prognosis? Has his condition permanently stabilized? Will his condition improve or deteriorate?
12. To what extent should the school provide rest periods for the child? How often should the child rest and what type of rest period should be provided?
13. Does the child's condition require any modifications in his diet? Should he eat light meals but eat often? Should any items be eliminated from his meals?
14. If medication has to be administered at school, what procedure does school personnel have to follow in order to fulfill this requirement?
15. Does the child need certain protective equipment, such as a helmet, in order to prevent him from hurting himself? If so, who will furnish this equipment?
16. If the child needs physical, occupational, and/or speech therapy, how often will these services be provided? Will these services be provided in school or will the child have to miss school?

17. Does the child need assistance in using restroom facilities? If so, how much assistance does he need?

These questions should serve as a sample of the type of modifications in the school program and the teacher's preparation which are essential for appropriate educational services for the physically disabled or chronically ill child. Without current information regarding the conditions of the child, the teacher will not be sure about which procedures to implement with the child. Answers to situations such as those posed above may also provide a school counselor with appropriate information for counseling the children. As the child matures and becomes more aware of the limiting aspects of his condition, he will need assistance, through counseling, in the continual process of development of his self concept.

Physical Modifications for Physically Disabled or Chronically Ill Children

Although the child who is physically disabled or chronically ill may not need a self-contained special classroom for his instructional program, many modifications will have to be made in the school building. These modifications may include the following:

1. Building ramps with appropriate slopes which will not be weather-slick at any time, to provide entry into the building.
2. Installing handrails throughout the hallways.
3. Lowering lavatories in the restrooms.
4. Widening doors of and enclosing toilets, lowering toilets and providing handrails within the toilet stalls.
5. Provision within the child's classroom or the school building for physical facilities required for rest periods.
6. Permitting the child the necessary time he will need if he has to move from one classroom to another.
7. Provisions of space for conducting physical, occupational, and/ or speech therapy.
8. Providing the child with the necessary time he will need to complete his assignments. His problems may cause him to write slower, read slower, or require brief periods of rest during the day.
9. Providing cars or buses with special equipment such as hydraulic lifts so the children may have easy access in and out of a means of transportation.
10. A teacher's aid who can help in caring for the physical needs of children who may need assistance.

11. Provision of special equipment in the classroom such as a special typewriter for those children who cannot write legibly by hand.
12. Training the teacher in the procedures to follow when a child has an epileptic seizure.

Of course, all children who are physically disabled or chronically ill will not require the entire modifications which have been listed above. However, if the school system is planning to provide a program which will include the majority of the children in the community having physical or medical problems, these factors must be considered carefully and planned in advance of opening the program. In the experience of one of the authors who assisted in planning and opening a school program for the physically disabled, all of these factors were considered and careful planning was completed prior to beginning the program.

Psychological Aspects of Physical Disability or Chronic Illness

The psychological aspects of physical disabilities or chronic illnesses are equally as important for school personnel to consider. A child who is or becomes disabled by reason of a physical difficulty or a chronic illness will have to make several adjustments during his life. As he grows older, the effects of his problem will begin to have more impact upon him and his functioning. For example, when he reaches the teenage years he may not be as mobile or physically active as his normal peer group, and may often be excluded from school activities such as dances, school plays, and school clubs. He will not be able to participate in physical education programs, or engage in athletics such as football, basketball, or tennis. These restrictions will cause the child to recognize time and again that he is, in some ways, different from his peer group and he may feel isolated and very inadequate. Counseling services will be required periodically throughout the lives of these youngsters to help them maintain adjustment to these situations. Classroom teachers will also have to focus on helping these children to develop appropriate hobbies so that their leisure hours can be meaningful and constructive.

Teachers should carefully plan activities such as field trips to insure that the physically disabled or chronically ill child may actively participate. The physical plant of the school should be constructed to provide these children with recreational and sporting activities and for possible development of interests as spectators of these types of activities. Class parties should also be planned thoroughly enough to include any child who may have a physical or medical problem. In brief, school programs need to include these children in as many activities as possible in order to help them become an integral part of the program, and of the school.

Selected Physical Disabilities and Chronic Illnesses

Medical descriptions of physically disabling conditions or chronic illnesses are not essential information for school personnel. However, descriptions of the ways in which physical functioning is affected are important. Medical doctors will generally provide this type of information upon request; therefore, school personnel can become knowledgeable about specific circumstances of a particular condition that a child may have. With this thought in mind, rather than discuss all of the possible conditions which may cause a child to be physically disabled or chronically ill, the authors have selected a few conditions which are more common among children.

Muscular Dystrophy

Muscular dystrophy is generally a progressive disease which causes the muscles to be replaced by fatty tissue. As the disease progresses, a child will become more disabled because he loses the use of his voluntary or skeletal muscles. The progressiveness of muscular dystrophy is often referred to as a wasting away of the muscles. The child becomes progressively worse, eventually must be confined to a wheelchair, and will usually die before reaching adulthood.

There is no cure for muscular dystrophy at the present time; however, research is being conducted by the National Institute of Neurological Diseases and Blindness in an effort to control and find a cure for this disease. Muscular dystrophy does not affect large numbers of children; however, school personnel will often have one or more children with this condition in the school program.

The child with muscular dystrophy will need special provisions, because he will generally be confined to a wheelchair, may often miss school and need homebound instruction. As his condition progresses he will require periodic counseling, physical therapy, and frequent rest periods during the school day (*Muscular Dystrophy: Hope Through Research* 1968).

There are presently over one hundred clinics in the United States which provide no-cost services such as diagnostic-services, follow-up care, and medical services. These clinics have been established through the efforts of the Muscular Dystrophy Associations of America, Inc. A few of the specific services provided through these clinics include the following: medical management, physical therapy, genetic counseling, education, and guidance in using community resources (*The Exceptional Parent* 1972).

Multiple Sclerosis

This is a disease which is also progressive, and generally does not afflict a person until he is twenty years of age or older, however, cases have been reported in children who are under fifteen. This is a disease which affects the central nervous system through the destruction of myelin which serves as a protective, insulating sheath around nerve fibers. As the disease progresses, the individual becomes more disabled; although, at times, he may appear to be improving (*NINDB Research Profile: No. 6, Multiple Sclerosis* 1967).

School personnel on the secondary level should be aware of this condition and the symptoms involved. Symptoms include such factors as difficulties in coordination, speech, and vision. Any child who consistently has symptoms of this type may not have multiple sclerosis, but his parents should be notified so they may seek appropriate medical consultation (Dunn 1973).

Cerebral Palsy

Cerebral palsy is one of the most common types of physical disabilities. A majority of these children will have multiple handicaps such as impairments in hearing, vision, speech, and intellectual functioning. Cerebral palsy is not a progressive disease, but it is a disorder which results in problems in motor coordination. Many children with this disorder will, therefore, have difficulty in mastering skills which involve fine or even gross motor abilities. This will include writing ability and using motor skills for carrying, sorting, and manipulating objects (Dunn).

According to Hopkins, Bice, and Colton (1954) the most common types of cerebral palsy are spastic and athetoid. They estimate that over two-thirds of the children who are cerebral palsied will have one of these two types of cerebral palsy. The other types of cerebral palsy, less common, are ataxia, rigidity, and tremor.

Dunn describes the motor involvement of the spastic child as follows:

Involuntary contraction of affected muscles when they are suddenly stretched—called stretch reflex—resulting in tenseness and difficult, inaccurate voluntary motion.

The child with athetosis will have the following motor difficulties:

Involuntary contraction of successive muscles resulting in marked incoordination and almost constant motion of the extremities. (Dunn, 1973).

Based upon these characteristics, school personnel should be aware of the extreme difficulties these children will have in performing motor skills. Working with these children will require patience, understanding, and special modifications in learning tasks in order to provide appropriately for their instructional program. For example, instead of requiring handwritten work or expecting the child to use his fine motor skills for writing lessons in the classroom, the teacher may have to permit the child with cerebral palsy to recite his lessons orally; or provide the child with a typewriter so that he may present written lessons which are legible and easier to manipulate.

Children who have cerebral palsy will require many modifications within a school program if they are to have success. Of course, there are some children with this disability who are so grossly limited that they cannot speak intelligibly, cannot move physically in a meaningful way, and are confined to a wheelchair; and they may also be blind or deaf. For such children a public school is usually not feasible, and some type of residential facility will be required for their care and training. If the child with cerebral palsy can attend the public school, he may require the services of a speech, physical, and/or occupational therapist. In fact, many of these children can progress if they are provided services from one or all of the therapists mentioned above during their early childhood years. Teachers will also have to make modifications in their programs because of the child's motor problems which have already been mentioned. The child may also drool excessively when speaking and special equipment will be required in order to preserve the child's classroom work (Robinson and Robinson 1965).

Epilepsy

Epilepsy is among the many disorders of mankind about which volumes of literature have been written. It is a disorder which has been frequently misunderstood, and a person with epilepsy has often been plagued with adverse social attitudes. Prior to the advent of drug therapy which has been responsible for improvements by way of partially or completely controlling one's seizures, many persons with epilepsy were prevented from participating in numerous events. For example, children with epilepsy were often excluded from school because of their seizures; and if permitted to attend school, they were not given the opportunity to participate in many of the school's activity programs. Persons with epilepsy have been feared, shunned, and treated very cruelly and, surprisingly, even in an enlightened society such as the United States, many of these attitudes are still prevalent today.

According to Robinson and Robinson epilepsy is characterized by the following:

> . . . recurrent attacks of unconsciousness, convulsions, stereotyped movement, and other miscellaneous symptoms. The types of attacks can be classified into several groups, but the patterns are not always distinct; numerous children show mixtures of symptoms. It is important to note that epilepsy in many children can be controlled medically with a high degree of success.

It is essential that classroom teachers know that a child has epilepsy. He also needs to know what medication the child is taking, how often the medication is required, and to what extent the child's seizures are controlled by the medication. Even if a teacher receives a report that a child's epileptic seizures are controlled by medication, he still needs to be prepared for the possibility of a child having a seizure in the classroom. The teacher must know what he can do for the child and how he can help the other children in the room understand the child's seizures. Of primary importance, the teacher must provide for the safety of a child during a seizure. A seizure which manifests severe activity is commonly referred to as a grand mal, and this is the type of seizure for which the teacher must be prepared to protect the child.

A grand mal seizure involves convulsions in which there is rigidity of the muscles. This activity immediately precedes the convulsive state in which the child will begin jerking and this stage is commonly referred to as the seizure. Many persons with epilepsy will have some type of warning prior to their seizure. The warning, referred to as the aura, may be in the form of a motor, visual, hearing, olfactory, or psychic process which actually forewarns the individual of an impending seizure. The seizure may start immediately after the aura or may be delayed long enough for the person to prepare himself for his seizure. Grand mal seizures seldom last long (possibly 30 seconds) and may vary in their frequency during any one day. The longer their duration, the more likely they will be followed by a period of deep sleep which is usually followed by disorientation and confusion on the part of the child. The grand mal is the most common type of epileptic seizure and may usually be controlled by proper medication (Kirk).

If a child has a grand mal seizure, the teacher should not try to restrain the activity, but instead help the child in the process of falling to the floor to insure that he does not injure himself, turn his head to one side, and try to provide comfort for him. He should also remove any sharp objects or any classroom equipment which is near the child so the child will not hit them during his seizure. Even though a majority of grand mal seizures are controlled by proper medication; the teacher should still be aware of the child's condition in the event the child forgets his medication, or needs new medication for the control of his seizures.

Other types of seizures include the petit mal, psychomotor, and Jacksonian. None of the seizures are as common or as severe as the grand mal. However, the teacher does need to be aware of the child with petit mal seizures. A child with this type of epileptic seizure may have brief periods of time during which he is inactive, he may stare into space, hesitate in his speech, or temporarily stop a motor activity. Seizures of the petit mal type may go unrecognized if the teacher is not alert to the child's behaviorisms. He may think that the child is not paying attention, is daydreaming, or just slow in his actions. One of the authors worked with a child who had petit mal seizures which were characterized by brief periods of inactivity during which the child stared into space. The seizures were as frequent as one or two every ten minutes and would last as long as ten to fifteen seconds per seizure. Without detection, this child would have consistently missed many aspects of the instructional program. Additional information regarding petit mal, psychomotor, and Jacksonian seizures is available in Robinson and Robinson, Kirk, and Cruickshank and Johnson.

Severe, Chronic Asthma

Asthma is a condition which affects many children. The more severe the asthma, the more likely it is that the child will need some type of special provisions in his school program. Asthma becomes more severe during specific seasons of the year such as the spring when many plants are blooming and there is much pollen in the air. The condition of asthma, "Is a disease of the bronchial tubes of the lungs marked by attacks of difficult breathing" (Kirk).

The main concern of educators with respect to the condition of asthma is that the child may miss school frequently or he may require hospitalization and have to receive his educational program in the hospital setting. Educators should also be alert to situations which may bring on an asthmatic attack, such as taking a group of children on a field trip to a location where ragweed is growing. An asthmatic attack is seldom very dangerous and a teacher should know about a child's medication for controlling this particular condition. A teacher should also be informed about any restrictions which might be placed on a child who has asthma and adjust his program accordingly.

Other Conditions

As mentioned previously, the authors did not intend to be comprehensive in a discussion of conditions which may be chronical illnesses or physically disabling. However, for the reader's individual research, a list is provided below of several conditions which have not been discussed in this chapter.

1. Crippling Conditions
   a. Muscular or Neuromuscular Impairment
      (1) Poliomyelitis
      (2) Spina Bifida
   b. Skeletal Deformities
      (1) Bone imperfections
      (2) Tuberculosis of the bones or joints
      (3) Osteomyelitis
      (4) Arthritis and myositis
      (5) Epiphysis
      (6) Polydactylism—Syndactylism
      (7) Congenital amputations
      (8) Fractures, burns
   c. Postural Defects
      (1) Postural foot conditions
      (2) Torticollis
      (3) Spinal Defects—Scoliosis, Kyphosis, Lordosi
2. Chronic or Special Health Problems
   a. Cardiac or heart anomalies
   b. Rheumatic fever
   c. Pulmonary tuberculosis
   d. Nephritis, nephrosis
   e. Hepatitis, mononucleosis
   f. Leukemia, other cancer
   g. Diabetes
   h. Malnutrition

From the preceding list, the reader should become aware that many conditions exist which may cause a child to be physically disabled or chronically ill. References which discuss many of these problems include Cruickshank and Johnson, Telford and Sawrey (1967), Kirk (1972), Lyght (1964), and B. Van Osdol (1972).

Nonpublic School Provisions

Homebound instruction and hospital teaching services are authorized through the majority of state departments of education, and may be administered through the state agency for education or a local public school system. Both of these programs are essential for children with physical disabilities or chronic illnesses because of the frequency with which they must miss school, and/or the lengthy intervals between their classroom sessions.

Homebound Instruction

Homebound instruction is provided for a child if he is confined to his home for a period of time and cannot attend the public schools. The absence from school must be over an extended period of time and cannot be because of some minor disability. Before a child can be placed on homebound instruction, a physician's report concerning the child's health is required and the local school system must usually apply for approval to have the child receive this type of service (*A Program of Education for Exceptional Children in Oklahoma* 1970).

Larger school districts generally have homebound instructors who are regular members of the teaching staff. A homebound instructor is similar to an itinerant teacher, except that he travels from home to home providing instruction to those children for whom his services have been approved. The number of children a homebound instructor can serve is usually limited by law and the number of hours the child must be instructed is also specified. Homebound instructors must serve as a liaison between the child and his regular classroom teacher. In this manner, the homebound instructor may help the child to progress in a manner similar to his classmates, and may also prepare the regular classroom teacher for the time when the child will return to his class program.

Hospital Teaching

Hospital teaching is somewhat different from homebound instruction; however, children with similar types of problems may be found in both settings. The hospital teacher is generally on the staff of the hospital, or if the hospital teaching program is quite large, the program may operate similar to that of an independent school system.

Hospital teachers must plan the instructional program around the medical services and treatment which has been scheduled for the child. If at all possible, teachers who serve in hospital settings must be strong-willed and convince hospital staff that the child's continuing education is important and should also be scheduled. If the child has to remain in the hospital setting for a long period of time and is not provided with appropriate educational services, he may then lose a year of school when he returns to his home.

A teacher in a hospital setting must be prepared to teach all subjects and all age ranges. In many instances, he may be the only teacher in the hospital, which will require a highly skilled person if the children are going to receive adequate instructional programs. Hospital teachers must also be innovative and knowledgeable in obtaining any special equipment that will be required in teaching children from a variety of backgrounds, grade levels, and age ranges.

Teacher Characteristics

A person who becomes a teacher of children who are either physically disabled or chronically ill must have certain characteristics if he is to be successful. From the descriptions of children and program modifications given previously it should be obvious that the teacher of children with these types of problems must be extremely patient. He must be innovative and capable of developing meaningful working relationships with other professional personnel. A teacher of these exceptional children must also be capable of discussing the children's problems with medical doctors and obtaining information from other professionals that will benefit the children.

Teachers of physically disabled or chronically ill children must be firm and sensitive. Because of the child's current problems and the possibility of his being overly protected by parents and family, the teacher has to know what he can realistically expect the child to do in the way of performing tasks and caring for his own physical needs. The teacher must also have the ability to work effectively with children who may have terminal conditions and know that their conditions, whether physical or medical, are terminal. Children who are rapidly becoming totally disabled may want to cease trying, often become discouraged, and may be overwhelmed with despair. The teacher will have to be aware of these conditions and have the training and sensitivity to handle these emotional situations. To accomplish these tasks and to avoid being discouraged in providing a meaningful program for children who are physically disabled or chronically ill, is a most difficult task.

Parent Counseling

The parents of children who are physically disabled or chronically ill will need periodic counseling services similar to those provided to the parents of other exceptional children. School personnel must be prepared to provide this counseling service to help the parents gain a better acceptance and improved understanding of their child. School personnel, including the principal and counselor, should also recognize that the parents of physically disabled or chronically ill children have been to many doctors, spent considerable periods of time in hospital wards, and sacrificed many material things in order to be able to provide financially for the special needs of their child. The particular condition of their child may be such that the parents are in serious financial difficulties and are emotionally drained. Sensitivity to the needs and emotional state of the parents is essential if school personnel are going to provide appropriate counseling services for them. Educators should also be knowledgeable about community resources which are available and will provide services to the children or to their parents. Knowledge of sources which can and will provide counseling services, special programs for the children, and possibly financial assistance for the parents will save the parents much time in searching for facilities, and considerable frustration from not knowing where they may turn next.

Organizations like the Shriner's have been most influential in making facilities available for children who are physically disabled. Other fraternal organizations exist which provide services for the children and there are also government agencies which can be helpful to these families. For example, although the program may not help their child, parents will be interested in knowing about the research which is being conducted by the National Institutes for Neurological Diseases and Blindness, and other service organizations.

Providing counseling services for parents which will help them improve their family relationships would be helpful. Recognizing that the parents may be restricted in their own social activities; because of the care which is required for their exceptional child, may help counselors to understand family situations which are very tense, and to relieve individuals who are most anxious and exhausted.

Services for the child who is physically disabled or chronically ill must be comprehensive and meaningful and should include all the members of his family. These children must be given every opportunity to develop their skills, interests, and their lives to the fullest extent possible.

Bibliography

A Program of Education for Exceptional Children in Oklahoma, Bulletin S.E. no. 7, Division of Special Education and the Oklahoma Curriculum Improvement Commission, Oklahoma State Department of Education, 1970.

Cruickshank, William M. and Johnson, Orville G. eds. *Education of Exceptional Children and Youth.* 2d ed. Englewood Cliffs, N.J.: Prentice-Hall, Inc., 1967.

Dunn, Lloyd M., editor. *Exceptional Children in the Schools: Special Education in Transition.* 2d ed. New York: Holt, Rinehart, and Winston, Inc., 1973.

Hamilton, K.W. *Counseling the Handicapped in the Rehabilitation Process.* New York: Ronald Press Co., 1950.

Hopkins, T.W.; Bice, H.V.; and Colton, Kathryn C. *Evaluation and Education of the Cerebral Palsied Child.* Washington, D.C.: Council for Exceptional Children, 1954.

Kirk, Samuel A. *Educating Exceptional Children.* 2d ed. Boston: Houghton Mifflin Co., 1972.

Lyght, Charles E., ed. *The Merck Manual,* 10th ed., Rahway, N.J.: Merck Sharp and Dohme Research Laboratories, 1964.

Muscular Dystrophy Association of America, Inc., *The Exceptional Parent* 1, no. 6 (April/May 1972).

Muscular Dystrophy: Hope Through Research, National Institute of Neurological Diseases and Blindness, National Institutes of Health, Bethesda, Md., 1968. Distributed through Washington, D.C.: U.S. Government Printing Office.

NINDB Research Profile: No. 6, Multiple Sclerosis. U.S. Department of Health, Education, and Welfare, Public Health Service, rev. 1967.

Robinson, Halbert B., and Robinson, Nancy M. *The Mentally Retarded Child: A Psychological Approach.* New York: McGraw-Hill Book Co., 1965.

Swack, Myron. "Therapeutic Role of the Teacher of Physically Handicapped Children." *Exceptional Children* 35, no. 5 (January 1969).

Telford, Charles W., and Sawrey, James M. *The Exceptional Individual: Psychological and Educational Aspects.* Englewood Cliffs, N.J.: Prentice-Hall, Inc., 1967.

Van Osdol, Bob. *Vocabulary in Special Education.* Moscow, Idaho: University of Idaho Research Foundation, Inc., 1972.

Wright, Beatrice A. *Physical Disability—A Psychological Approach.* New York: Harper and Brothers, 1960.

PHYSICAL DISABILITIES AND CHRONIC ILLNESSES
Study Sheet #1

1. Discuss the psychological impact of physical disabilities and chronic illnesses.

   a. Impact on the child.

   b. Impact on the parents and family.

   c. Impact on school personnel.

PHYSICAL DISABILITIES AND CHRONIC ILLNESSES
Study Sheet #2

1. Choose one condition which is physically disabling or a chronic illness and describe this condition using the following format:

   a. Name or condition.

   b. Physical symptoms.

   c. Effect on physical performance.

   d. Effect on learning performance.

   e. Ways in which this condition can be prevented, controlled or improved.

'With a little help, I can see and hear many things.'

6

The Sensorially Impaired—
Vision, Speech, and Hearing

THE VISUALLY IMPAIRED

Definitions and Estimates of Prevalence

For sensorially impaired children, educational as well as other legal procedures are determined by definitions which have been specifically adopted for such purposes. Deviations from that which is considered normal vary in scope. In order to meet the needs of children who are visually impaired, certain criteria for exceptionality have been determined.

According to Telford and Sawrey (1967), blindness is usually defined as follows: "Visual acuity of 20/200 or less in the better eye with proper correction, or a limitation in the fields of vision such that the widest diameter of the visual field subtends an angular distance no greater than 20 degrees." Criteria within this definition were established by the American Foundation for the Blind. This definition means that a person with this impairment must be at a distance of twenty feet in order to read the standard type which a person with normal vision can read at a distance of 200 feet. A restriction in the field of vision means that a person may have normal vision for an area on which he can focus, but his field of vision is so restricted that he can see only a limited area at one time. This is usually referred to as "tunnel vision."

Another definition of blindness is based on the degree of useful vision that is retained by the individual, or in terms of the media which he is able to read. In such an instance, Dunn (1973) reports that blind children include children who have little remaining useful vision; therefore, they must use braille for purposes of reading.

The determination of eligibility for services which are available for blind persons through agencies or states is usually based on two characteristics of vision, which are visual acuity and field of vision. If corrected vision in the better eye is 20/200 or less the individual is considered to be blind. The second characteristic for determining blindness pertains to the condition in which a person's visual field is restricted to an angle no greater than 20 degrees as the widest diameter (Dunn 1973). These definitions are referred to as legal blindness or economic blindness.

Educators have also used these definitions for placement of children in special classes. Therefore, children with 20/200 vision or less are placed in self-contained classes for the blind; and children with a vision of 20/200 and upwards but less than 20/70 were eligible for placement in classes for the partially sighted, which are seldom found today. However, such definitions are not practical in terms of all education, because children with limited visual acuity make different uses of their abilities.

One of the most generally accepted characteristics for the partially sighted child is a visual acuity of between 20/70 and 20/200 in the better eye after maximum correction. Further stipulations are made regarding the methods used to educate children with this type of visual problem. These children retain relatively little residual vision and can read only very large print or possibly regular print under very special conditions.

Abel (1958) as reported by Cruickshank and Johnson (1967) has described five categories or degrees of visual acuity. They are as follows:

1. Total blindness, or light perception, or visual acuity up to but not including 2/200: would be unable to perceive motion or hand movements at a distance of three feet.
2. Motion or form perception or visual acuity 5/200: would be unable to count fingers at a distance of three feet.
3. Visual acuity up to 10/200: would be unable to read larger headlines of a newspaper, but would be expected to have some travel vision.
4. Visual acuity up to 20/200: would be unable to read 14-point or smaller type but would be expected to read large headlines of a newspaper.
5. Visual acuity of 20/200: would be able to read 10-point type, but insufficient vision for those daily activities for which vision is essential.

The state of Oklahoma (S.E. Bulletin No. 8 1971) accepts students as legally blind for special services whose best corrected vision is 20/200 or less. A child is eligible for special class placement if he has a corrected visual acuity of 20/70 or less in his better eye.

It seems to be generally accepted that the incidence of blind and partially sighted individuals is one of the lowest among the different exceptionalities. However, the incidence of mild visual defects is very high. Consequently, the authors estimate that one-fourth of all school children have some visual defects. A majority of these defects are easily correctable and do not require special educational or vocational considerations.

The statistics related to the prevalence of blindness and partial sightedness tend to be undependable. Part of the difficulty in collecting reliable data in this area, as reported by Hoover (1964), may be ascribed to a lack of uniform definition of blindness or visual impairment, and part to the fact that visual acuity is not determined by standardized methods.

The prevalence of blindness is often dependent on the characteristics of the culture involved. The rate may be higher in some areas, such as Asia or Africa, because of poor medical care and malnutrition. As medical services improve, the rate of incidences may go down for children and up for the aged, because average life spans are increasing. Therefore, the types of visual difficulties would also be reflected in the ages of those involved, because older people are more susceptible to varying types of visual difficulties.

The means most widely accepted for estimating the prevalence of blindness in the United States is the Hurlin method, which was based on studies of blindness in North Carolina and included the criterion of legal blindness presented above. Race and age factors within the various state populations served as a guide for Hurlin's estimates of blindness. The rates of prevalence for different states varies from slightly over one per 1,000 to almost four per 1,000 population. Using these estimates, more than 400,000 persons in the United States were blind in 1965 (Hurlin 1953 and 1962). For current estimates of blindness in the United States in 1972, this figure could approach almost 600,000 (Wilson 1965).

According to Dalton (1943) the incidence of mild visual defects affected approximately one-fourth of the school population. A survey which was taken in California involved over 5,000 children and indicated that 22 percent of the elementary children and 31 percent of the high school students had visual defects. The majority of these problems were so mild, though, that they required no special services because the vision defects were corrected.

Assuming that the criterion for blindness is a corrected vision of 20/200 or less in the better eye, then it is estimated that there is one blind child in every 3,000 school age children. The partially sighted population, using the criterion of a visual acuity of between 20/70 and 20/200, is estimated to be one in 500. As a total group, a conservative estimate is that approximately .0009 of all school age children need special educational facilities for the visually impaired. Two-thirds of these children are educationally partially sighted and the remaining one-third are educationally blind. Based on a current estimate of more than 53 million school children, there would be approximately 16,000 educationally blind and 32,000 partially sighted children who could benefit from special education services (Telford and Sawrey and Dunn).

Methods of Identification

Identifying children with gross visual defects is much easier than identifying those children who have less obvious difficulties. The child who is partially sighted is often not identified until some time during the elementary school years when the need for visual acuity becomes important in order to accomplish certain academic tasks.

In many instances, the observation of behaviors may cause a teacher to become aware of some suspected visual difficulty. Some of the more common symptoms associated with visual impairment are listed below. These symptoms were selected from Winebrenner (1952).

1. Has chronic eye irritations as indicated by watery eye or by red-rimmed, encrusted, or swollen eyelids.
2. Experiences nausea, double vision, or blurring during or following reading.
3. Rubs eyes, frowns, or screws up the face when looking at distant objects.
4. Is overcautious in walking, runs infrequently, and falters for no apparent reason.
5. Is abnormally inattentive during chalkboard, wall chart, or map work.
6. Complains of visual blurring and attempts to brush away the visual impediments.
7. Is excessively restless, irritable, or nervous following prolonged close visual work.
8. Blinks excessively, especially while reading.
9. Habitually holds the book very close, very far away, or in other unusual positions when reading.
10. Tilts the head to one side when reading.
11. Can read only for short periods of time.
12. Shuts or covers one eye when reading.

Of the various formal tests used to screen visual impairment, the Snellen Test is the most widely used because it can be easily administered. The test consists of a chart with rows of E's which are printed in different sizes and placed in various positions. A distance designation is assigned to rows of letters of a specific size. For example, at a distance of 20 feet, persons with normal vision can read the 20 feet row. If one can read correctly the letters on this row at this distance, he has 20/20 vision. Deviations from an ability to read correctly the letters at specified distances provide an indication of visual impairment.

The Snellen E chart should be used as a screening device for the possibility of visual problems with all school age children. However, this test is not appropriate for attempting to determine all visual impairments. For example, a telebinocular is a measuring instrument that is easy to use. It assesses visual skills in the areas of depth perception, vertical imbalance, lateral imbalance, and distant and near point fusion. It can be very helpful in determining a child's visual skills which are needed for reading and other close work. Another means of identifying children with visual impairment is the Massachusetts Vision Tests which consist of a monocular vision acuity test, plus a sphere test, and the Maddox Rod Test. The Massachusetts Vision Tests are generally considered to be more effective in measuring visual difficulties than the Snellen E Chart (S.E. Bulletin No. 8, Oklahoma 1971).

Children suspected of having a visual difficulty should be referred to an ophthalmologist or other eye specialists. The schools or other agencies that work with children may do limited screening of vision, but specific diagnosis should be made by a professional eye specialist. For any child who has a visual impairment, recommendations should be made to the parents for them to return the child to the eye specialist frequently in order to provide periodic checks for possible progressive disorders.

Characteristics of the Visually Impaired

A totally blind child is often seen as showing a lack of animated facial expression, often having blank looking or disfigured eyes, and one who displays a general awkwardness in his ability to handle himself in space. The child who is partially sighted may be seen as a child who wears thick lens or holds objects unusually close to his eyes in order to see them.

However, using general physical appearances in order to differentiate between the sighted child and the visually impaired child is not always possible. The visually impaired child may have organic impairments in addition to his visual problem; however, the incidence of multiply handicapped, visually impaired children is infrequent. Visually normal children may also have organic impairments which are similar to those of children having visually limited ability, and these impairments may be because of problems such as prematurity, malnutrition, or German measles.

A common difficulty found among blind or partially sighted children is related to gross motor performance. Obviously, the child with a visual impairment may have difficulty in areas such as mobility. Buell (1950) indicates that these children tend to be deficient in physical skills and general physical coordination. Environmental conditions may be the primary factor which results in difficulties in gross motor performance because the visually limited child is seldom encouraged to participate in physical activities. The visually impaired child will be deficient in imitation of skills, skipping, running, and other childhood activities. He may not be encouraged or have a desire to explore his environment and thus the development of his physical skills will be limited. As the child grows older, he may prefer to sit rather than participate in physical activities because he has been consistently warned of the many dangers which might exist in his environment. He may need to be encouraged and assured that his performance in normal activities, in which he is capable of functioning, will be beneficial.

Fine motor skill development may be deficient in children who are visually impaired. Deficiencies in this area of functioning will usually be evident because the child may have had limited activity in the manipulation of small objects, such as playing with building blocks, reaching and grasping objects for visual inspection, and learning the functional use of his hands. His inability to see these objects will cause the child to have fewer experiences and practice which is needed for the development of his fine muscles.

Independent travel will also be an area in which the visually limited child will be restricted. Consistently bumping into sharp objects or falling over objects will cause the child to have less desire to travel in his environment. Mobility of the visually impaired child may be affected by other handicaps which could involve his other senses. The importance of the auditory sense becomes apparent. Because his visual sense is limited, he may have to depend upon his auditory sense to provide him with clues about his environment and stimulation to move. Other senses may also become important in providing the necessary motivation for such a child. In some instances, persons around the visually impaired child may be overprotective of him which may increase his anxieties relative to mobility problems.

Being hampered somewhat in his ability to learn through visual imitation may cause the visually impaired child to suffer some major restrictions in the acquisition of knowledge. He is unable to learn through simple imitation of visual cues as does the normally sighted child. His parents and teachers must patiently teach him simple childhood skills, because he is unable to acquire these skills by himself. He must also be taught how to use his other senses to his best advantages.

The visually impaired child will experience many difficulties in the normal educational environment. He may have extreme problems in reproducing or interpreting written communications. His limited early childhood experiences with concrete objects, which aid the child's learning skills for discrimination of sizes, shapes, and colors probably will cause the child to have difficulties with abstract ideas. Some of the problems he may encounter with abstract ideas will have to do with factors such as distance, height, speed, and applying appropriate language to a complex problem.

The emotional needs of the visually impaired child do not differ from those of the sighted child. However, because of the many problems which were mentioned previously, his emotional growth and developmental processes may be severely affected by obstacles to which the child is subjected. Anxious parents may often overprotect their child if he has visual defects, which places restrictions on his normal desires for independence. Special help and counseling may be necessary for the parents of a visually impaired child in order to help them cope with the special problems that their child will encounter. Of course, the parents will also encounter many problems themselves in learning to care for their child, and counseling services will be periodically needed for the parents.

The inability to participate in physical activities such as playing sports, going on school field trips with his classmates, playing at school recess, learning to dance, and being included in physical education courses may cause the visually impaired child and his family to be faced with periods of serious emotional stress and anxiety. Experiences which will result in stresses of this type will vary considerably among individuals who are visually impaired. The inner resources of the child and of the members of his family will determine how well these periods of stress are handled. Other factors which will influence the extent to which emotional stresses and anxieties are met successfully will depend upon how successfully previous encounters have been, and how well the child and his family have been prepared to cope with problems of this type.

Experiences which result in emotional stresses and anxieties may also depend upon when the child became visually impaired. For example, if a child is visually impaired from birth; he may have less difficulty in adjusting to his disability than the child who becomes seriously visually impaired later in life. The child who was born with good vision will have to adjust his view of himself from one who was capable of certain activities to one who is now, because of his visual impairment, less capable of specific activities. This process may require more time and patience on the part of the child and his family. For the visually impaired child who once had good vision, adjustment will involve accepting a certain amount of dependence from others; whereas prior to his disability, he may have been completely independent in performing certain activities or skills.

Attempts to distinguish differences in the emotional adjustment of visually impaired children based on the time of onset of the impairment cannot be determined by hard and fast rules. For example, a child who is born blind or with a serious visual impairment will have difficulties in skills such as learning to eat, playing with toys, dressing himself, exploring his environment, and caring for his personal needs. His parents may become discouraged and quite exasperated in their attempts to teach him and play with him. During their efforts, the child will not respond to them with visual recognition, bright smiles, or other facial expressions, and the parents may unavoidably resent the lack of emotional responses from the child. Thus, they may do everything for the child, or neglect him and cease trying to help the child. During the child's stages of early development, the parents should seek training and counseling for the purpose of guiding them in caring for, understanding, and teaching their child. Without this training and counseling, the child may be the one who suffers by becoming an individual who is overly-dependent or neglected to the extent that he is, for all practical purposes, helpless.

Restrictions in physical activities and overprotection of the blind child may result in the development of certain characteristics which have no social or functional purpose. The child may rock his body, roll his head, move his hands before his eyes, or poke his fingers in his eyes so often that these behaviors become a part of the child's characteristics. Other handicapped children may also exhibit these same characteristics which are not limited solely to visual handicapping conditions. Blind children who develop these characteristics will generally require training in order to eliminate them. With appropriate guidance regarding activities in which the child can perform, teachers and parents can be helpful in providing an environment which will help the child develop more functional characteristics (Cruickshank and Johnson).

If blind children or seriously visually impaired children learn to use their other senses appropriately they can become very sensitive to small cues in their environment for a source of information and guidance. However, in comparison to normally sighted children, the visually impaired child is usually not superior in the use of his senses. Similar to training which is appropriate for learning academic skills, the blind child can be taught to listen closely to environmental stimuli and learn how to use these sounds for determining distances and possible obstructions to his mobility. Abilities such as these are not, however, innately superior in visually limited children (Telford and Sawrey).

Indications of significant educational retardation may be evident when one compares a blind child to children with normal vision of the same chronological or mental age. This difference is not necessarily a lower general intellectual functioning among visually impaired children but may be the result of a lack of appropriate educational services. Children with severe visual problems will have more difficulty learning abstract concepts and learning through the use of Braille, large print type; or audition will tend to cause these children to learn at a slower rate. Visually impaired children may have medical problems which cause them to miss school frequently and they may not start school at the age of six. All of these factors contribute to his problems in learning and, thus, one may conclude that the significant educational retardation of visually impaired children is multidetermined (Dunn 1973). Of course, this does not mean that the blind child cannot be mentally retarded, emotionally disturbed, or below average in his general intellectual functioning. Genetic factors may influence his intellectual functioning and environmental situations may contribute to the development of severe emotional problems. The authors have worked with several children who were blind, deaf, and mentally retarded; and several instances of multiple handicaps among the visually impaired have been reported in the professional literature.

Overview

Blind children were the first handicapped group for whom special provisions, such as residential centers and day school classes, were made, although the prevalence of blindness is comparatively smaller than other handicapping conditions. Visually handicapped children do not differ significantly from normal sighted children in physical appearance; although they may display certain characteristics often associated with nervous or mentally retarded children. They also tend to fall behind in certain areas of cognitive learning and in arithmetic.

The visually handicapped child may encounter some difficulty in making social adjustments; but, as a rule, they do not exhibit special characteristics or personality types. The difficulties they encounter are related to their desires for independence and their needs for a certain degree of dependence because of their disabilities; and because of a tendency toward feelings of anxiety about moving around in an unfamiliar environment which is full of potential hazards.

The overall intelligence level of the visually impaired child does not differ significantly from that of the child with normal vision. Those individual intellectual deficits that do occur may often be associated with another handicap. Generally, the basic intellectual capacity of blind children can be compared to that of the general population.

THE HEARING IMPAIRED

Definitions

The term "deafness" is often commonly used to refer to either total or partial loss of hearing. However, more recently, the term "hard-of-hearing" has been used to replace the phrase "partially deaf."

The types of problems faced by partially hearing or hard-of-hearing children may be completely different from problems encountered by children with complete hearing losses. Therefore, careful considerations must be made in discriminating between the two groups of children with such different hearing impairments.

Social, educational, and medical factors are the criteria used to determine the extent to which one's deafness is a problem. For example, the social criteria involves adequate communication skills, and without these skills the deaf child will have serious problems. Communication problems will usually exist if the hearing loss exceeds 80 decibels. If the decibel loss is less than 80; an individual may still have severe communication problems; however, he may learn communication skills to the extent that he will be considered as a hard-of-hearing child. Determining whether an individual is deaf or hard-of-hearing will also depend upon his ability to learn how to use a hearing aid. The medical criteria for determining the effects of a hearing loss is based on the decibel loss which the child suffers (Davis and Silverman 1966).

In making a distinction between "deaf" and "hard-of-hearing" children, it is necessary to point out that very seldom does an individual have *complete* loss of hearing. Many individuals will show ⁓ne degree of residual hearing as measured on an audiometer; however, the ability to use residual hearing is a primary factor in discrimi-ˀetween deafness and hard-of-hearing.

ˌosed definitions for the hearing impaired were prepared in ˌhe Committee on Nomenclature of the Conference of Ex-f American Schools for the Deaf. These definitions are still ˌre reported by Davis and Silverman as follows:

Deaf: Those in whom the sense of hearing is nonfunctional ˌor the ordinary purposes of life. This general group may be divided into two smaller groups which are determined by when the loss of hearing occurred.

a.   The congenitally deaf: Those who were born deaf.
b.   The adventitiously deaf: Those who were born with normal hearing but in whom the sense of hearing became nonfunctional later through illness or accident.
c.   The hard-of-hearing: Those in whom the sense of hearing, although defective, is functional with or without a hearing aid.

Pauls and Hardy (1953) indicate that the following classification of hearing loss is based on the necessary intensity (loudness) in decibels (db) before an individual is capable of detecting the presence of sound.

20-40   db loss = Mild
40-60   db loss = Moderate
60-75   db loss = Severe
75-100 db loss = Profound

An intensity of about 70 decibels, or about 48 decibels above the normal speech-reception threshold, is indicative of an average intensity for conversational speech. According to Newby (1964) this means that a person with a loss of 30 decibels who is using a hearing aid would barely be able to hear conversational speech. The individual would, of course, miss much of what is said because many speech sounds would be made below his threshold for speech.

Telford and Sawrey indicate that a definition of deafness or hard-of-hearing also takes into consideration the quantitative aspects of the loss. This factor typically differentiates hearing loss as it is measured audiometrically in terms of decibels. Such a loss refers to the deficit in the better ear for the frequencies in the speech range. The White House Conference on Child Health and Protection (1931) utilized the age of onset of the hearing loss as the main criterion for distinguishing between the deaf and the hard-of-hearing. This conference defined deaf children as those persons who are born with a hearing loss which prevents the maturational acquisition of speech; as those persons who acquire deafness before language and speech are developed; and those persons who become deaf shortly after speech developed, and consequently, lost their language skills. Even though these definitions are old, they still seem to be applicable to children who are hearing impaired.

In SE Bulletin No. 8, Oklahoma (1971) the hard-of-hearing child is one who has a hearing loss which has not prevented him from acquiring speech and language in the normal manner, which may be described as imitating what he hears. However, the authors realize that an individual with this type of hearing loss experiences difficulty in auditory reception. Therefore, he may not hear all of the speech sounds distinctly and may confuse, substitute, or omit sounds. He is, though, still capable of oral communication and is able to master language to some degree.

Cruickshank and Johnson expand the classifications of hearing loss offered by Rushford (1964) and give an indication of what might be expected relative to language growth at each level. These classifications are generally the same regardless of the source of information. Most audiometers used to test hearing use standards that were set by the American Standard Association (ASA) in 1951. Their standards were based on a survey of normal hearing taken in 1937. More recently, however, new standards were set by the International Organization for Standardization (ISO) allowing an extra 10 decibels for each level of hearing acuity compared to ASA's standard of 0 decibels for normal hearing. Therefore, the new ISO standards consider a 10 decibel loss to be within the normal range of hearing. The classifications referred to earlier are as follows:

Group A—Mild Hearing Loss: 15-30 db (ASA), 25-40 db (ISO) in the better ear across the speech range. Those children who have a hearing loss in this range usually learn speech spontaneously in the normal manner and are considered to be on the borderline between those with normal hearing and those with a significant hearing impairment. They are unable to hear certain speech sounds and what they hear is slightly diminished in volume. Children with a mild hearing loss require special help so that they can maintain what speech and language skills they have learned.

Group B—Hard-of-hearing: 35-60 db (ASA), 45-70 db (ISO) in the better ear across the speech range. Such a loss is distinctly a handicap. The child may be able to learn language with the help of amplified sound, but will encounter difficulty in following group conversations. He may have a limited vocabulary and may be easily confused by words with more than one meaning. What he hears is more diminished in volume. The child's speech will reflect his distorted hearing and will be characterized by numerous articulation problems, consisting of distortion, omissions, and substitution of consonant sounds. For example, he would not be able to distinguish between the k-t-p or b-d-g, etc. Special help would be required in order to establish good speech patterns and full language development.

Group C—Borderline Severely Hard-of-hearing-Severely Deaf: 65-75 db (ASA), 75-85 db (ISO), above 500 (Hz) frequency range in the better ear across the speech range. The spontaneous development of adequate language and intelligible speech will not be developed by children with this range of hearing loss. They may make numerous grammatical errors and tend to use a more concrete vocabulary. As in the previous group, they will have some degree of difficulty in comprehending words with more than one meaning. They also show much distortion in their articulation. Amplification and intensive special training is necessary for these children.

Group D—Severely Deaf: 80-95 db (ASA), 90-105 db (ISO) in the better ear across the speech range. Children who fall in this range of hearing loss do not develop speech spontaneously. The types of speech which the children will hear are mainly speech pitch patterns and the vowel sounds. Even with amplification, these children would hear conversations as a whisper. They would need amplification and an educational program specifically planned for deaf children.

Group E—Profoundly Deaf: 95 db-no response (ASA), 105 db-no response (ISO) above 500 Hz in the better ear across the speech range. Even with amplification, these children hear only sensations which are of the noise type. They require intensive training and education by special education teachers who are trained to teach deaf children. Education must start during the preschool years if these children are to learn speech and language adequately. Without special aids, these children are unaware that someone is talking.

One may go beyond these classification systems in order to gain a fuller understanding of the impact of a deaf child's language problems. At a recent conference (1970) on Vocational Education for the Handicapped, Howard Wyks who was the vocational principal of the Marie Katzenback School for the Deaf in Trenton, New Jersey, proposed that deaf children should be considered as a part of the disadvantaged population. His proposal was based on the premise that English for deaf children may be considered as a second language. As the severely hearing impaired child progresses through school, language becomes more difficult for him; therefore, he must have educational experiences which relate communication and computational skills to pertinent areas of employment.

Estimates of Prevalence

Davis and Silverman report a Silverman (1960) estimate that 5 percent of school age children have hearing levels outside the range of normal, and that one or two out of every ten in this group (of the 5 percent) require special educational attention. A percentage estimate for today would reflect a more accurate count, but according to O'Neill (1964) there were approximately 300,000 children and 2,300,000 adults in the United States, who were considered hard-of-hearing. Also, because of the aging process, the incidence of hearing difficulties would tend to increase each year if the age of the population is considered.

S.E. Bulletin No. 8, Oklahoma (1971) suggests that because of some confusion in arriving at an acceptable definition and an adequate criterion for assessment, it is difficult to arrive at an accurate estimate of the number of children with auditory problems. However, it is felt that most surveys show an incidence of 1.5 percent of the total population have some type of hearing impairment. Estimates from other authorities may run as high as 4 to 5 percent of the population.

The reader should note that deafness or hearing impairment may be found in any subpopulation group within the United States. There is no particular group in whom deafness is more prevalent, and severe hearing impairments may be the result of a variety of factors such as genetic causes, rubella, prenatal influences, or injuries.

Methods of Identification

In more severe cases where a child is auditorially handicapped, it is possible to identify the handicap by behavioral symptoms alone.

One research report, Curry (1954), indicated that teachers do only slightly better than chance in selecting those students in their rooms who have some type of hearing loss. Therefore, in a majority of cases involving those children with mild to moderate hearing losses, it is necessary to use more formal means of identification.

Several tests have been devised in an attempt to assess hearing losses. Many of the tests which are in existence were devised prior to the development and sophistication of the pure-tone audiometer. Although no longer widely used, a few of these older methods employed such test devices as tuning forks; one's ability to hear conversational speech; the tick of a watch at specified distances; and the use of noisemakers such as bells or wood blocks. These methods only provided rough estimates of the possibility of a hearing loss because of variances in environmental testing situations such as outside noise factors, the lack of appropriate acoustics, the shape and size of the testing room, and even the extent to which the tester had normal hearing (Newby).

The most frequently used electronically controlled device for testing hearing is the pure-tone audiometer. The audiometer produces tones of varying frequency (pitch) and intensity (volume), which cover a wide range. This machine is carefully calibrated to give out "pure" tones at each frequency selected, ranging from 125 cycles per second (cps) to 8,000 cps. The volume is controlled by an attenuator which is usually calibrated in 5 db steps. The test consists of systematically presenting a series of tones that vary in pitch and volume. The person being tested hears the tones through a set of earphones, one ear being tested at a time. The subject is asked to indicate either verbally, by using hand signals, or pressing a buzzer when he can hear the tone that is being presented to him. The results are then plotted on an audiogram, giving an indication of the individual's ability to hear a tone at each of the frequencies presented.

The pure-tone audiometer is commonly used in the public schools to screen children in order to find those who may have a hearing impairment.

Another type of audiometer has been devised to test from ten to forty children at one time. This special device is a phonographic audiometer which will accommodate any number of headphone receivers that is desired up to a total of forty. Special recordings utilizing both male and female voices are then played through the headphones. One ear is tested at a time. The voices, reading digits or words, grow gradually less distinct until only those with normal or superior hearing acuity are able to hear what is being said. The children are to respond by filling blanks, checking words from a list, or by drawing a picture of the object that has been named (Newby).

Moss, Moss, and Tizard (1961) report another special test which may be used to test an individual who is suspected of malingering or is severely retarded, or very young. Such a test uses the Galvanic Skin Response as an indicator of whether or not an individual has heard a presented sound. Initially the individual must be conditioned to respond by pairing a tone with a small electric shock, to which the individual responds. His responses are indicated on a special machine. If proper learning has taken place, the individual responds in the same manner when the tone is presented by itself, provided he is able to hear the tone. Such a device is more commonly used under special circumstances.

If the use of these instruments indicates that a child has a hearing impairment, the child should be referred to a medical specialist who can determine if the loss can be corrected by surgery or by the use of a hearing aid. The medical specialist who is trained in the area of the anatomy of the ear and hearing is the otologist. Public schools may also have an audiologist on the staff who can appropriately assess a child's hearing by using one or both of the audiometers previously described. The audiologist should also be trained to know the special types of assistance or training which will benefit the child. The audiologist should establish good working relationships with the otologist, since they will often work as a team in diagnosing a hearing problem, working with the child's parents, and specifying a training program.

Characteristics of the Hearing Impaired

All children at birth, whether deaf or of normal hearing, go through the same steps of language development. They experience emotion, cry, gurgle, and laugh. However, the child with a severe hearing loss or profoundly deaf child will eventually slow down in the area of speech development referred to as babbling. This is the stage of speech development when the child with normal hearing is concentrating on reproducing sounds he has made or sounds he has heard others make. The normal child gains a sense of satisfaction in hearing himself make funny noises. He also gains some pleasure from the way some sounds feel as they are made, as in the "m" sound, and from the reactions he gets from significant adults around him. For the deaf child, much of this experience is missing. If a child is unable to hear the sounds that he or others make, he may lose interest in making sounds. Rather than repeating favorite sounds, he utters random concoctions of sounds. In some cases, he may be self-stimulated to reproduce sounds that are kinesthetically pleasing as in the "m" sound; however, for the deaf or hard-of-hearing child, speech development will suffer at this point. He may also become handicapped in other areas of development because he is unable to respond to or react to sounds in his environment.

For children with less severe hearing losses, speech may be slower in developing, but a hearing loss may often go unnoticed until the child has entered school; and poor articulation, chronic inattention, failure to respond when spoken to, confusion when given directions, or other common symptoms of a hearing loss become more apparent. If a child has other handicaps such as a physical disability, or mental retardation, hearing losses may also often go undetected because of the primary problems or symptoms of the other handicaps.

Symptoms of a Conductive Loss

It is not possible to specify with accuracy, the symptoms that are always associated with a conductive hearing loss. However, certain generalizations can be made. For example, if an individual has a conductive type hearing loss, he may not be aware of external noises around him and he is generally able to hear himself well through bone conduction. Therefore, he may speak consistently in a relatively quiet voice, omit some inflections in his speaking pattern, and make it difficult for others to hear him.

The individual with a conductive hearing loss usually has no impairments in his speech discrimination skills. In a noisy environment where normally hearing individuals tend to raise their voices, he will be able to hear the loud voices and perhaps not hear the surrounding noises. He is able to tolerate loud voices of an intensity that would be uncomfortable for individuals with normal hearing. The conductive hearing loss acts as an ear plug, thus protecting the inner ear. He also tends to have about the same degree of loss for all frequencies, however, he may hear the higher frequencies better than lower ones.

A person with a conductive hearing loss may frequently complain about subjective noises in his head. These noises may be focused in one or both ears, or throughout the head. This is usually caused by an increased awareness of sounds caused by normal bodily processes; whereas, the individual with normal hearing is more aware of the many sounds which come from the environment (Newby).

Symptoms of a Sensori-Neural Loss

Newby relates that the individual with a sensori-neural hearing loss involving the ability to perceive sounds may not be able to hear himself speak; and, thus, he may speak in a very loud voice when such intensity is inappropriate. Because of his inability to hear his own voice, he is unable to judge how loudly he is speaking. It should be pointed out; however, that in many cases, those children with either type of hearing loss learn how to regulate their voices using other cues from their environments.

Difficulty with speech discrimination is much more common among individuals with a sensori-neural type hearing loss. Primary problems are in the area of discriminating high frequency sounds, and particularly if these sounds are produced with weak intensity. Words which sound similar but have different meanings may be most difficult to discriminate. He may be able to hear normal speech, but he will experience difficulty in understanding what was said. Part of this difficulty may be because he fails to hear initial or final sounds of a word and hears only the vowel sounds. This individual will experience great difficulty in his ability to hear in noisy surroundings. External noises will interfere with his ability to perceive normal conversations or other types of verbal productions. The person with a sensori-neural hearing loss may also complain of consistent buzzing noises in one or both ears and in his head. Obviously, his hearing problems will be more intense than those of the person with a conduction type loss (Newby).

In summary, it is often difficult to tell whether or not an individual has a hearing handicap unless the loss is severe. In many cases, the physical appearance is not altered. Certain behavioral symptoms may give an indication that a hearing loss could be suspected. However, specially designed tests utilizing mechanical devices should be administered to the child suspected of having a hearing loss in order to determine if such a loss exists and in order to differentiate between the type of loss and severity. The most commonly used device is the pure-tone audiometer which may be used for screening purposes.

THE SPEECH IMPAIRED

Definitions

"Speech is defective when it deviates so far from the speech of other people that it calls attention to itself, interferes with communication, or causes its possessor to be maladjusted" (Van Riper 1964).

In order for speech to be defective, there must be a listener who makes such a judgment. Speech that is conspicuous may depend on the age of the individual involved. Young children, when learning how to talk, make many types of speech errors such as, "wabbit" instead of "rabbit." If the same types of speech errors were made consistently by an older child or an adult, that individual's speech would be considered defective. Adults suffering certain types of mental or physical shock following a severe accident, or war action, may develop speech impairments. Thus, it is possible for a speech defect to arise at any time in life.

If the way an individual speaks (such as using a peculiar voice, hesitations, or distortions) causes a lack of communication, his speech is unintelligible and defective. Facial contortions which are often seen in the child who stutters or the individual with cerebral palsy, may also be considered defective. In such a case, the listener may be paying more attention to the facial distortions than to what is being said. In the case of the individual with cerebral palsy, his inability to control facial muscles may interfere with articulation which may cause several problems that impede communication. The individual who is unable to talk, for one reason or another, is also penalized in his ability to communicate. He may develop a system of gestures to replace words; however, if another person were not in constant contact with this type of gesturing, he would have a great deal of difficulty in interpreting this method of communication. Therefore, the impaired person's effective communication is limited.

Speech is also considered defective when a person becomes so concerned about it that he becomes handicapped socially or vocationally. Emotions can greatly affect the flow of speech and the ability to communicate. The child who stutters often becomes so concerned about his speech problem that he avoids situations where he must speak. This often creates another emotional problem for the individual, and a vicious cycle is set in motion. Similar reactions may be observed in those with other types of speech difficulties.

Another definition cited by Telford and Sawrey (1967) offers similar implications regarding defective speech. "Speech is considered to be defective when the manner of speaking interferes with communication, when the manner of speaking distracts attention from what is said, or when speech is such that the speaker himself is unduly self-conscious or apprehensive about his way of speaking." Once again the listener and his interpretation plays an important part in determining whether or not speech is defective; except in the instance where the speaker himself is concerned to such an extent that he is unable to communicate.

Estimates of Prevalence

It is difficult to pinpoint the prevalence of speech disorders, usually because of the different criteria used by the investigators, the areas sampled, and the interpretation of what constitutes defective speech. On a general basis, however, the authors estimate that from 5 to 10 percent of all school children have some type of speech impairment.

Telford and Sawrey cite findings by two committees of the American Speech and Hearing Association (1952, 1959) which independently estimated that a minimum of 5 percent of school-age children have defects of speech sufficiently serious to warrant speech correction or therapy, and that an additional 5 percent suffer from noticeable but less serious defects. The present authors do not believe that a percentage breakdown of the different types of defects would be pertinent information, because of the rapidly changing population and the availability of services for handicapped children.

Methods of Identification

Many indications of speech defects may be discussed by parents or by the classroom teacher. These cases should be referred to speech and hearing clinics or other professional people. Systematic speech screening procedures are in effect throughout most of the public schools, but thorough diagnostic evaluations are usually made when a more severe type of speech defect is involved. A battery of tests, including a complete physical and dental examination, an assessment of intellectual level, an audiometric evaluation of hearing, and, in some cases, a psychiatric examination should be given.

Telford and Sawrey report that there are several scales and tests which can be used to screen speech or aid in assessment (Barker and England 1962; Fletcher 1953). Some of these are the Wood Index of Defective Articulation, The Templin-Darley Screening and Diagnostic Tests of Articulation, and the Boston University Speech Discrimination Picture Test. There are also specially scaled phonographic recordings of defective speech available. These are graded in terms of severity and the individual's speech may be compared with the samples (Curry et al. 1943; Perrin 1954).

Characteristics of the Speech Impaired

In some cases, those with speech defects have other disabilities. Those with more severe speech problems include the mentally retarded, brain-damaged, or those with structural deformities such as cleft palate or cleft lip. However, there is another group of children whose only problems are their speech impairments. They are otherwise physically and intellectually normal, which is in contrast to those whose speech impairments are associated with other handicaps.

Although most of the individuals with a defect in speech are found to be physically normal, generally 10-15 percent of the children with the more serious types of speech defects also have other physical disabilities. On tests of motor proficiency, children with a speech impairment perform slightly below normal children (Jenkins and Lohr 1964).

The incidence of speech defects is higher for those children who are either visually or aurally handicapped. Children who have speech defects generally seem to have difficulty in the area of language proficiency, which may affect their overall intelligence. There appears to be some evidence that possibly shows that these children frequently fall below the norm in measured intelligence because, as stated earlier, speech defects are more commonly associated with mental retardation. A person must possess a certain intellectual capacity if he is ever able to learn proficient speech.

Speech disorders are often accompanied by emotional problems. In a society that places value on the ability to communicate orally, the child with a noticeable speech defect is sometimes heavily penalized or rejected. The one group that is most markedly affected is the stutterer. Those with other types of speech disorders are also needlessly ridiculed by those who do not understand the problems involved. It should be noted, though, that the child who has speech problems as a result of emotional trauma should receive emotional therapy primarily, and speech therapy secondarily.

The authors believe that the readers should be aware of normal speech developmental patterns and the different characteristics of defective speech. Therefore, the authors' following brief descriptions are offered only as introductions to impaired speech. Further study in these areas may be pursued in speech and hearing courses.

Speech Development

Speech development begins with the birth cry. Throughout the early months of life, the baby begins to experiment with sounds, producing a majority of vowel sounds. This also is a time when the muscles, as well as the lungs, needed for later speech are exercised and strengthened. Swallowing is also used to develop the skills necessary for the production of certain speech sounds, such as the "k" and the "g."

The stage of babbling begins early in life, usually around the eighth week. This stage consists of the production of various vowel sounds and with the production of various consonant sounds such as the "g," "b," and "m." These sounds are fairly easy to produce and are a part of the gurgling and other sounds made by the baby. This type of vocal play is easily reinforced by the attention given to the child from others in the environment. Babbling continues until about the fifth to sixth month when the type of vocal play involved begins to become more purposive. Sound production is also pleasing to the child, although a majority of the speech sounds uttered are randomly selected. The child doesn't need to be able to hear in order to enter this stage of speech development.

During the second six months of life the child begins to repeat heard sounds, and the lalling stage in speech development is begun. Sound production is associated with hearing and in producing sound a child is beginning to learn how to control his environment through speech.

The echolalia stage usually begins during the ninth or tenth month of life. During the lalling stage the child is inclined to repeat sounds that he has heard himself make, but during the echolalia stage he begins to imitate sounds that he has heard others make. His repertoire of sounds is increasing and he is able to form more sound combinations. Hearing acuity is vital to this stage of development, because the child must be able to hear sounds produced by others in order to develop speech.

True speech generally appears around twelve to eighteen months. The child is able to make certain sound combinations at will and does so for a purpose. He is also able to comprehend certain speech such as "no-no" and will respond motorically. Beginning vocabulary usually consists of nouns which are important to the child. Later, verbs enter the vocabulary, followed by adjectives and adverbs. Pronouns are next with articles and prepositions coming last. Parts of speech, though, are often omitted or used incorrectly as the child begins to learn language. By the age of one year, the child should have a vocabulary consisting of two to three words. By age two the vocabulary should contain nearly 300 words, and the child should be able to put together simple two- or three-word sentences. The acquirement of vocabulary then increases rapidly. The three-year-old child should have a vocabulary of approximately 800-900 words; but by age six, growth in vocabulary generally slows down.

Articulatory Defects

Defects in articulation are the most prevalent of the speech disorders. Errors in articulation are characterized by omissions, substitutions, distortions, and additions of speech sounds. Although many such errors are commonly found among children who are just learning to talk; speech is considered defective if they persist at a later age. It is felt that a child should be capable of producing all of the speech sounds (consonant and vowel sounds, including blends, dipthongs, etc.) accurately by the age of 7-7 1/2; unless there is some physiological or psychological cause, such as defects in the articulators (larynx, teeth, tongue, lips, hard palate, soft palate, jaws, or nasal cavity) or a fear of communicating with others.

Omission of speech sounds occur when a child leaves out a sound in a word, such as pay for play, or pease for please. Such errors are very common in young children who are not yet capable of producing blends of two consonant sounds. Certain sounds may also be omitted from the beginning, middle, or end of words.

Substitutions of speech sounds involve the replacement of one consonant sound for another. For example, a child may substitute the "w" for the "r" sound in the word "rabbit." Some children may be able to produce a sound in one word, yet substitute another sound for the same sound in another word. For example, a child may be able to say the word, "yes," correctly; but substitutes the "l" for the "y" sound in the word, "yellow." He may substitute the "f" for the "th" in the word, "tooth"; and the "p" for the "f" in the word, "fork." Such errors are often inconsistent in that the child may be able to produce the sound, but has not stabilized the use of the sound in speaking.

Distortions of sounds are probably more noticeable in the child who is said to have a lisp. The sibilant sounds, "s" and "z," usually take on a mushy characteristic. In a frontal lisp, the voiced or unvoiced "th" sound is also substituted for the "s" or "z" sounds. In the lateral lisp, air is forced out the sides of the mouth and the "s" and "z" take on the characteristics of the "sh" or "zh" sounds.

Another type of distortion is referred to as lalling. In this case the "r" and the "l" sounds are usually affected, because of misplacement of the tongue. However, the "t" and "d" sounds may also be affected. Distorted sounds are often caused by improper manipulation of the articulators, possibly caused by poor learning.

Some children may attempt to add a sound to a word. For example the word, "please," may become "puhlease"; or the word, "hanger," may become "hangger." This type of error frequently occurs in words that have a blend in them.

As mentioned earlier, omissions, substitutions, distortions, or additions of speech sounds may occur in either the initial, medial, or final position in a word, or may occur consistently in all three positions. Errors in articulation often may appear to be very inconsistent.

Some of the causes of articulatory defects may be attributed to poor speech models in the home or environment, mental retardation, poor muscle coordination or control, emotional conflicts, organic anomalies, or structural defects involving the articulators, or related to hearing impairments and auditory perception difficulties.

Voice Defects

Defects which involve the voice usually include deviations of pitch, quality, or intensity. When pitch is involved, the individual may speak in a voice that is too high, too low, a monotone, or suffer from pitch breaks often associated with the onset of puberty. When a teenage girl speaks in a voice that is so low that she attracts attention to herself; she is using an inappropriate pitch level for her age and sex.

Some children speak so softly that they are difficult to hear. Others may speak too loudly, consequently inappropriately, for a situation. In either case, a hearing impairment may be suspected. It is also possible that the child has learned to speak loudly in order to be heard over the noise of other sounds in the environment, such as those sounds made by several brothers and sisters, by TV and/or radio, etc.

Defects in voice quality include hypernasality, denasality, breathiness, or hoarseness and huskiness. In normal speech, a certain amount of nasality is required for the proper production of certain speech sounds such as the "m," "n," and the "ng" sounds. However, for other speech sounds, it is necessary to close the nasal passage in order to prevent excessive nasal resonance. The individual who seems to "talk through his nose" is involved with hypernasal speech. This type of speech is often characteristic of the child with a cleft palate; or the child who has some degree of paralysis of the soft palate and is unable to affect the necessary closure of the nasal passage during speech. In some cases, improper speech may be caused by a poor speech model.

In denasal speech, the individual may sound as if he has a cold in his head. There is a complete lack of the nasal resonance necessary for certain speech sounds. In such cases, the cause of denasal speech may be attributed to occlusions to the nasal passages as when the adenoids are swollen or infected in some way.

In some children, an unusual amount of hoarseness may be noticed. If this condition appears to be persistent, an examination of the throat should be recommended, because this type of voice defect may be caused by the growths of nodules or polyps on the vocal cords. These growths, caused by improper use of the voice or by straining the cords, pose a difficulty common to those individuals who use their voice a great deal. With help, though, such individuals may be retrained in the proper use of the voice.

The individual who appears to be out of breath when he speaks may also be retrained in a more effective way of speaking. Breathiness involves both tension and quality difficulties.

Defects in Rhythm

The most common speech difficulty that comes under this heading is stuttering. Stuttering is characterized by blocking, repetition, or prolongation of speech sounds, words, phrases, or syllables. Physical tension or facial or other types of bodily distortion may also be observable.

Although difficulties in the rhythm of speech are fairly common to some degree in most of the population under various circumstances, the individual who becomes a stutterer becomes more emotionally involved because of his nonfluency. Many children experience such nonfluency during the process of developing speech; however, as they become more proficient, such nonfluencies disappear. If they do not, the child may be regarded as a primary stutterer. This usually means that the child experiences a certain amount of nonfluency in his speech; but he is not yet concerned about his speech and has not yet adopted any gestures to help him initiate speech, or avoidance reactions to speech. With some help from a speech therapist, this individual may often be helped to overcome his periods of nonfluency.

However, as more people begin to notice nonfluent speech and call attention to it, the individual may soon experience much tension and anxiety toward speaking, and he adopts various means of initiating speech such as stamping his foot, hitting a table, or moving some other part of the body. Facial grimmaces may become apparent as may other signs of physical strain and tension. In some cases this individual may attempt to avoid speaking situations, thus jeopardizing social and vocational or educational opportunities.

It is fairly safe to say that no two people who stutter are alike in their patterns of stuttering; except in the fact that they are having difficulty in their rhythm of speech. There are many instances when the stutterer may go for seemingly long periods with fluent speech; while at other times he may not be able to communicate at all. In many cases the stutterer is able to sing or recite poetry without a single period of nonfluency. The stutterer may be able to speak to certain people freely, with little stuttering; yet may be unable to talk to other people without becoming hopelessly involved in nonfluent speech.

The emotions of the individual who stutters are deeply involved. It is important that those who come into contact with a child who has nonfluent speech become informed about the various aspects surrounding this speech disorder. After the speaker begins to think of himself as being a stutterer, the anxiety surrounding speech becomes self-perpetuating and a vicious cycle is established. The speaker feels anxious about his nonfluent speech so he inevitably becomes nonfluent. Then, he becomes more aware of his nonfluent speech, and consequently becomes more anxious, etc. There are several theories regarding the cause of stuttering. However, no one, as yet, has discovered a satisfactory answer to this relatively unique phenomenon.

According to Cooper (1973) most studies pertaining to stuttering indicate that two out of three persons who have the problem of stuttering will recover spontaneously. Cooper has developed "The Cooper Chronicity Prediction Checklist for School Age Stutterers: An Inventory for Research" which is one approach to use in predicting recovery from stuttering. He also reports that his inventory may assist a speech clinician in identifying variables which have a cause-effect relationship to stuttering. These variables include the following: chronicity and family history, chronicity and severity, chronicity and duration of stuttering, and chronicity and stutterer's attitudes. Further research with this inventory may prove very beneficial to speech clinicians.

Delayed Speech

Delayed speech usually refers to a marked retardation in the child's ability to use language or to communicate. The child may frequently substitute or omit sounds. He usually uses simple words and phrases rather than sentences and may use a vocabulary that consists primarily of nouns and verbs. In some cases, he may show no interest in speech at all; and not only will not attempt to speak, but will often not listen to speech. In such a case, the child may attempt to communicate by the use of gestures.

If a child has not acquired the use of a small vocabulary by the time he is 18-24 months old, there may be reason to suspect some degree of speech retardation. If a child is not using simple two- or three-word phrases by the time he has reached thirty months, he should be referred to a physician or to some other type of specialist to determine if there is some type of physical cause for the delay in language development. Of course, if a child has been ill frequently throughout infancy, such a rule may not apply as there may be retardation in speech because of factors related to the child's illness.

There are several possible causes of delayed language. One is mental retardation. The retarded child is usually slower in developing in all areas of physical activity. Coordination is often poor, especially in areas that require fine motor skills such as in speech. These children have difficulty in the area of articulation, and in higher level aspects of speech such as perceiving, thinking, and remembering.

Another cause is based on emotional disturbance. In some cases, a child may develop a fear of communicating with others. For some children, the act of not speaking is a powerful means of controlling the behavior of others in their environments. Under this category the child who becomes voluntarily mute may be considered as speech defective. In such emotionally involved cases a child may have gone through the normal stages of speech and language development and then suddenly stopped talking. Such cases may often be related to some event in the life of the child that has caused him to stop talking. Small children also may go through negative stages in which they do not respond well to communication. As they grow, there are so many demands placed upon them that the pressures become momentarily unbearable, and they may learn to react by not speaking. In this way they can maintain some control of the situation.

Autistic children would also come under this category. These children are often so sensitive to their surroundings that speech or communication is threatening to them. This type of speech problem is very complex and usually involves a child who does not desire to relate to people in any way. Although such children may be taught to speak through good therapeutic assistance, they usually exhibit other marked differences that place them in a category by themselves.

In other cases, delayed speech may be caused by a lack of appropriate stimulation in the environment. A child must be able to hear speech and have a reason to communicate before he can be stimulated or motivated to speak. If his needs are met without using speech, he will not develop speech as quickly as others. In some environments, children are often discouraged from speaking for various reasons. Demands may be made on the child regarding speech that are not possible for him to meet, causing much pressure on the child who may then associate speech as being an unpleasant experience.

Brain injuries may also be responsible for a delay in language development. Certain areas of the brain are responsible for the proper development of speech skills. If any of these areas are damaged, such as that which is responsible for the movement of the articulators; speech may be more difficult to acquire.

A final possibility for the cause of a delay in speech is that of a hearing impairment. If a child is physically unable to hear speech; he will not feel motivated to speak. The child may also have difficulty in perceiving speech, which may be caused by other types of auditory problems.

Delayed Language

Many of the causes attributed to delayed speech may affect the child in the area of language. When brain damage is present, the child may have difficulty in understanding speech, to perform the motor act of speaking, or to learn how to read and write. He may also have similar difficulties if a brain lesion occurs after language has been learned. The degree of difficulty the child experiences is dependent upon the extent of the brain damage. Milder forms can often be observed in the child who experiences great difficulty in learning how to read, commonly known as dyslexia and alexia. Another child may experience his primary handicap as an inability to express his thoughts; although he is capable of comprehending what is said to him. Still another child may experience difficulty in several areas, which make communication a very arduous task.

Cleft Palate Speech

Cleft palate speech is usually characterized by a very nasal quality of speech; and often includes mild to severe distortion of certain speech sounds, such as the plosives; which require the build up of a certain amount of air pressure in the mouth before the sound can be produced. Other speech sounds may also be affected in different ways.

A cleft or opening may occur in several places in the mouth or nasal passages. A cleft may involve the hard palate, the soft palate, the hard and soft palate, the lips, the jaws, or the nose. These openings are generally caused by the failure of these areas of the mouth to close completely during growth and development in the early stages of pregnancy in the mother. Another type of cleft exists where there are no visible signs of an opening; yet a child exhibits the same type of cleft palate speech. In such a case, the cleft may be just under the skin covering of the hard or soft palate, where it involves the bony structure between the oral and the nasal cavity.

The peculiar nasal quality characteristics of cleft palate speech is caused by the fact that air cannot be blocked off from the nasal cavity as is necessary for most of the sounds in normal speech. In most cases, these clefts can be surgically repaired. However, the child may continue to have some difficulty with speech.

Cerebral Palsy Speech

In speech associated with cerebral palsy, brain damage may cause extreme difficulty in the control of the muscles which are necessary for the production of speech sounds. Although in some cases, the speech muscles may not be affected; a majority of those children with cerebral palsy do experience a handicap in this area. The individual is usually unable to control such things as speech rate or rhythm, and the accurate production of consonant sounds. Speech is often jerky, or very labored, and slow. The voice is also affected because the child may not be able to control the pitch and quality of the sounds.

Speech Defects Associated with Hearing Impairment

A child unable to hear speech of others clearly may exhibit speech defects, usually in articulation, but sometimes in voice production as well. His voice may be either too loud, or too soft, or show a lack of inflection, which gives a monotonal quality. Depending on the type of hearing impairment present, the child may have a mild articulation defect, may show retardation in the development of speech and language skills, or may not be able to develop speech at all without special training. The type of articulation problem that exists is generally determined by the type of hearing loss.

In summary, individuals with speech defects include those people whose speech is conspicuous or unintelligible; or is unpleasant to the speaker. There are many degrees of speech handicaps ranging from mild articulation problems to more severe speech problems, which are associated with cleft palate or cerebral palsy. In many cases, a speech defect can easily be identified. There are also special tests available which have been devised to evaluate speech. Although those with speech defects may be physically normal in appearance, speech defects are often associated with other handicaps.

EDUCATIONAL PROGRAMS
The Visually Impaired

Educational objectives for visually impaired children do not differ from the objectives for normally sighted children. The primary difference in educational programs for visually impaired children will be the ways in which programs will meet the objectives; obviously, there are some visually impaired children who may require special vocational training, teachers who are specially trained, and special equipment within the classroom (Telford and Sawrey).

Classrooms for visually impaired children must be equipped with various tools, which provide other than visual cues. Emphasis is usually placed on learning through listening. Children also must be trained to use tactile skills, and encouraged to engage in appropriate physical activities. Thus, he has the opportunity to develop needed social skills.

It must be decided as soon as possible whether a visually handicapped child is to use Braille as his primary means of learning, or if the child is to use both Braille and large print books. The child who is not totally blind must be encouraged to use his residual vision as much as possible.

Training in the use of a Braille typewriter or a Braille stylus and slate is also essential for the visually handicapped. The slate and stylus is composed of two metal strips between which is placed a sheet of paper. A stylus is used to punch holes in the paper using the Braille alphabet. In some cases, where the visual deficit is less severe, the child may be taught a minimum usage of pen and pencil.

Additional special equipment and other resources which are necessary for visually impaired children include such items as the following:

1. Tape recorders
2. Record players
3. Special resource or itinerant teachers
4. Braille typewriters and/or a Braille stylus
5. Special calculators
6. Rulers and slide rules
7. Compasses and protractors
8. Relief maps and globes
9. Special large print books
10. Magnifying devices

Classrooms for blind children must also be carefully designed and advantageously located. Special care should be taken in the arrangement of each room in order to facilitate movement; and in some cases make possible a sight-saving program. Therefore correct illumination, either natural or artificial becomes an essential factor. The classroom must have ample space for special materials, which are usually larger and more cumbersome than those found in regular classrooms. Care should also be taken in the selection of furniture to be used in a special classroom.

When a sight-saving program is being utilized, special considerations should be given to the placement of the teacher's desk and other pieces of equipment. Chalkboards should be of a lighter color so as to reflect light. It should be noted that sight-saving classes are older concepts of education and today's education should reflect a curriculum that requires the children to use their residual sight. Sight activities are not harmful to the sight-defective child. In fact, maximum use of one's residual sight is recommended for educational growth.

Partially sighted children usually should be encouraged to remain in the regular classroom as much as possible. They are also educated and prepared for life in much the same way as the normally sighted individual. They are encouraged to use vision to its maximum, learn to read and write, and acquire as much education as possible by normal means. In some cases there is a need for a slight adjustment in curriculum and the use of special equipment; but otherwise, education for partially sighted children may follow that of normally sighted children.

If partially sighted children remain in the regular classroom; one of the special provisions should be the seating arrangements. Allocations must be made to place these children closer to information centers such as the chalkboard. They also must have the freedom to move around the classroom to get closer to the special equipment and materials. In general, partially sighted children should be included in as many of the activities provided for the normally sighted children as possible.

The Hearing Impaired

Ewing (1960) indicates that because of the problems involved, it is preferable to educate the deaf and the hard-of-hearing children in separate rooms or by different means. The differentiation between deaf and hard-of-hearing children is usually based upon the ability to learn and understand speech. Totally deaf children must depend almost entirely on visual and other cues; but children with little residual hearing need some auditory training in order to make maximum use of their hearing. Therefore, the mixing of hard-of-hearing children with deaf children may cause the hard-of-hearing children to manifest deaf characteristics and fail to utilize their residual hearing.

Some deaf children will need special devices which offer amplification systems. The classroom should be designed to reduce those sounds which would interfere with amplification of desired sounds. Walls, ceiling, floors, and other openings must be specially designed or treated for this purpose. The location of the room is also important in reducing or eliminating extraneous, distracting noises. Special soundproofing materials should be used on the walls and ceilings. Lighting is another consideration in the special class, because deaf or hard-of-hearing children must depend on visual cues for much of their learning. S.E. Bulletin No. 8 Oklahoma (1971) recommends the following list of equipment for use in the classroom for deaf or hard-of-hearing children:

1. All the equipment provided in the regular classroom
2. Sense training equipment: Montessori equipment or a suitable substitute; colored yarn, balls, or ribbon for matching color; children's jigsaw puzzles

3. Equipment used in teaching speech reading; small table and chair so the teacher may sit with her lips on eye level with the child
4. Equipment for instruction in reading and other visual subject matter; chart racks for picture and word charts, picture cards; picture dictionaries; textbooks with simple language and large print; opaque projector; slide or film projector; 16mm projector; bulletin boards on children's eye levels
5. Piano
6. Records for acoustic training
7. Instruments for rhythms; bells, drums, cymbals, horn, tambourines, etc.
8. Television
9. Work books
10. Audiometer—pure-tone

The hard-of-hearing child who remains in the regular classroom should have a hearing aid if necessary and should be seated close to the teacher and in such a manner that he would be able to use lip reading skills. The use of concrete objects whenever possible helps the hard-of-hearing child grasp abstract ideas. Pictures may also be used to illustrate the meanings of words, especially if they are similar in sound.

A classroom that consists only of hearing impaired children, may possibly use a group hearing aid which stimulates both ears. Also, tape recorders and record players in which the intensity level can be controlled may be beneficial in auditory training. Although there are special visual aids specifically designed for use with the aurally handicapped, the teacher can still make her own materials based on the needs of the children.

The Speech Impaired

In most public schools across the country, a speech correctionist is available to work with children who have relatively mild speech defects. Those children who have more serious speech difficulties are usually referred to special speech clinics. The speech therapist generally does not work in a regular classroom. Rather, she uses a small room equipped with a mirror to accomodate anywhere from one to six children at a time. Special equipment is generally carried from one school to another, and usually includes materials which are prepared specifically to suit the needs of children involved in a speech therapy program.

A relatively comfortable room with pleasant surroundings is a very essential facility. In some cases, special equipment such as a tape recorder may be desirable. Other commonly used items may be obtained from the school, such as tongue blades, speech improvement cards, blowing equipment, practice devices, and educational toys and games. A place to keep therapy case records is also an important consideration.

RESIDENTIAL FACILITIES

Programs for the Visually Impaired

Residential schools for the blind involve an intensive care program, which hopefully provides a homelike environment. In many facilities the children are encouraged to go home as much as possible; and arrangements are made for special students to attend local public schools. The public schools should enable the students to get broader educations by taking courses that are not regularly offered in the residential schools. One of the primary concerns of residential schools is maintaining the student's contact with the general community, because they need to be able to live in a sighted-society also. Presently, nearly all states make special provisions for educating visually handicapped children. Either special schools are provided by the state, or arrangements are made to have these children educated by other agencies (Cruickshank and Johnson).

Programs for the Hearing Impaired

The residential school was one of the first types of facilities for educating deaf children. Several residential schools are in operation, but there has been a decrease in the number of hearing impaired children being sent to such special schools. Deaf children, like other children, need contact with the hearing environment.

There are several advantages and disadvantages associated with special programs and the needs of each particular child must always be considered. The trend today, however, is for the aurally impaired child to remain in the community and attend public schools if adequate provisions are available to him.

COMMUNITY SERVICES

The Visually Impaired

Barnett (1955) indicates that the vocational needs for the visually handicapped are usually inadequately met. Even though visually impaired people may be vocationally trained; they still have difficulty in finding appropriate employment. It is estimated that less than half of the blind individuals capable of working are doing so, and only about 20 percent of those who could function in a sheltered workshop are doing so.

Training programs to prepare the blind with employment skills are usually not available. In most cases, the blind person learns employment skills in the same situations as the visually sighted. However trained, though, the blind or partially sighted must compete with sighted persons for jobs, and combat the prejudices of some employers.

Sheltered workshops probably employ more visually handicapped people than other facilities do; but the employment outlook is not totally bleak, because many companies accept visually handicapped employees and integrate them into jobs where sighted people also work (Telford and Sawrey).

The Hearing Impaired

Lunde and Bogman (1959) indicate that the aurally handicapped are employed in almost all of the major occupational areas. However, there are usually fewer in the higher professional, managerial, and clerical and sales areas, which may be because of the greater demand for communication skills involved in those occupations. A larger proportion of this group is employed in the crafts or in semi-skilled types of employment, and a smaller proportion work as unskilled laborers; but there are indications that approximately 85 percent of the deaf workers have successful vocational careers.

Every state has a vocational division, which is responsible for the training of or working with the hearing handicapped for the purpose of preparing them to become self-supporting citizens. A list of occupations for which these individuals can train may be obtained from the United States Office of Education, Vocational Division. Similar information may also be obtained by inquiring at local state offices of rehabilitation.

SPECIAL TRAINING FOR TEACHERS

The Visually Impaired

Generally many of the same requirements necessary for the normal classroom teacher apply to the teacher of the visually handicapped. Personality attributes, including the ability to get along with people and in some cases the ability to counsel with parents is important. The special class teacher must also be able to withstand the physical and mental trauma that may be present in working with exceptional children.

In addition, the special teacher should have a broad general educational background and courses in special techniques and procedures for teaching the visually handicapped. Coursework also should include study in the behavioral sciences, developmental psychology, and practicum experience with exceptional children. The teacher also should continue his educational experiences by maintaining an awareness of methods and procedures and materials that are constantly being developed.

The Hearing Impaired

Once again, the teacher who works with deaf or hard-of-hearing children must have a good general educational background. In addition, the teacher should be competent in the areas of parent education, special techniques, methods and materials necessary in educating the hearing impaired, and in cooperating with other professionals involved in the educational program of these impaired individuals. This teacher must be aware of the physical and emotional demands often made when working with exceptional children.

Those teachers who work in special schools may be required to meet the state's certification requirements for special education. Special training in methods and techniques for teaching the aurally impaired, as well as experience in working with exceptional children, may be required.

Because many hard-of-hearing children are enrolled in the regular public classroom, the regular classroom teacher may be called upon to become oriented to the needs of the child with a hearing impairment. (Certain suggestions are found in Cruickshank and Johnson):

1. The handicapped child should be placed in such a location that he is close to the teacher and has his back to the light so he is able to use visual clues.
2. The teacher must make sure she has the child's attention before giving assignments or directions.
3. The teacher may need to rephrase a new idea in several different ways when it is first presented to the child.
4. Other children should be helped to understand the handicap.
5. The handicapped child should be included in as many extracurricular activities as his classmates so that he feels that he belongs to his group.

The Speech Therapist

The speech teacher is a specialist who usually works outside the regular classroom. One of the primary tasks involved in therapy or speech correction is the identification of speech and language problems, and then applying the necessary remedial procedures. In order to meet certification standards, most states require stringent academic preparation, plus supervised practical experience in working with speech impaired children.

Van Riper indicates that the speech therapist must be patient, have a sense of humor, have ingenuity in preparing materials and adapting techniques, and be able to work closely with others who come into contact with the children on their caseload, including parents. A very important attribute which should be developed if it is not already possessed by the therapist is that of empathy. It is necessary to understand how the child with a speech defect feels about his problem.

Children with speech defects or voice defects are usually referred to the speech therapist. The therapist also screens certain grades each year to evaluate the speech of each child in the public school, and selects those who are in need of speech correction. The therapist selects a caseload, usually 75 to 100 students, each of whom is seen every week. These students usually work with the therapist in groups of from three to seven. A majority of the cases seen by the public school speech therapist are generally mild, consisting of articulatory defects which improve rapidly. The therapist also works with children who have voice disorders, or with stutterers. In some cases the therapist may go into the regular classroom and give the regular classroom teacher suggestions on how to improve the speech problems of those children who may need only simple treatment. This procedure is often the case in making a follow-up check on children who have been dismissed from the regular caseload.

The speech therapist may cover three to five schools each week, from which she selects the students with whom she will work. She also has some time alloted to work on records, which must be kept on each child, and time to counsel with parents or other professionals when necessary.

Many speech therapists take courses in different areas of special education as part of their academic preparation, as the speech therapist is usually considered a special education teacher. Minimum regulations for certification are required in every state.

Bibliography

"A Program of Education for the Exceptional Children in Oklahoma," S.E. Bulletin no. 8, prepared by the Special Education Section and the Oklahoma Curriculum Commission, 1971.

Barnett, M.R. "Current Problems of the Blind." In *Special Education for the Exceptional*, vol. 2, Edited by M.E. Frampton and E.D. Gall. Boston: Porter Sargent Publishers, 1955.

Buell, Charles. "Motor Performance of Visually Handicapped Children." *Journal of Exceptional Children* 17 (December 1950).

Cooper, Eugene B. "The Development of a Stuttering Chronicity Prediction Checklist: A Preliminary Report." *Journal of Speech and Hearing Disorders* 38, no. 2 (May 1973).

Cruickshank, William M. and Johnson, G. Orville, eds. *Education of Exceptional Children and Youth.* Englewood Cliffs, N.J.: Prentice-Hall Inc., 1967.

Curry, E.T. "Are Teachers Good Judges of Pupils' Hearing?" *Journal of Exceptional Children* 21 (1954).

Dalton, M.M. "A Visual Survey of 5,000 School Children." *Journal of Educational Research* 37 (1943).

Davis, Hallowell, and Silverman, R. Richard, eds. *Hearing and Deafness.* New York: Holt, Rinehart, and Winston, 1966.

Dunn, Lloyd M., ed. *Exceptional Children in the Schools: Special Education in Transition* 2d ed. New York: Holt, Rinehart, and Winston, 1973.

Ewing, A.G., ed. *The Modern Educational Treatment of Deafness.* Washington, D.C.: The Volta Bureau, 1960.

Hoover, Richard E. "Toward a New Definition of Blindness," in *Blindness, 1964.* Washington, D.C.: American Association of Workers for the Blind, 1964.

Jenkins, E., and Lohr, F.E. "Severe Articulation Disorders and Motor Ability," *Journal of Speech and Hearing Disorder* 29 (1964).

Lunde, A.S., and Bogman, S.K. *Occupational Conditions Among the Deaf.* Washington, D.C.: Gallaudet College Press, 1959.

Moss, J.W.; Moss, M.; and Tizard, J. "Electrodermal Response Audiometry with Mentally Defective Children." *Journal of Speech and Hearing Research* 4 (1961).

Newby, Hayes A. *Audiology.* 2d ed. New York: Appleton-Century-Crofts, 1964.

O'Neill, John J. *The Hard of Hearing.* Englewood Cliffs, N.J.: Prentice-Hall Inc., 1964.

Pauls, Miriam D., and Hardy, William G. "Hearing Impairment in Preschool-Age Children." *Laryngoscope* 63 (June 1953).

Telford, Charles W., and Sawrey, James M. *The Exceptional Individual: Psychological and Educational Aspects.* Englewood Cliffs, N.J.: Prentice-Hall, Inc., 1967.

Van Riper, Charles. *Speech Correction: Principles and Methods.* 4th ed. Englewood Cliffs, N.J.: Prentice-Hall, Inc., 1964.

Wilson, John. "The Blind in a Changing World: The Extent, Causes, and Distribution of Blindness," in *Blindness 1965.* Washington, D.C.: American Association of Workers for the Blind, 1965.

Winebrenner, D.K. "Finding the Visually Inadequate Child," *Visual Digest* 16 (1952).

Wyks, Howard. "Deaf Children are Disadvantaged." Paper read at Vocational Special Education Workshop, June 1970, at Texas Tech University.

SENSORY DISABILITIES
Study Sheet #1

1. Distinguish between the different roles of the regular classroom teacher and the special education teacher in providing services to children who are sensorially disabled.

SENSORY DISABILITIES
Study Sheet #2

1. In what ways can a classroom teacher support and enhance the services provided by a speech therapist?

2. Among children who are visually impaired, hearing impaired, or speech impaired, which group is the most educationally deprived? Discuss and defend your position.

'I do better work each day!'

7

Children with Learning Disabilities

DEFINITION

Learning Disabilities is a term that is compatible with the educational system. Through the years during which this term has become popular, educators have seen a number of different nomenclatures attached to this specific area of disabilities. One will occasionally happen upon terms such as minimal brain dysfunction, specific learning disabilities, perceptually handicapped, perceptually immature, dyslexia, word blindness, hyperkinetic syndrome, hypokinetic syndrome, attention syndrome, clumsy child syndrome, aphasia, and dysgraphia, all of which are subsidies within the area of learning disabilities. The authors do not believe that there is an equation between any of these and the term learning disabilities. The child may be dyslexic but this does not necessarily mean he is categorized as a learning disabled child. Also, if the child is categorized as a learning disability child, it doesn't necessarily mean that he possesses all of those particular handicaps.

The learning disabled child may have difficulties in some area of reading. He may have difficulties in arithmetic and writing. He may have behavioral problems. There is a number of manifestations that could pertain to this child. This particular child is not a mentally retarded child. He is not a child who has severe hearing problems. He is not a child who has severe sight problems. He is not a child who has severe motor involvement. A severe motor involvement may mean such limits as a cerebral palsy child would have. The learning disabled child has average or above average mental ability, but he is probably performing academically below his mental ability and he may have secondary emotional, social, or cultural kinds of problems that may be quite disruptive to the classroom and at home.

The field of learning disabilities is relatively new and this newness is exemplified by the diffuse number of definitions used to describe these children. A few of these definitions will be referred to in this chapter for the purpose of illustrating different views of Learning Disabilities. It is not the purpose of the authors to indicate a single preferred definition. Minskoff (1969) cites the following definition from The National Advisory Committee on Handicapped Children:

> Children with learning disabilities means those children who have a disorder in one or more of the basic psychological processes involved in understanding or in using language, spoken or written, which disorder may manifest itself in imperfect ability to listen, think, speak, read, write, spell or do mathematical calculations. Such disorders include such conditions as perceptual handicaps, brain injury, minimal brain dysfunction, dyslexia, and developmental aphasia. Such terms do not include children who have learning problems which are primarily the result of visual, hearing, or motor handicaps, of mental retardation, of emotional disturbance, or of environmental disadvantage.

Whittlesey's (1969) definition also includes children with certain specific motor problems, defects in coordination, and visual-motor difficulties. Thus, the defect may lie in the perceptual, integrative, or expressive areas. His definition *excludes* children with obvious defects such as cerebral palsy, mental retardation, emotional disturbance, defects in vision, or decreased hearing.

Cruickshank (1966) indicates that irrespective of the terminology, some children experience a disturbance of some sort in normal cephalocaudal neural maturation in different stages of development, either perinatally, prenatally, or postnatally. This disturbance may result in an inability to progress normally in various sensory modalities, which cause these children to characterize visual-motor, audio-motor, and/or tactual-motor deficiencies. It appears that the great majority of children with brain injury manifest coordination problems in gross-motor and fine-motor movements. Therefore, they appear to be clumsy in skills which involve dexterity and coordination such as cutting with scissors, cutting while using a knife and fork, lacing shoes, or writing with a pencil.

Learning disabilities usually refers to one or more significant deficits in the essential learning processes and requires special education techniques for remediation. Kass and Myklebust (1969) also indicate that generally children with learning disabilities manifest discrepancies between academic expectations and actual achievement in one or more areas, such as spoken, reading, or written language, and in mathematics, and in spatial orientation.

From the Kansas Association for Children with Learning Disabilities pamphlet (Morrison 1971), Hellmuth in Special Child Publications (1971) indicates that the learning disabled child may be a student, usually a boy, who performs significantly below his grade placement and general intelligence level in reading and spelling. This child does not exhibit measurable neurological defects or loss of visual or auditory acuity. This child also is not mentally retarded, cerebral palsied, nor does he possess other obvious defects. Academically this child is unable to acquire at a normal rate, through the general curriculum a proficiency in reading and spelling which corresponds to his general ability; and this is true even when good instructional procedures are used. This child may show minimal neurological signs which the authors believe are common knowledge to special education professionals, such as right-left disorientation, impaired motor control, perseveration, time disorientation, perceptual-motor and visual-motor problems, hyperkinesis, impulsive actions, short or no attention span, mixed laterality, directionality problems, unusual reading and writing posture, impaired two-point discrimination. Hellmuth indicates too that behavioral or emotional problems will exist by late grade three. He also indicates that psychometric testing yields a typical wide scattering of subtest scores even though the student's I.Q. score is in the normal or above normal range. The authors have also noted the spread in the subtest scores of many children tested for learning disability classes.

Recently there has been considerable pressure from certain disadvantaged, socioeconomic groups to place the culturally, socioeconomically deprived youngster within the confines of the learning disability definition. The authors do not agree with this inclusion, because there has to be an educational objective for learning disabilities that is meaningful and functional. If the gates are opened to include many different educational-socioeconomic problem areas, the training objectives would not be consistent with present learning disability definitions; moreover, it appears that the learning disability category of education would be expanded to such an extent that learning disability school programs would become a dumping-ground for all educational problems. Like it or not, professionals have categories of exceptionalities and these categorical concepts can be functional if schools maintain an educational guideline structure which is in keeping with the total school program.

Estimates of Prevalence

Estimates of prevalence depend on the criteria and cutoff points used, whether these be in the form of learning quotients, or achievement level discrepancies. The prevalence range suggested by Kass and Myklebust is from 3 to 5 percent of the school population. There may be overlapping among different areas of the handicapped in which some of these children are currently being serviced in other special education programs.

There is controversy and difficulty in defining learning disabilities because the minimal brain dysfunction category is not popular with many pediatric-neurologists, and since brain injury is not an accountable ailment, no exact figures exist on the number of these children. A general estimate seems to indicate that at least 5 percent of the United States school children possess learning disabilities. Major interest in the learning disability area is of very recent origin and there is still confusion among professionals as to terminology and identification. Therefore, estimates of incidence seem to depend on individual interpretations of the scope of the category and may vary from 5 to 20 percent of the total school population.

Methods of Identification

Identifying children with specific learning disabilities should be accomplished as early as possible. It is vital that preschool and first grade teachers be aware of the major signs and symptoms and have information concerning referral sources where extensive evaluations can be made.

The preschool and first grade teachers can use an individual record sheet for each child. This record sheet should contain a list of characteristics which may be indicative of learning problems. An example by Slingerland (1969) would be as follows:

1. Attention span
2. Behavior and Social Relations
3. Indications of Mental Growth and General Maturity
4. How crayon or pencil is held
5. Family pattern or handedness or language difficulties, if known
6. Language
7. Preferred and avoided activities
8. Coordination
9. Writing of name
10. Handedness

In parent conferences the teacher can learn when the child began to talk, to walk, to develop hand preference (if he has done so); how directions are understood and followed at home; if he is able to express himself verbally with ease or if he is frustrated by inadequate expressive efforts. The regular class teacher will have a number of learning disabilities children in her classroom and she will be valued as a part of the identification process. It is suggested that all teachers become aware of the identification procedure for learning disability children. There are some clues emitted by these children which are easily recognized, and the regular class teacher, if aware of these clues, will be a referring agent.

Standardized tests can be administered to aid in the evaluation of general abilities. Such tests as readiness tests, perceptual tests, I.Q. tests, and achievement tests are suggested evaluative techniques.

Continued experience with learning disabilities in children may reveal identifiable symptom complexes. Kirk and Bateman (1962) suggest three common symptoms that could be used to identify learning disabled children:

1. All are retarded or disordered in school subjects, speech or language, and/or manifest behavior problems.
2. None are assignable to major categories of exceptionality such as mental retardation or deafness.
3. All have some presumed neurologic basis (cerebral dysfunction) for their manifested disability or disabilities.

In some schools it is common practice to use group screening for children who are suspected as high risk for learning problems. Each child's learning characteristics are described, and the information is produced for the necessary intervention-instructional programs aimed at prevention of learning disabilities.

Rice (1970) indicates (from Dunn 1968) that there are three facets of an effective evaluation process:

1. Make a study of the child to find what behaviors he has acquired along the dimension being considered (language, cognitive skill development, motor skill, etc.).
2. Develop samples of a sequential program designed to move him forward from that point.
3. Demonstrate the method by which he can best be taught material.

An important thing to remember in diagnosis is that one needs to estimate realistically how much each individual child can learn, under what circumstances, and with what materials. Each child must be programmed on his own level of functioning.

Characteristics

A number of characteristics are observable by the classroom teacher and by the parent which may aid them in getting some implication that their child or children are involved in learning disability or perceptual problem areas. These children will have a tendency to do reversals on numbers or letters, such as b's and d's, p's and q's. They also may have inversions of numbers, such as writing 17 for 71. Some of these children have mirror writing. They may write something upside-down-backwards, hold a mirror up and you can see perfect writing.

There will be some possible coordination problems. A child may appear awkward, may frequently trip over his own feet, or bump into things. One should be careful to distinguish this child's awkward conditions from the child who may be acting-out and has no learning problem. Learning disabled children will have problems in audio-discrimination with such sound-alike words as dime and diamond. This situation is not a hearing problem, but it is an auditory inability to discriminate certain sounds and categorize these sounds.

These children may have a perseveration problem. Perseveration does not mean the same thing as persevering. Persevering is great. This is what a child does on a task if he stays with the task until it is completed. The child who perseverates is the child who will do a task, and he will do it, and he will do it again, and he will do it again, and he will do it again, and he will do it again. There is no end to the task. Many times he will start a task; erase it, and start over, erase and start over, erase and start it over. He will do two or three lines, erase it and start over; get mad; tear up the paper; break the pencil; and never complete a satisfactory task.

This child may also be hyperactive. A hyperactive child is one who has difficulty in screening out the stimuli that come to him. You may be sitting in a room while you are reading this chapter and there may be noise around you such as the shuffling of papers. The door may slam. You can hear the air conditioning or heating system. Somebody is making noise in the other room, but this isn't distracting to you. You are able to screen out these extra stimuli. This particular learning disabled child isn't able to screen out the excessive stimuli. These things involve his environment at all times; consequently, the excessive stimulus creates a very short attention span. He becomes engaged with the task at hand and as he tries sorting through the task he cannot sort out the stimuli that keep bombarding him. Therefore this child is involved in a very serious kind of academic problem. If he is unable to sit at his desk and do the arithmetic, the reading, the writing, or whatever school task is required of him because of the bombarding stimuli, he then becomes a problem to himself and to the teacher.

Learning disabled children will sometimes have very poor handwriting, art work, and drawing. The inability to coordinate eye-hand movements are indications that these children will have trouble performing on group tests of intelligence or achievement. Of course, it should be obvious that if this child has reading problems, he will not do well on a group-administered test. Therefore, adequate assessment of the child's learning strengths and deficits will require an individual test battery.

A situation that may be quite noticeable with learning disabled children is in their general performance. In their general environment they will appear brighter than the tests show them to be and teachers get indications that tell them that this child is not retarded, but that there is just something missing, and the teachers know that he can do these things if he has the right kinds of opportunities. This feeling is also evident with the child himself. He will have a kind of feeling which says to himself, "Well, I know I can do this, I'm just as smart as the other kids, I know I can do it. But something is wrong and for some reason I can't do it." This is a child who has poor perception of time and space. He may get lost easily. He might not be able to tell time. He gets confused in physical locations and can't understand where he is.

Teachers and parents should use concrete kinds of demands upon these children, or even singular kinds of demands. A parent might say, "Get out of bed and come to breakfast," rather than, "Get up from bed, put on your shoes and your clothes, and go brush your teeth, and wash your hands, hang the towel up, make your bed, pick up your clothes, come in and eat breakfast." By the time the child receives all these orders he is so busy trying to sort them out, he gets confused, and he probably ends up unable to do any of them. Sometimes a child may look at his teacher in a very confused kind of manner after he has been given a long list of orders, because he is having problems trying to sort out all of the information.

Poor perception may cause the child problems in categorizing and associating. For example, the teacher may show him four flying objects such as a bird, helicopter, an airplane, and a kite and then toss in a turtle and an automobile and a baseball. Now if the teacher asks the child to put these together, those objects that are similar, he may not be able to sort out the objects—the four objects that are flying objects. He may toss in a ball or he may toss in the turtle.

These inconsistencies can be tragic in the academic setting. The child may recognize a word today and not recognize the word the next day. Teachers may not use consistent teaching methods and this is a very important aspect to this particular child because he lacks perceptual consistency. He has the inability to perceive an object as having different qualities or varying properties such as size, position, and shape. He may look at a capital "A" and a small "a" and these are just not recognized as being the same object. He looks at a firetruck from the back, from the front, and from the side, and he is unable to recognize it from all angles as a firetruck. This inability to recognize an object from any view causes consequent problems when this child goes to school. He is faced with books that have different size print, different colored letters, different kinds of types in the letters, and other kinds of varying qualities.

There are also a number of emotional-affective kinds of characteristics that are observable to the teacher and parent from this particular learning disabled child. This is a child who has the inability to control affect, in other words, he overreacts to stimuli. He may have an inadequate impulse control. As an example: a child may work for a period of time on a school task, maybe a picture, a painting, or writing assignment, and at the end of this task he loses control of himself and becomes quite emotional, with crying outbursts and ridicule of himself and others. He simply does not have the ability to control the affective tones involved with the completion of the tasks.

This is a child who embellishes the task at hand whether he's reading a story out loud or whether he's telling a story or whether he is adding details to pictures. It's something like the perseveration mentioned earlier in this chapter and it just seems that the child cannot stop himself. He may start a story and then he keeps the story going, going, and going. The suggestions for the teachers and parents at this particular point would be that one should not appear interested and agree with the child's embellished story and continue listening; nor should one reject the child and tell him to shut up, stop adding to the story, and call him a liar. Instead of either agreeing or rejecting, one should try to detour the child down another avenue of conversation.

Learning disabilities children will have a very low frustration tolerance. Many times if they don't get immediate success on a task or if they don't get the results they desire immediately they may react similar to one in a paranoid state of affect. They will attack the object or the person who they feel is hindering the situation. As an example, a boy doesn't get the immediate success he wants from drawing a picture. He may attack the picture and rip it up or break the pencil. He may attack the teacher, because the teacher didn't give him the grade that he needed or wanted on this particular assignment. The emotional procedure of avoiding failure is to attack the failing situation. The teacher may attempt to help a child or correct his papers to show him where he made a mistake and the child will try to avoid this situation by attacking the teacher with such language as, "You're stupid and everybody's stupid and I don't want you to look at my paper."

A child may not respond to any of the demands that the parent or teacher makes and this way the adult becomes upset and the child gets even with the parents and teacher. Parents and teachers should maintain or at least try to control this situation simply by being aware of the child's tensions. The adult should be alerted to the emotional build-up within the child and realize that the child is beginning to reach the end of his toleration point. He can no longer tolerate the task at hand. He can no longer tolerate the teacher or himself. He's about ready to blow a fuse. Parents and teachers should learn to recognize these clues before the explosion, then they would naturally avoid having a lot of trouble with the child.

Children with learning disabilities come to the attention of the schools by way of any of a number of characteristics. Clements (1966) selected ten of the most frequently cited characteristics of learning disabled children. In order of frequency they are listed as follows:

1. Hyperactivity
2. Perceptual-motor impairments
3. Emotional lability
4. General orientation defects
5. Disorders of attention (e.g., short attention span, distractibility, perseveration)
6. Impulsivity
7. Disorders of memory and thinking
8. Specific learning disabilities in reading, arithmetic, writing, and spelling
9. Disorders of speech and hearing
10. Equivocal neurological signs and electroencephalographic irregularities.

Myers and Hammill (1969) state that the characteristics observed in children with specific learning disorders may be divided arbitrarily into at least six categories:

1. Motor activity: hyperactivity, hypoactivity, incoordination, and perseveration
2. Disorders of emotionality
3. Disorders of perception
4. Disorders of symbolization: receptive-auditory, receptive-visual, expressive-vocal, and expressive-motor
5. Disorders of attention: excessive attention and insufficient attention
6. Disorders of memory.

Cruickshank and Johnson indicated that Rappaport lists three major response patterns of brain-injured children, each of which he subdivides. His grouping includes the following:

1. Inadequate Impulse Control or Regulation
   a. Hyperactivity
   b. Hyperdistractibility
   c. Disinhibition
   d. Impulsivity
   e. Perseveration
   f. Lability of affect
   g. Motor dysfunctions
2. Inadequate Integrative Functions
   a. Perceptual difficulties
   b. Conceptual difficulties
3. Defective Self-concept and Narcissistic Hypersensitivity
   a. Low frustration tolerance
   b. Flight from challenge
   c. Overcompensation
   d. Control and manipulation of others
   e. Negativism or power struggle

The Kansas Association for Children with Learning Disabilities pamphlet (1971) presents Hellmuth's outline of the characteristics of children with learning disabilities as follows:

I. Behavioral
   A. Mixed laterality—The child is dominantly neither right nor left sided. This includes hands, feet, and eyes.
   B. Delayed responses—There is a noticeable and unusual time lag in responding to questions or stimuli.

C.   Inconsistency—The child tends to respond to the same stimulus one way one time and a different way at another time.

D.   Distractibility
   1.   An abnormal fixation to unimportant details while disregarding the essentials.
   2.   A blurring or inversion of background and foreground, where the main subject may blend with the background or the background itself may become the focus of attention.

E.   Hyperactivity—A forced, undirected response to stimuli. A drive that compels the child to act, to flit from one thing to another, that makes him unable to withstand countless stimuli which the normal child disregards.

F.   Quiet, daydreaming, phlegmatic behavior—This is the opposite extreme from the hyperactive child. Sometimes referred to as hypoactive.

G.   Emotional lability—The child may be "highstrung" irritable or aggressive, but change quickly from high temper to manageability and remorse. He may be panicked by what would appear to others as a minimally stressful situation; however, some of these children are of sweet disposition and even-tempered even in the presence of a frustrating inability to perform academically.

H.   Disinhibition—Lack of emotional control, easy laughing or crying which may persist beyond reasonable limits.

I.   Catastrophic reaction—Extreme helplessness, despair or anxiety experienced when a child is confronted with a task beyond his ability, usually accompanied by intense crying.

J.   Extreme irritability and intolerance of discipline.

K.   Aggressive, antisocial, or uncontrolled behavior.

L.   Aimless, random movements—May "paw the air," wave arms, shuffle feet, etc.

M.   Impulsiveness—Cannot keep from touching and handling objects, particularly in a strange or overstimulating environment.

N.   Short attention span.

O.   Perseveration—The persistent repetition or continuance of an activity once begun, especially if the child has experienced success or pleasure. This may be characterized by difficulty in shifting from one activity to another, or the inability to start or stop a series; also, the persistent repetition of questions over and over even though they have been carefully answered.

    P.   Meticulosity—An exactitude demanded by the child who must have everything "just so."

    Q.   Abnormal clumsiness or general lack of coordination, either gross or fine movements, or both.

II. Speech

    A.   Transposition of syllables—as "aminal" for animal.

    B.   Reversals of syllables—as "Jofe" for "Joseph."

III. Language or Reading

    A.   Jumbled language or disturbed syntax—as "Mother, me to the store" for "Mother and I went to the store."

    B.   Word-finding difficulty—The child just cannot "call up" a word he wants to use. Similar to "having a word on the tip of the tongue, but can't say it."

    C.   Inability to separate a whole into parts or to combine parts into meaningful whole. The child may recognize the word "bus" as a whole but cannot put "b" with "us" to form the word. Likewise, he may be able to recognize the letters or syllables, but cannot break the word down into its component parts.

    D.   Letter substitutions

        1.   Inversions—as V for A

        2.   Reversals—as b for d, ma for am

        3.   Similar letters—as he for h

        4.   Random substitutions—as ro for m

    E.   Word substitutions—was for saw, top for pot, etc.

    F.   Distracted reading—skipping, jumping words.

    G.   Slow recognition of words.

    H.   Omission of words, phrases, and sentences.

    I.   Definite deficiency or retardation in reading—Two or more years behind age-grade placement is significant for most elementary school pupils.

IV. Writing and Drawing

    A.   Inability to form letters or digits correctly—starts at wrong direction in marking, forms in segments, etc.

    B.   Difficulty in staying on or between the lines.

    C.   Difficulty in judging how long or how tall a letter is.

    D.   Disturbance in spatial relationships—Difficulty in identification or matching of shapes—rotation or distortion of drawings of geometric designs. To compensate for poor performance the child may make innumerable and meticulous tiny strokes of the pencil in his drawings.

    E.   Reversal of letters or digits.

V. Intelligence

    A.   Apparently of normal, potentially normal, or superior intellect.

    B.   The child who "is bright enough but just can't learn."

    C.   Verbal intelligence appears to be better than performance intelligence. May have a good vocabulary and can readily learn things read to him. Has difficulty "figuring out things."

Each of these learning disabled children is unique. The child who is afflicted with just some of these characteristics may have a very difficult task of conforming to the demands of home and school. When provided with understanding, compatible instruction, and attention, many of these children are able to fit naturally into regular public school classes and develop their potentials as happy, productive citizens.

Hyperactive Children

"The hyperactive child" is a broad category covering children who have four main problems: overactivity, distractibility, impulsiveness, and excitability. The degree of a hyperactive child's problem varies greatly; at one end of the spectrum there are boys who don't do school work up to the expected standard because they can't concentrate, and at the other there are boys who are aggressively antisocial and cannot be kept in a regular classroom. Most children who are called "hyperactive" are somewhere in-between these two extremes.

The problem is a common one: probably about 5 percent of all grade school children have difficulties of this kind. Many more boys than girls are hyperactive. The origin of the problem is not known at present. For most of these children the difficulty is probably that they are at one end of the normal range of activity level; in other words they are like children who are unusually tall or heavy. In a small minority of cases (about one out of ten) there is evidence that the child had an injury or an illness which affected his brain and

Reprinted by permission of *Expectations,* vol. 2, no. 4, September/October, 1972, from an article, *For Parents of Hyperactive Children,* by Mark A. Stewart, M.D.

which is probably related to the onset of this difficulty. There is no evidence at all that lack of love, absence of parents from the home, or other unfortunate experiences, cause children to be overactive, though these things might make a hyperactive child's problems worse.

Symptoms

Overactivity is a term used to cover the following kinds of behavior: unusual energy, needing less sleep than other children, inability to sit still in the classroom or at meal times, talking a great deal, talking out of turn in class, being unusually loud, wearing out clothes and shoes faster than other children, inability to keep from touching other children in class and interfering with them, disrupting classes by clowning, etc.

Distractibility refers to not getting work done in school, not being able to persevere with homework, daydreaming, being easily distracted from projects by outside stimuli, being unable to listen to stories or attend to TV programs, leaving projects unfinished, tuning out teachers and parents when they try to give directions, being unable to play card games or games such as Monopoly through to the end.

Impulsiveness covers: running out in the street or riding a bicycle in front of cars, jumping into the deep end of the pool without knowing how to swim, being unable to save up money for something that is badly wanted, letting out secrets or saying things that are known to be rude, saying "sassy" things to the teacher to show off, doing dangerous things on the spur of the moment, etc.

Excitability means such things as being easily upset, having a low frustration tolerance, not being able to take "no" for an answer or to accept delay, having a "short fuse" and getting into fights over little things, getting wound up and excited around other children, and crying more than other children.

Other important difficulties for the hyperactive child are: having a low opinion of himself, being unpopular with other children, fighting, rebelliousness, and learning problems.

Hyperactive children often do not get along well with other children of their own age. This may be because they are silly and immature in their behavior, or because their behavior in class turns the other children off. As a result hyperactive children may develop a "chip on the shoulder" attitude; this leads to further trouble because of a vicious circle. Other kinds of behavior which stem from this difficulty with other children are clowning in class to impress other children, trying to buy friendship with money or candy, telling boastful stories, fighting and bullying.

Because of their impulsiveness, hyperactive children may get involved in lying, stealing, playing with matches or setting fires, vandalism, and sometimes such things as running away from home or truancy.

Treatment

There are some very important things that parents can do which will help their hyperactive child to be happier and to behave better. There are also some specific treatments which doctors may give children with this problem. Commonly physicians treat hyperactive children with stimulant drugs, such as Ritalin or Dexedrine. Paradoxically these drugs make children calmer, less active, and better able to concentrate. Successful drug treatment also shows the child that he can succeed in school. It is important for parents to understand that the prime target of drug treatment is their child's difficulty in school, and that another approach is best for changing behavior at home. The person who can best tell whether the treatment is doing any good is the child's teacher, and direct reports from the teacher are the basis on which the physician can judge whether his treatment is doing any good.

WHAT CAN PARENTS DO TO HELP? THE MOST IMPORTANT JOB FOR THE PARENTS IS TO SEE THAT THEIR CHILD DOESN'T GET DISCOURAGED AND BEGIN TO THINK OF HIMSELF AS A PERMANENT FAILURE. AT THE SAME TIME THEY MUST KEEP UP A FIRM DISCIPLINE.

For Parents

The principles of raising a hyperactive child aren't different from those for a normal child, but the frustrations and disappointments are much greater. Naturally parents blame themselves for their child's misbehavior, and grandparents, neighbors, and teachers often help to make parents feel inadequate and guilty. These feelings may in turn lead to arguments and quarrels between the father and mother of the child, and unhappiness of the other children in the family. Again, CHILDREN ARE NOT HYPERACTIVE BECAUSE THEIR PARENTS HAVEN'T LOVED THEM OR DISCIPLINED THEM ENOUGH. Probably they were born that way, for reasons we don't understand. Parents also feel guilty when they lose their tempers and beat their hyperactive child severely. This isn't the right thing to do but it is forgiveable because few parents have been taught

how to raise normal children, let alone hyperactive. TRY NOT TO
FEEL GUILTY ABOUT THE WAY YOUR CHILD IS.

Principles of Raising a Hyperactive Child

1. You have to love and accept your child as he is. Perhaps you
can change some of his behavior for the better, or perhaps he can,
but he needs to be accepted for what he is, and loved in spite of his
faults. Some aspects of his behavior are so much a part of his nature
that it is fruitless to try to change them. Restlessness, fidgeting, and
talking all the time can be contained for short periods, but they will
find an outlet. It is better to accept this kind of behavior and channel
it, rather than to try to stop it. Similarly you should work around his
short fuse, his impatience, and his lack of perseverance rather than
clash with him over these shortcomings.

The problems of hyperactive children seem never ending in the
grade school age, but there is no need to be gloomy about the future.
As these children grow into their teens they do become less active
and better able to concentrate and stay with things. It seems likely
that they may always be somewhat more restless, impulsive and so
forth, but these qualities, which give them so much trouble in school,
may have advantages in adult life. An abundance of energy, a desire
for action, an outgoing attitude toward people, and an ability to
make up your mind quickly are real assets in some walks of life.
Many successful businessmen, engineers, physicians, salesmen, and so
on have been hyperactive children. If your child grows up in a stable
and well-organized home, the chances are very good that your hyperactive child will be a happy and successful adult. Much of the behavior that gets a hyperactive child into trouble during his grade school
years would not be a problem were it not for the pressures and
restrictions of our urban life, and the failure of our schools to come
to grips with the fact that children come to school with different
kinds of temperament as well as different levels of intelligence.

2. Hyperactive children need to be treated with a firm but
kindly discipline, first as normal children do, only more so. One of
the major difficulties of a hyperactive child is that he is more impulsive and impatient than a normal child, and it takes him longer to
acquire self-control. He therefore has a greater tendency to get into
mischief and this may lead him into serious misbehavior. At the same
time he is high-spirited, curious, active, and perhaps aggressive; you
can therefore expect him to be pushing at the limits of what his
parents and teachers will allow all the time. Unless these limits are

clearly defined, and firmly enforced, he will often be getting away with things and learning to flout authority.

On the other hand when parents try to apply the usual rules to their hyperactive child, they may find that they spend their entire time scolding him, thereby making life miserable both for him and themselves. It seems best to ration the rules for the hyperactive child, and to tell your other children openly that you are doing this because the hyperactive one has a problem. This should not involve giving up any important rules (always letting parents know where he is, coming straight home from school, doing homework promptly), but should be relaxing on less important rules, (keeping his room tidy, being neat with his clothes, and good table manners). Father and mother should get together and agree upon the really important rules; these should be as few and as general as possible, and should allow some flexibility; and these rules should be firmly enforced.

Hyperactive children need closer supervision because of their inability to control their behavior. Partly this can be achieved by companionship with a child; the father can share activities with the child and through his presence keep him out of mischief. Using the same principle a child can be kept out of mischief by having him in organized activities that will appeal to him, such as athletic programs at the Y.M.C.A. This supervision cannot be maintained all the time, and there will be times when the child has to be punished for breaking rules. Punishment should take the form of being deprived of a treat or a privilege (TV programs, candy, riding his bicycle) and to be effective it should be given out as soon after the offense as possible. When children become very upset and angry in your company, they should be given a choice of shaping up or of going to their room for a period; this time away from the family or their friends is the most effective way to treat outbursts of temper. On the whole punishment is a weak way to influence a child's behavior, and it may even backfire by reinforcing behavior. Some children misbehave persistently knowing that they are going to be punished, the reason being that they would rather have their parents angry and upset than have no attention from them. Rewarding good behavior is the strongest way to influence a child's behavior, but parents and teachers tend to take good behavior for granted and show an active interest only in bad behavior. We need to catch children being good, particularly hyperactive children who seldom get rewarded for good behavior in the ordinary course of things. It is also important to reward children for beginning to do things right, rather than waiting for them to do things exactly the way you asked them to do. Love and praise are great rewards; little presents or treats can make your love more concrete. Keep a supply of dime store toys for this purpose, or take time to play a game with your child.

3. Your child's opinion of himself. He always feels trouble at home and at school; often disliked by other children, his teachers, and even you at times. The hyperactive child is likely to have a very low opinion of himself, and to react with resentment, or silly bids for attention that only make matters worse. Building up his morale is a crucial job for the hyperactive child's parents.

Parents can find other areas of success to compensate for the difficulties that a child has in school. Hyperactive children may be particularly good at working with their hands, selling things such as Boy Scout candy, handling animals, or at sports. *Parents must do everything they can to involve their hyperactive child in activities in which he can succeed.*

Team sports are usually difficult for hyperactive children because of the complicated rules and the necessity for waiting your turn. Sports such as swimming, gym, or wrestling are more likely to capture the hyperactive child's interest. Boy Scout activities and Y.M.C.A. activities are very helpful, and as the child grows older he should be given the opportunity to meet physical and social challenges such as are required in camp counselors. Preparation for being junior camp counselors (lifesaving courses at the "Y" for example) is an excellent way to boost a boy's morale.

It may be difficult to involve children in outside activities because they tend to give up easily and because they've experienced failure and rejection before. The way around this is for the child's father to be involved in the same activity, and for him to do it with his son as a recreation.

The most basic and important factor in preserving a child's morale is that parents should enjoy being with their hyperactive child and doing things with him. No child will ever think more highly of himself than his parents do: if they're not interested enough to spend time with him, or if they spend their time scolding him and never seem to enjoy being with him, he is going to think poorly of himself.

Hyperactive children have a tough time in school because they are called on to do the things that are hardest for them, namely sitting still and paying attention to the teacher or working on assignments. They are criticized or disciplined for these problems though they have little or no control over them. A common judgment made on hyperactive children in school is that they could do better if they would only try. Remember not to be too hard on your son when he comes home from school; it is likely to have been a long hard day for him. Do not push the issues of good grades and his school performance. Some parents find it hard to accept anything less than the best school performance from their children; they forget that success in school is not the only thing that determines success in adult life.

4. Specific Problems. *Overactivity:* There should be definite limits set on the amount of boisterous and loud behavior that you are prepared to accept within your house. When your child goes beyond these limits he should be told that he must either calm down or go and do his thing outside or in the basement, or in some place that is acceptable to you. Besides this, and having reasonable standards for behavior at the dinner table and in company, there is not much point in trying to control activity; you should live with the restlessness in front of the T.V. set, or the continual squirming while your child reads a book. On the other hand you and he will be much happier if his activity can be channeled into constructive outlets. When he plays iceless hockey, trampolines, goes out running with his dog, or wrestles at the Y he is enjoying being active, and probably building up his self-confidence; meanwhile he is not irritating you with aimless fiddling around.

Short attention span and inability to persevere. Whether your child is working on building a model or doing a homework assignment, he will do much better if the work is divided up into small units. In other words he can do a few of his problems, or put a few pieces of a model together; bring what he has done to you for your approval; stretch his legs, and go back in a few minutes and start over again. It is best that he not work on his own, because he will be subject to all sorts of distraction and have nobody to bring him back to the work in hand. If he works in your presence, you can encourage him, bring him back to the short piece of work he has to complete, and reward him with praise and recognition when he has finished each unit. You should always insist that he finish any project for the simple reason that completing a model or finishing a game, rewards him for persistence. If he never finishes anything, he will never experience the reward of seeing something through and he simply won't learn this habit.

Unfortunately much schoolwork is boring and repetitive, but there are some ways that parents can help to increase children's interest. A number of teaching machines are available for helping children to learn grade school arithmetic and language skills, and these are designed in ways that appeal to children who have short attention spans. In a more general way parents can help to promote their children's interest in school by cultivating shared interests. For example, an interest in the history of frontiersmen can become a joint interest of a boy and his father, and can be encouraged by visits to museums, old houses of pioneers, forts, Indian mounds, and so forth. Father and son can watch T.V. programs related to this interest together, and perhaps plan related games or build models together. In this way a father draws his child into an interest which will give reading and social sciences more meaning.

Written work is probably the child's greatest hang-up in school. The understanding teacher will reduce written assignments for a hyperactive child to the absolute minimum, and not fuss about the neatness of the work turned in. Parents should follow this example, but do what they can to encourage the child to make frequent use of his writing skill. For example, they should encourage him to write short letters to a favorite relative, or to a pen pal; he should also write off for catalogues, maps, tourist guides and so on. Whatever he writes and brings home from school should be recognized and praised, not taken for granted. He is likely to try to do his writing in a great hurry, and therefore to make a number of careless mistakes. Usually he will then get upset and want to throw the whole thing away. For this reason a parent should be around when he is doing this work, and try to slow him down and encourage him. He should use strong paper which will take a lot of erasing, and parents need a stock of the kinds of erasers used by typists. When a child is not too sure about his spelling it may be best to have him check words with parents before he writes them down. During this kind of work parents have a golden opportunity to gently brainwash the child with the idea that he should check his work at least once after he has finished. Probably nothing will prevent hyperactive children from making careless mistakes in arithmetic and writing, so that it is important that they learn to check their work.

Getting upset or wound up easily. Prevention is the art here, rather than treatment. Hyperactive children do get very wound up around a group of other children, and this has a number of implications. For example, birthday parties had better be out of doors, or in some place like the basement where it won't matter to you that things get a bit out of hand. It is a mistake to take a hyperactive child on a long shopping trip with your other children because when he gets bored he is likely to start stirring them up. One of the most important preventive measures you can take is to school your other children not to respond to the hyperactive child's irritability, teasing, and bickering. This is asking a lot of your other children, and you should be sure to let them know how grateful you are when they manage to keep the peace in face of provocation.

When your child begins to be upset you should take him out of whatever situation he is in and try to get him back to the situation and help him. Leaving him to go on trying to handle the situation on his own, and telling him to shape up or calm down, usually results only in his getting more and more frustrated. When your child has gotten beyond himself in being upset he should be taken to his room, or some other room where he can be on his own, and told to wait there until he feels he can behave in an acceptable way again. He should never be allowed to win his way in a dispute with you by having a temper tantrum, even when you are in some public place and it is mortifying to have him screaming and acting up. Buying peace by giving in to a child reinforces his tendency to have a tantrum the next time that he wants something and you don't want to give it to him.

Impulsiveness. This is a very difficult problem to work on, but it can be influenced through close supervision and the direct teaching of self-control. Riding a bicycle recklessly in the streets, and guessing wildly at words that he doesn't know when he is reading, are two good examples of impulsive behavior. The one can be handled best by very close supervision of the child's first trips around streets in the neighborhood, stern instruction in the rules of traffic, and rehearsing the natural consequences of his ignoring these rules. This means that when a child is first riding his bicycle, his father should ride with him and see that he stops properly at stop signs, stays on the right hand side of the road, gives signals and so forth. Whenever the child fails to observe these rules the father should patiently go over what are the likely consequences of his ignoring the rules when a car happens to come along. The first few times that the child rides his bicycle on his own he should be asked to recite what are the most important points he has to remember when he is riding in the streets; for example what he does when he comes to a stop sign. The idea behind this is to get him to instruct himself about the rules, and build a system for self-control. The same method can be applied to reading. The difficulty is that the child doesn't take the time to figure out a word, and because of his hurry tends to guess. At school and at home he can be coached gently in the idea of slowing down, stopping to think about a word that he does not recognize, and sounding it out to himself until he hits on the right word for the context. This can be made into a sort of game where the child is induced to say to himself . . . STOP, THINK, LOOK . . . or some similar short message. Again the idea is that he should learn to instruct himself in order to regulate his behavior.

Whenever this doesn't involve physical danger children should be allowed to face the consequences of their impulsive behavior. For example, if a child dashes out to school on a very cold day without a coat on he should be left to face the consequences of getting cold. He may learn something from this experience himself, but will not get anything from having his mother chase after him with his coat. Some kinds of impulsive behavior are best prevented altogether. Money should never be left lying around on the kitchen table or on top of father's dresser where it may be picked up by the child without the parent being sure that anything has happened. Each time the child does this and gets away with it, the habit is reinforced. The answer then is that all money should be put away in safe places; this includes your other children's savings banks, purses and wallets. The same kind of preventive measure should be applied to matches, gasoline for the lawn mower and so forth. Lying cannot be handled in this way, but can be discouraged if parents emphasize to the child that owning up to having been in mischief will not be followed by punishment for the mischief. In other words self-incrimination will be recognized, and the act of telling the truth will be rewarded by forgiving the original sin.

Aggressiveness. This is best handled by the parents setting an example of calmness, and particularly by their avoiding physical punishment, and by encouraging the child to have normal friendly activities. The more he can find friends who are like himself and enjoy physical activity and competitiveness, the less he will resent other children and pick fights with them. Within the house your child should be rewarded when he has a peaceful day and does not bug his siblings, and his brothers and sisters should be rewarded for not responding to his trouble making. When he does get into fights he should be left to face the consequences, whether this is being beaten up by another or having an angry parent complain about his bullying a smaller boy.

Summary. Your hyperactive child will have the best chance of growing up happily if you accept him for what he is, believe in his future, help him as best you can with his specific problems, set firm limits to his behavior, and most of all if you enjoy his company. This is a difficult undertaking for you, and you should feel no shame if you need help and encouragement for yourself. On the contrary it is important that you let your physician know your own difficulties, and unburden yourself about your disappointments and frustrations. That is what he is there for.

The authors agree with the text of Dr. Stewart's statements, and believe that he has offered some valuable information relative to hyperactive children. This information should be quite helpful to parents and teachers alike.

Educational Provisions

There are numerous kinds of methods and procedures suggested for working with these children in this particular day and age. However, education is still in somewhat of an experimental area as concerns these children. There is very little evidence of research which indicates static procedures or techniques for learning disabled children. It was only a few years ago that authorities thought that these children could not stand the stimuli that were in the classroom and offered recommendations to discard bulletin boards, distractible objects, and bright curtains. In other words, keep a bland room, and keep the toys out of sight, because these children could not tolerate these stimuli. The authors have noticed recently in visiting classrooms and talking with teachers that these forms of stimuli aren't necessarily disturbing the children. The authors have gone into classrooms which appear to be total chaos, not as a result of the bombarding of the stimuli, but because of the teacher's inability to tolerate the situation. The authors, also, have gone into other classrooms in which the teachers had beautifully decorated rooms. There were all kinds of stimuli existing and the children were performing beautifully, which indicates that the most important factor in this situation may be the teacher's ability to maintain the class, rather than how much stimuli were coming in from the outside.

Presently the authors believe that there are varying success factors in the learning disability area. A suggestion to parents and teachers would be for them to go with that which is an advantage to them and their particular children. The main thing to be realized at this point is that all methods and procedures that are indicated for a learning disability child are not appropriate for all learning disability children. Some children will need specific kinds of things that will not work with other children. The same for each child is like saying everyone must be aware of and appreciate the same model car—that nobody has a choice. There are no individual needs to be considered. This is not the way the world rotates. Some things work for some children and some things work for other children. Some methods of rearing children work for some parents and the same methods don't work for other parents. Therefore, one should not be conclusive and say that there is a specific panacea for the learning disabilities child.

No single or best approach to teaching the learning disabled child is recognized today. General practice in the education of the learning disabled child in the public school setting has not followed systematic methodologies or specific practices of teaching to overcome specific disabilities which affect learning. Modification has been in terms of what is taught rather than how it is taught.

Some good educational practices to use with these children may be to influence the environment of learning, to realize a concept of individual differences and differentiated education, to develop techniques and methods for remediation of the faulty learning process, to realize an experiential framework, to experiment with and manipulate ways of learning, and to manifest a concept of education for total life adjustment.

Heckrel and Webb (1969) indicate that if a school is setting up a program for the learning disabled child there are three basic steps that must be followed:

1. It involves the identification of those children who are not learning by normal techniques.
2. The diagnostic orientation must be integrated with treatment procedures.
3. Educators have the task of developing an effective school program that serves the learning disabled child by providing special help and curriculum adjustments for as long as the child requires them.

After the teacher knows each child well enough to set realistic goals for the student's accomplishment of skills, a daily plan of activities may be devised. The activity schedule should not be rigid. The class needs a variety of activities throughout the day. The day's first activities should focus on the child's area of greatest difficulty. Effective supervision is mandatory.

Because the learning disabled child may have faced constant failure, more attention must be directed toward developing self-motivation than would be necessary for the ordinary child. The goals must be simple and concrete, rather than abstract and complex.

Provisions for helping disabled children may or may not include the establishment of a self-contained classroom situation in which the children receive all of their instruction from *a* special teacher. Special tutoring may be necessary for some children, and the remaining part of their school time may be spent in the regular classroom or in a part-time special class placement with emphasis placed on each child's specific learning problem.

Objectives

The educational objectives indicated by Rappaport (1969) are as follows:

1. View this child as a total, integrated organism that needs a total, integrated program in order to have the most effective opportunity for learning.
2. Insure the consideration of all aspects of his developmental growth and performance within his education program.
3. Acknowledge learning opportunities to be present both before and after school hours, so that more than classroom conditions are considered, and so that the teacher is not charged with the sole responsibility for the child's habilitation.
4. See this child not only as a pupil, but also as a member of a family and of society, with the result that the home and the community assume their responsibilities in providing adequate and appropriate learning environments.

Hellmuth (1971) as quoted by the Kansas Association for Children with Learning Disabilities (Morrison 1971) indicates the following goals and objectives:

1. Provide special educational programs which will bring *each child with learning disabilities* back into the main stream of the regular educational system at the earliest possible time.
2. Provide for early detection of learning difficulties on the kindergarten and preschool level, so that these children who have learning problems may be channeled into a program best designed for their individual needs.
3. Implementation of special education programs for children who manifest learning disabilities in every school district within the state.
4. Development of consistency in quality of programs and facilities throughout the state for education of *children with learning disabilities.*
5. Educate the public to understand and support better care for these children.
6. Help parents to understand and accept such children.

7. Stimulate research in the areas of learning disabilities.
8. Aid both state and national legislative processes to obtain funding for special education.

Hopefully long term educational objectives for a child with learning disabilities should be to assist the child in actualizing his potential and help him become an effective and integral part of society. Short term objectives should be directed toward enabling the child to achieve academically, to attain social maturity, to be able to communicate, to care for himself, and to function emotionally within a framework acceptable to the public schools and his environment.

The ultimate goal is to provide the learning disabilities child with an opportunity for total self-realization, to enable him to achieve dignity through his abilities and accomplishments. Also, the ultimate objective for these children is to remediate their problems and return them totally to the regular school program. Presently there seems to be a general opinion that over 90 percent of the children will return to a regular pattern of schooling. It should be noted, though, that parents and teachers should not set a time limit on the return schedule. Some children may remediate in six months, others in one, two, or three years, and on. Do not set a plan in effect that controls a schedule for all children's remediation. Consider each child separately.

An overall educational structure should include careful planning and control of time, space, materials, and techniques relative to the developmental needs of each youngster. This comprehensive planning should enable the child to experience the opportunity to succeed and overcome his previous failures.

Services for Learning Disabilities Children

If the concept of individualization is accepted, then there are several major elements which must be incorporated into the educational program. Current research presented by Cruickshank and Johnson offers the following suggestions:

1. Rappaport's relationship structure—the ability of the teacher to understand the child sufficiently well at any given moment, through his verbal and nonverbal communications, to relate in a way which aids the child's development of impulse control and other ego functions.
2. Environmental structure—the classroom must be a nonstimulation environment, and the room should be smaller than the

standard sized classroom because as space increases, so stimuli increase; as space decreases, the stimulus value of space also decreases.

3. Program structure—consistency is very important and it is essential that the daily program be structured with sufficient similarity from day to day to provide a pattern for adjustment and a setting wherein satisfying predicition can be practiced by the child.
4. Structured teaching materials—it is in the structure of the teaching materials that the child's peculiar needs can be met directly.
5. Motor training—there should be daily motor training, usually accomplished on an individual basis, for approximately thirty minutes. This child usually demonstrates incoordination of gross-motor and fine-motor movements.
6. Language development and speech therapy—daily speech and language development, under the supervision of a skilled speech therapist who understands the problems of speech in neurologically handicapped children, is a requisite.

These children need to be provided with immediate psychological, educational, neurological, and other determined evaluations. Space and facilities at each school should provide flexibility for special programs. This would include items, such as mobil partitions, audio-visual equipment, and other teacher desired materials. Teacher's aides should be available for service as special education teachers so that each child may receive the needed individual instruction. It is suggested that there should be one teacher per six students in programs for children with learning disabilities without a teacher's aide, and one teacher per ten students with a teacher's aide. In no case should there be more than ten students in one self-contained classroom. Many states have school laws that control class enrollment, and these controls usually maintain a maximum of ten students in each class.

The Multidisciplinary Approach

A multidisciplinary team of specialists more nearly matches a comprehensive theory of learning disabilities than does a single specialist or group of specialists working in isolation. Problems related to severe learning disabilities are many and tend to reveal themselves in interrelated clusters. Landreth (1969) suggests, "Present research indicates that certain physical deviations, brain injuries and defects, speech and hearing defects, emotional problems, and reading difficulties all frequently occur concomitantly in the learning disabled child."

While the causality or exact sequence of occurrence for many children has never been satisfactorily established, it is recognized that the combinations of specific deficits that a child may have are infinite. A multifaceted disability presents a complexity which must be matched with nothing less than multifaceted remediation, the kind of remediation that only a team approach can provide. Theoretically speaking, therefore, the team approach is an attempt to match the dynamic team structure.

Landreth (1969) also indicates that success of team cohesiveness depends upon a number of factors: a common commitment to similar professional beliefs, personal factors of openness and security, presessions, and adequate time.

Referrals are usually made by a school counselor or a classroom teacher, sometimes parents refer their child. After they are referred, they should be given a comprehensive battery of tests to determine the child's position or problems in intellectual development, emotional development, reading, speech, and hearing. The parents are interviewed. The information gained should be assembled and evaluated at a joint staff meeting. The team members then make recommendations which seem most beneficial for each child. Records of evaluation and recommendations are sent to the child's school and are discussed with his parents.

Pediatric Examination

It is very essential for the pediatrician to communicate directly with school personnel. School personnel, and particularly the classroom teacher, can often provide the pediatrician with valuable information about the child—areas of strengths and weaknesses behaviorally, academically, and socially. Direct preliminary communication in seeking school observations as part of the child's total evaluation enables one to have a better understanding of the physician's findings and recommendations.

Clements indicates that the basic role of the pediatrician includes the following areas of involvement: (1) to detect any disease process, physical handicap, or sensory impairment which might deter the learning process; (2) to insure that all necessary studies and consultations are obtained and to coordinate them in a meaningful and organized manner; (3) to provide interpretation of the findings to the parent and to the schools, when necessary; (4) to assess development status periodically and to provide anticipatory counseling for the parents so the adequate plans for appropriate school placement can be made to help avoid prolonged frustration, disappointment, and the secondary emotional problems resulting from prolonged school failure; (5) to provide periodic reevaluation, ongoing support, and medical management for the child, and appropriate counseling for the parents.

The authors suggest the following guideline for a comprehensive report on the suspected learning disability child. This guideline is not recommended as a static profile. The different needs of each child, school, teacher, and other professionals may call for additions to or deletions from this list.

Pediatrician Report

I. Family information
    A. Parent-family review
        1. Socioeconomic history
        2. Domestic-emotional stability
        3. Age and health of parents
        4. Intellectual functioning of parents
        5. Sibling information
    B. Parents' previous concern and referral history
    C. Parents' acknowledgement and understanding of the problem
II. Physical Examination
    A. Gestation period
    B. Prenatal, neonatal, perinatal and postnatal period conditions
    C. Maturational history (sat, walked, talked)
    D. Specific unusual accident or illness situations
    E. Pediatrician's observations of child's examination behavior
    F. Results of physical examination should reflect all areas of vision, perception, and coordination that may cause potential learning problems
    G. Electroencephalogram (if needed)
III. Educational Information (if available, may be added)
    A. School achievement and behavior records
    B. Present functioning level
    C. Intelligence Quotient Range
IV. Summary
    A. Relative diagnosis and prognosis
    B. Treatment recommendations for the child, parents, teachers, and siblings

Psychological Examination

The psychological examination should be considerate of many aspects and levels of functioning. The examination will consist of a comprehensive evaluation. No single test should determine the fate of the child. Each psychologist has his favorite evaluation techniques, and the results of his testing will be only as good as is his ability to test and interpret. Therefore, one must realize that many degrees of testing exists. The following list contains some of the tests which are commonly used in testing children who are suspected of having learning disabilities problems:

I. Testing Instruments
    A. Wechsler Intelligence Scale
    B. The Raven Progressive Matrices
    C. The Peabody Picture Vocabulary Test
    D. The Bender Visual Motor Gestalt Test
    E. The Berry Development Test of Visual Motor Integration
    F. The Horst Reversals Test
    G. The Wepman Auditory Discrimination Test
    H. Wide Range Intelligence Test
    I. The Frostig Visual Perceptual Test
    J. Illinois Test Psycholinguistic Abilities

Social History

It is recommended that the task of collecting domestic (home) information should be the responsibility of a social worker.

I. Social-Economic History
    A. What is the cultural socioeconomic performance of the family?
    B. Is this child accepted into the family structure?
    C. What level of marriage and emotional stability exists?
    D. Do the family relationships reflect a functional environment?
    E. What community standards and educational aspirations does this family have?
    F. Indicate the intellectual functioning range of the family.
    G. How involved have the parents been in home-school communication?
    H. Indicate the educational level of achievement of the parents and siblings.
    I. Do the parents realize or reflect a problem?

Teacher's Report

The following areas of information should be the teacher's responsibility. The authors believe that a good teacher will be aware of many of the behavioral and educational manifestations of the child's performance. Therefore, the teacher is the one person who should be able to report accurately the child's performance levels in the different areas of his school program.

I. Teacher Communication to School and Parent
   A. State what you see as the child's learning problem.
   B. Don't postpone or magnify the problem.
   C. Don't give false hope, be positive as well as negative relative to the child's level of growth. Don't mislead the parents, help them to understand what is said.
   D. Don't use a "brain-injury" vocabulary. Speak toward education remediation.
   E. Don't be defensive; the parents will supply you with information if you give them the opportunity.
II. Teacher's Educational Evaluation
   The teacher needs to be aware of the characteristics of the learning disabilities child in order to report the following information:
   A. The academic areas of learning problems.
   B. The degree of perceptual, conceptual, categorization, visual and audio discrimination, and symbolization involvement.
   C. The degree of aphasic or communication deficiency (speaking, listening, writing).
   D. The effect that the learning problem has upon the child's total education program.
   E. The effect that the learning problem has on the emotional and social growth of the child.
III. Teacher's Observation of Child's Physical Condition and Hygiene
   A. Is the child obese?
   B. Does the child appear to be malnourished?
   C. Does the child appear to have eaten before school?
   D. Is the child clean and well groomed?
   E. Does the child appear to be fatigued?
   F. Does the child have visual problems?
   G. Does the child have auditory problems?

H.   Are speech or language problems evident?
I.   Does the child indicate confused left-right body dominance?
J.   Does the child have coordination problems?
K.   Are there other noticeable physical problems?
L.   Is attendance regular?
M.   What appears to be the child's general maturational level?

IV. Teacher's Observation of Attitude and Behavior
A.   Is he distracted easily by visual or audio stimuli?
B.   Is he destructive, hostile, belligerent, or cruel?
C.   Is he hyperactive or hypoactive?
D.   Is his frustration tolerance low?
E.   Is he stubborn, uncooperative, or undependable?
F.   Is he emotionally in control of his general behavior?
G.   Is school a pleasant situation for him?
H.   Is task application evident?
I.   Does he distract other children?
J.   Does he utilize his time well?
K.   Does he complete his work? (on time, late, not at all)
L.   Does he consistently leave his position or desk?
M.   Is a short attention span evident?
N.   Does he demand attention from the teacher or from other children?
O.   Does he appear to be in fantasy land (dreamworld)?
P.   Does he relate to peer and teachers adequately?
Q.   Does he have a poor self-concept or self-image?
R.   Is he a sad and unhappy child?

V.   Teacher's Observations of the Educational History
A.   Is his home-school communication desirable?
B.   Is he a consistent school problem?
C.   Has he repeated a school grade?
D.   Does he have a history of individual tutoring?
E.   Is there a general interest and motivation lag?
F.   Does he receive speech therapy?
G.   Is his reading comprehension confused?
H.   Does he have jerky eye movement when he reads?
I.   Does he attack reading through basic phonics and word analysis?
J.   Is he deficient in reading, math, and spelling?
K.   Is his vocabulary compatible with his sex and age range?
L.   Does he have difficulty in defining words?
M.   Does the child have a history of reversal problems?

N. Does he invert numbers and confuse letters?
O. Does he appear confused when given directions?
P. Does he call objects by the wrong names?
Q. Does he have proficiencies in other school areas?

The team approach should enable the teacher to have the advantages of many different disciplines. This multidisciplinary approach should consist of an optometrist or ophthalmologist, a reading specialist, a child psychiatrist, a speech and hearing therapist, a dentist, a social worker, a pediatric-neurologist, the parents, and the school personnel.

Degree and Certification Programs for Teachers

There is somewhat of a general consensus that the teacher of learning disability children should be a master teacher. The McCarthys (1969) indicate that it has not been demonstrated that either years in school or number of degrees increases one's success in teaching children with learning disabilities. They believe that what is acquired during training, not how long training takes, is the critical variable. The authors agree with McCarthys' statement that it is the proficiency of training that is important, but the different trends should be interesting to note.

Cruickshank (1966) indicates the following information relative to current certification trends:

Certification requirements for school personnel in the United States have been published biennially since 1951. In 1964, one state, California, required five years of preparation for beginning elementary teachers. The fifth year had to be completed within the first five years of employment. Forty-five states required the bachelor's degree; five states required two, but less than three years of college work; and one state required less than two years. Nine states mandated the completion of a fifth year for secondary school teachers, thus indicating a trend in requirements which in time will probably be expected also of elementary teachers.

Another important trend is the effort to overhaul and improve the "approved-program" approach in which a specific number of course credits will be required in specified subject areas. This approach is now in use in forty states.

A third trend among the states is toward the strengthening of the academic preparation of teachers in the areas of general education requirements. In some states this is done by increasing the academic requirements in general, while reducing the course credit required in professional education courses. In other states the trend is toward requiring concentration in one field for an academic major and a minor in education.

Cruickshank continues by indicating that still another significant trend is toward the use of the National Teachers Examinations as a qualifying hurdle. Generally this exam would be in addition to the completion of the approved teacher education program for certification or as a supplement to accreditation. Cruickshank also tells that there has been an increase in the trend toward state acceptance of the certification standards proposed by the National Council for Accreditation of Teacher Education, and also for reciprocity of certification among states.

Good programs for the preparation of teachers for learning disabilities seem to plan a diversity of experiences, including training in assessment, remediation and research, participation in public school classrooms and clinical settings, and contact with a variety of children with learning problems, and their families as well. Adelman (1970) has shown that the forms these experiences take can be categorized into five types of activities: (1) academic—including lecturers seminars, and readings; (2) individual participation and supervision; (3) sensitivity training groups; (4) meetings; and (5) demonstrations.

In general, these programs may be characterized as having been prepared from the standpoint of achieving a positive commitment toward meeting the needs of the individuals in the program, the needs of the field of education, and the needs of society. Such a programmatic commitment and such experiences tend to produce an atmosphere wherein the trainee learns to appreciate and accept the full responsibility of his professional role. Specifically, the professional role should be concerned with the following responsibilities (Adelman): (1) to participate in service (e.g., training, teaching, consultation) activities which will have a direct impact on improving the educational opportunities for children with learning disabilities; (2) to participate in research activities designed both to evaluate and improve such service and, more generally, to increase our understanding of the etiology; (3) to relate such understanding to the basic theories of instruction and learning. The product is an individual who is able to become effectively and creatively involved in service, training, and research; (4) to increase our understanding of the diagnosis, remediation, and prevention of learning disabilities.

Adelman continues by indicating the need for a core program or unit which is divided into seven areas, as follows: (1) the developmental and learning processes and the relationship of these processes to instruction—here the focus would be on the interrelationship between instruction, development, and learning of both normal and abnormal individuals, emphasizing the pertinent facets of sensory, perceptual, motoric, linguistic, cognitive, social, and emotional development; (2) a conceptual model of the assessment procedures; (3) basic theories of instruction—including emphasis on principles related to effecting motivational and attitudinal changes; (4) the effective use of other human resources—clarifying both the potential value and limitations of such resources; (5) the development of the skills necessary for understanding and carrying out research; (6) the development of personal skills required for professional effectiveness; and (7) a systems analysis of the key variables involved in classrooms, schools, and their environs.

After completing the core program, graduate students who want to specialize in the area of learning disabilities would be required to take courses which develop necessary on-the-job skills. These might include assessment techniques, curriculum development, general principles and techniques of remedial instruction; special principles and techniques related to teaching learning disabled children, research design, and techniques of supervision and consultation.

The teachers of learning disabled children may be taught by a three-step training program: (1) introduction of a concept or technique, that is, teaching a specific idea or skill through discussion and demonstration; (2) supervised practice; and (3) follow-up feedback and consultation.

Requirements for Teachers

In selecting a teacher for the learning disabled child there are basic guidelines which can be followed by observing certain characteristics of elementary teachers who are to become specialized education teachers. Cruickshank has suggested the following guidelines:

1. Identify those teachers from kindergarten through third grade who everyone agrees are outstanding teachers.
2. Watch them work with children—in formal planned visits, in informal drop-in observations, and in marginal day-to-day contacts.
3. Select from among them those who really enjoy teaching.
4. From the outstanding primary teachers who enjoy teaching, select those in whose classrooms the following conditions prevail: (a) the children all understand what they are doing and

why; (b) all children feel reasonably sure that they will succeed at the task assigned; (c) the children know what instructional aids, materials, and resources are available and can use them correctly and independently without interrupting the teacher or class; (d) possible behavior problems are anticipated and prevented by redirecting a situation which could lead to trouble; (e) children move individually and as groups from one activity to another without confusion or loss of purpose; (f) the interests and efforts of the children are invested in the achievement of a task rather than in pleasing the teacher; (g) the teacher sometimes makes a mistake, and when she does, the children call it to her attention and help her to rectify the situation with the same good humor and tolerance which they enjoy when they are found in error; and (h) children with special problems know what their problems are and know that the teacher and class understand and are willing to help, and even though they still "goof" sometimes they feel certain that they are improving.

5. Select those who: (a) are secure in their dealings with principals, supervisors, psychologists, medical consultants, and parents; (b) are interested in and willing to try new ways of dealing with old problems; (c) are enthusiastic about experimentation and (d) are highly motivated to work with children who have special problems.

Teachers who meet those requirements can be somewhat assured of success after they have received adequate specialized training, provided that during the initial phase of their adjustment to meeting new requirements they maintain good health, have no major family crisis, and do not feel pressured to take courses to meet certification requirements in an area not directly related to their new assignment.

Characteristics of Teachers

Some of the characteristics of a good teacher are true self-respect, maturity, proper sensitivity, a well-integrated identity, and abundant frustration tolerance. The teacher should be trained both in specific techniques and skills, and also how to use himself and his own behavior to aid in the children's growth.

Cruickshank states that a good teacher must possess the following attributes: (1) be successful in small group instruction; (2) be skilled in one-to-one teaching situations; (3) have much patience; (4) have an experimental point of view and a willingness to try new methods; (5) be able to accept slow progress of children; (6) be able to establish warm relationships between self and children; (7) feel comfortable in a structured teaching situation; (8) be verbal to the point where he can maintain strong relationships with representatives of related disciplines.

Parent Counseling

The concept of the total child must be administered to the parents. Many times the parents are consistently aware of all the negative aspects of their learning disabilities child and fail to open the door to the positive growth that presently subsides within the child. It should be noted, then, that the counseling of the parents must be concerned with the total life implications of the child's learning disabilities problem.

If the teacher is the counseling agent, he must make himself aware of all the ramifications of the different disciplines which are concerned with the child. If a school counselor is the counseling agent, then, that person must likewise become an integrative part of the team approach and be aware of the idiosyncratic behaviors which are common to this child and his family.

The parents should be given the opportunity to share the information relative to the child's problems. The counseling session should not communicate a secretive, avoiding, detached atmosphere. The session should be a time of affective-intellectual sharing.

Rappaport has expressed the need for the following conditions:

> In the counseling session focus should be on the needs of the parents. Parents also need the opportunity to air their anxieties and to raise questions. In attempting to explain why their child has problems, the counselor should share neurological, medical, and all other information factually, but in a fashion that makes sense to the parents. Parents must know that if the professionals have not as yet identified all the causes of brain dysfunction, they cannot blame themselves for their child's problems. Parents should also be helped to realize that etiology is important only as a means of defining the appropriate habilitative program. Identifying the etiology is not meant to stigmatize or to indict them as being biologically or in any other way inferior.

The parents must be aided in making themselves aware of their aspirations for the child and whether these aspirations are compatible with the level of growth of the child. Many times parents feel the pressures of the traditional school program and are unable to rid themselves of the anxieties brought about by their child's failing. Consequently, more pressure is applied to the child to get back into the normal academic and social world, and this additional pressure causes the child to deteriorate even more rapidly.

Parents hold back many frustrations in their attempts to create a successful functioning level for their child, and the relief of these frustrating situations should be the common goal shared by the parents, the school, and the counselor. The counselor must be able to give guidelines to the parents which will enable them to structure a world for their child that is pleasant and comfortable. The counseling session must provide the parents with the clues to the child's behavior, and the kinds of reactions and feedback to the child that will help him become an accepted member of the family and school.

Rappaport relates that parents should want their child to be a person in his own right rather than an extension of themselves. Also, parents should not feel uncomfortable with their child's learning and behavioral disorders. They should recognize their child's need for structure and consistency, which would enable them as parents to conduct their lives and household in a manner that is organized, but not rigidly compulsive.

Parent counseling may be a time-consuming program, therefore the counselor needs to provide situations which will meet the individual needs of the parents. Some parents are knowledgeable about the learning disabilities problem and could work well in a group counseling session. Information could be shared directly with other parents, and each could lend emotional support to the other. They would be able to express themselves in a nonjudging, noncensoring, and non-blaming environment. The counselor, of course, would have to be skilled enough to lead the group toward a desired goal. Certain members of the group should not dominate the session; therefore, the counselor would have to assert some direct control at times.

Individual sessions may be the need of other parents, and this time must be provided for them if they are to achieve an adequate level of home-school growth. Many different problems will be emitted by the parents and it is important that the counselor not seek closure on these problems until they have been thoroughly defined and discussed. All potential ramifications of subsequent problems must be explored. The parent is not in need of additional confusion; therefore the counselor should not create problems by introducing areas of discussion which are wholly unrelated to learning disabilities and academic-social remediation.

Quite likely, one of the most important aspects of the counselor's role is merely to be available to the parents and to be aware of the problem. False hope or false information would be the epitome of poor counseling.

Published Materials

There are many materials that can be used in teaching the learning disabled child. The following is a list of companies where various materials and tests can be obtained to aid the teacher.

AAHPHER Youth Fitness Test Manual (1967 revised edition). President's Council on Physical Fitness, 1201 16th St., N.W., Washington, D.C. 20036.

Autokinetic, Inc., Box 2010, Amarillo, Texas 79105. Various reading and penmanship materials.

Bell & Howell Company, 7100 McCormick Road, Chicago, Illinois 60654. The Language Master and various other materials.

Better Reading Foundation, 52 Vanderbilt Ave., New York, N.Y. 10017. Children's Digest and Humpty Dumpty, periodicals.

Burns Record Company, 755 Chickadee Lane, Stratford, Conn. 06497. Square Dances—Album D, and other records.

Colgate Palmolive Co., Professional Services Dept., 740 N. Rush St., Chicago, Illinois 60611.

Continental Press, Elizabethtown, Pa. 17022. Instructional Materials for Exceptional Children by Eichler and Snyder (1958) and other materials.

Cuisenaire Corporation of America, 12 Church St., New Rochelle, N.Y. 10805. Cuisenaire Rods (1958).

Dev. Learning Readiness, Western Division, McGraw-Hill Book Co., Manchester Road, Manchester, Mo. 63011.

Eye Gate House, Inc., 146-01 Archer Avenue, Jamaica, N.Y. 14435. Various filmstrips.

Garrard Publishing Co., Champaign, Ill. 61820. "The Happy Bears" story reading pad by E.W. Dolch (1956) and other materials.

Highlights for Children, 2300 W. 5th Ave., Columbus, Ohio 43212. A periodical.

Ideal School Supply Co., 11018 South Lavergne Ave., Oak Lawn, Illinois 60453. Magic Cards and other materials.

The Judy Company, 310 N. 2nd St., Minneapolis, Minnesota 55401. Judy-See Ques.

Lyons and Carnahan, c/o Rand McNally & Company, P.O. Box 7600, Chicago, Illinois 60680. Auditory and visual discrimination.

Milton Bradley Co., Springfield, Mass. Link Letters, Uncle Wiggley Game, and other materials.

Puzzles and Patterns, Matt G. Glauach and Donovan Stoner, Steck-Vaughn Co., Austin, Texas.

Science Research Associates, 259 East Erie St., Chicago, Illinois 60611. Basic Reading Skills Workbook (1963) and other materials. Reading Laboratory and Kindergarten Math.

Scott, Foresman and Co., East Lake Ave., Glenview, Illinois 60025. Basic Reading Skills Workbook and other materials.

Steps in Teaching Language for the Deaf, Volta Bureau, 1537 35th St., N.W., Washington, D.C.

Teaching Aids and Toys for Handicapped Children by Barbara Dorward, Copyright 1960 by the Council for Exceptional Children, NEA, 1201 16th St., N.W., Washington 6, D.C.

Teaching Resources Corp., 100 Boylston St., Boston, Mass. 02116.

Tiny Tots Publishing House, Inc., 5483 N. Northwest Highway, Chicago, Illinois 60630. Various materials.

Whitman Publishing Co., Racine, Wisconsin. Picture Word Book, Simple Objects to Color, and other materials.

Tests

American Guidance Services, Inc., 720 Washington Ave., S.E., Minneapolis, Minn. 55414

Minnesota Pre-school Scale (Goodenough, Maurer & Van Wagenen)

Peabody Language Development Kit (Dunn & Smith)

Peabody Picture Vocabulary Test

Verbal Language Development Scale (Mecham)

Vineland Social Maturity Scale

Consulting Psychologists Press, 577 College Ave., Palo Alto, California 94306. Marianne Frostig Developmental Test of Visual Perception.

Language Research Associates, 175 E. Delaware, Chicago, Illinois 60611. Wepman Auditory Discrimination Test.

Illinois Medical Book Company, 215 West Chicago Ave., Chicago Illinois 60610. Illinois Test of Psycholinguistic Abilities (McCarthy & Kirk).

Bureau of Educational Research and Services, Extension Div., State University of Iowa, Iowa City, Iowa. Templin-Darley Articulation Test.

The Psychological Corporation, 304 East 45th St., New York, New York 10017

Arthur Point Scale of Performance Tests, Revised Form II

Bender Visual Motor Gestalt Test

Benton Revised Visual Retention Test

Eisenson's Examining for Aphasia (2nd Edition)

Goodenough-Harris Drawing Test

Harris Tests of Lateral Dominance

Minnesota Test for Differential Diagnosis of Aphasia (Hildred Schuell)

Vineland Social Maturity Scale, Revised (Doll)

Psychological Test Specialists, Box 1441, Missoula, Montana 59801

Full-Range Picture Vocabulary Test (Ammons & Ammons)

Memory-for-Designs Test (Graham & Kendall)

Quick Test (Ammons & Ammons)

Scott, Foresman & Co., 1900 East Lake Ave., Glenview, Illinois. 60025 Bryngleson & Glaspey Articulation Test Cards

Bibliography

Adelman, Howard S. "Graduate Training in the 'Speciality' of Learning Disabilities: Some Thoughts," *Journal of Learning Disabilities* 3, no. 2 (February 1970).

Clements, Sam D. *Minimal Brain Dysfunction in Children.* NINDB Monograph no. 3, Public Health Service Bulletin no. 1415. Washington, D.C.: U.S. Dept. of Health, Education, and Welfare, 1966.

Cruickshank, William. *The Teacher of Brain-Injured Children.* New York: Syracuse University Press, 1966.

———, and Johnson, G. Orville. *Education of Exceptional Children and Youth.* Englewood Cliffs, N.J.: Prentice-Hall, Inc., 1967.

Heckrel, John R., and Webb, Susan M. "An Educational Approach to the Treatment of Children with Learning Disabilities." *Journal of Learning Disabilities* 2, no. 4 (April 1969).

Kass, Corrine E., and Myklebust, Helmer R. "Learning Disabilities: An Educational Definition." *Journal of Learning Disabilities* 2, no. 7 (July 1969).

Kirk, Samuel A., and Bateman, Barbara. "Diagnosis and Remediation of Learning Disabilities." *Exceptional Children* 29, no. 2 (October 1962).

Landreth, Garry L. "Complimentary Roles of the Pediatrician and Educator in School Planning for Handicapped Children." *Journal of Learning Disabilities* 2, no. 2 (February 1969).

Learning Disabilities Due to Minimal Brain Dysfunction. Bethesda, M.: National Institute of Health, 1970.

McCarthy, James J., and McCarthy, Joan F. *Learning Disabilities.* Boston: Allyn and Bacon, Inc., 1969.

Minskoff, Gerald. "Notes of Federal Activities in Learning Disabilities." *Academic Therapy* 5, no. 1 (Fall 1969).

Morrison, Dr. James. Kansas Association for Children with Learning Disabilities, pamphlet, 1971.

Myers, Patricia, and Hammill, Donald D. *Methods for Learning Disorders.* New York: John Wiley and Sons, Inc., 1969.

Rappaport, Sheldon R. *Public Education for Children with Brain Dysfunction.* Syracuse: Syracuse University Press, 1969.

Rice, Donald B. "Learning Disabilities: An Investigation in Two Parts." *Journal of Learning Disabilities* 3, no. 3 (March 1970).

———. "Learning Disabilities: An Investigation in Two Parts." *Journal of Learning Disabilities* 3, no. 4 (April 1970).

Slingerland, Beth H. "Early Identification of Preschool Children Who Might Fail." *Academic Therapy* 4, no. 4 (Summer 1969).

Stewart, Mark A., M.D. "For Parents of Hyperactive Children," *Expectations,* ACTION for Brain-handicapped Children Inc., St. Paul, Minnesota 2, no. 4 (September/October 1972).

Whittlesey, Dr. Wes. "Introduction to Children with Learning Disabilities." Position Paper, Director of Pediatric Services, Oklahoma State Department of Health, April 1969.

LEARNING DISABLED CHILDREN
Study Sheet #1

1. Give an educational definition of learning disabilities.

    a. In what way or ways does this definition distinguish a learning disability from other learning problems?

LEARNING DISABLED CHILDREN
Study Sheet #2

1. Describe a few educational and behavioral symptoms of the learning disabled child.

   a. Educational

   b. Behavioral

LEARNING DISABLED CHILDREN
Study Sheet #3

1. Describe the various ways in which a child can exhibit hyperactivity.

2. Briefly describe how the child's hyperactivity may interfere with his learning.

'Please don't leave me alone.'

8

The Emotionally and Behaviorally Maladjusted

DEFINITION

Many theories of personality, child behavior, and remediation presently exist within the framework of a definition-seeking study of the emotionally or behaviorally disturbed child. The authors' experiences have indicated that it is extremely difficult to find a perfect definition for the disturbed child. A definition must be relevant to the many different cultures, societies, and moral values. Any one single definition doesn't seem to be consistent with the needs of all professionals or theories of treatment.

Kessler (1966) has indicated the following guidelines as referral criteria for disturbed children:

1. Age discrepancy. There are ages by which most children have outgrown particular habits and behavior.
2. Frequency of occurrence of the symptom must be considered. One should be concerned when the symptomatic behavior is aroused under minimal stress, which means it occurs very often.
3. The number of symptoms is an obvious consideration. The more symptoms, the more the child is disabled. However, one should not rely exclusively on the criterion of multiplicity of symptoms to judge the extent of psychopathology. It is possible for a single symptom to work so efficiently that all the child's anxieties are taken care of at once. All of his problems may be bound up in the one phobic situation so that there is no spillage into other areas.
4. The degree of social disadvantage is an inevitable determinant of parental concern about children's symptoms. It is easy to see a vicious circle at work where the symptom's effects may tend to perpetuate the symptom.
5. The child's inner suffering is often overlooked. It is often assumed that the child's opinion of himself is based solely on the

spoken statements of others. So, if the parents are tolerant, and outsiders do not know about the symptom, the parents may feel that the child will not be upset about it. But children are quite capable of judging themselves. And though he may not verbalize his inner distress, he often reveals it to someone who knows him well.

6. Intractability of behavior is implied, in part, in the criterion of frequency. The persistence of symptoms, despite the efforts of the child and others to change them, is the hallmark of so-called behavior disorders.

7. General personality appraisal is the most important criterion, and the most difficult. This criterion has to do with the child's general adjustment, rather than with isolated symptoms.

Before one is able to describe abnormal or different behavior, one should have some workable concepts of normal behavior. If one were to describe normal behavior, a judgment must be made concerning one's own values, his immediate environment's values, and national or worldly values. Children are unable to live in a static world today. Their environment and cultures are constantly changing, and the children must learn to switch from one role of behavior to various different roles. Behavior and values which are acceptable in one school or city may not be tolerated in another school. Values of the child's home or community may not be acceptable in his school; therefore, this child must learn early in life that he will have to play many different roles of behavior.

Apparently one of the most serious concerns for behavior deviations is that which prevents a child from maintaining a normal pattern of intellectual, social, and emotional growth in the public schools. Schools have achievement records and tests which supposedly determine normal ranges of progress for various academic subjects. Therefore, certain expectations exist for children with particular age ranges. Rubin, Simson, and Betwee (1966) indicate that children can be identified as failing to make appropriate and significant progress in certain well-established and accepted areas of accomplishment, such as at school. They also feel that necessary patterns of adaptation for any given age period may be defined, and deviance from these may be a useful guide to the identification of maladaptation.

Many definitions of disturbed behavior appear to center around the child's inability to maintain himself adequately in the home, school, and community. Buhler, Smitter, and Richardson (1966) have indicated that in psychological terms, a problem is a hindrance that may disrupt the continuity of the processes within an individual or a group. An example would be a child's problem in school which disrupts the classwork, the desirable cooperation of the group, and/or the child's own ability to function.

Kessler writes that the criteria for judging a child's need for help should be considerate of three behaviors—progression, fixation, and regression. The authors are in agreement with Kessler's view that a child is growing, changing, and developing, and as a consequence of this interaction with his world his behavior is constantly changing. The changes in behavior, though, may be indicated by either a static display, which in effect will cause the child to regress because he cannot maintain proper peer relations if he does not move forward; or he actually may manifest serious regressions, which will result in a significant lag in growth; or he will move forward toward maturity and acceptable growth. Hopefully, of course, all children will move forward in an acceptable way of life. Realistically, though, one must realize that some children will manifest behaviors that cannot be tolerated in their schools, homes, and communities.

One must always be aware that some children can succeed in one or more areas (e.g., school) of life, but may be completely debilitated in another area (e.g., home or neighborhood). Therefore, the child's *total* level of functioning must be considered when determining a definition of a disturbed child. Consequently, the authors' experiences have indicated that a definition for an emotionally and/or behaviorally disturbed child must reflect a child's inability to function compatibly with the total environments in which he must live. A definition which appears to encompass these environments would be one which defines the emotionally disturbed child as a one who cannot emotionally, intellectually, and socially function in a manner that is acceptable to his peers, teachers, parents, and legal authorities within his school, home, and community environment.

Prevalence of Emotionally Disturbed Children

It would be an impossible task to determine the actual prevalence of children within the boundaries of the United States, who are categorized as emotionally disturbed children. Kessler suggests that statistics about the number of children who possess personality disorders have little significance, because each researcher's criteria for defining these children would be somewhat different. The authors believe that there isn't a means at the present time which would enable all behaviorists to tabulate emotionally disturbed children under the same set of criteria. Consequently, estimates of prevalences within the United States population will range from 1 to possible 15 percent of all school children.

McCaffrey and Cumming (1969) report studies suggesting an expectancy that 5 to 10 percent of all children manifest emotional disturbances. They did indicate, though, that one should be aware of the fact that emotional disturbances reported in single surveys may subside within relatively short periods of time, and that other disturbances will progress to fixed and accumulative patterns of academic and social failures. Jones (1960) also assumes that definite figures of prevalence are not possible, but he does believe there to be little doubt that both incidence and prevalence is high. Jones also indicated that the Subcommittee on Juvenile Delinquency of the United States Senate recently found that 10 percent of school age children need psychiatric treatment.

Presently many professional estimates agree with a number of other association reports concerned with mental health problems. It appears quite likely that these different reports, even though possessive of different criteria, have indicated a fairly close estimate of prevalence. This prevalence seems to fall consistently within the 5 to 15 percent range—a conservative range, but one that is in apparent agreement with many different behavioral professionals.

Methods of Identification

Dupont (1969) lists Eli M. Bower's report on a California State Department (1955) study concerned with early identification of emotionally disturbed children. Specifically, the study was aimed at discovering the extent to which a teacher-centered procedure might be employed for identifying disturbed children and the extent to which information about children ordinarily obtained by the classroom teacher may be used. The teacher was not involved in the study, until the psychiatrist, psychologist, or counselor in each participating school was asked to identify some children who were or had been in treatment by the clinical staff for their emotionally disturbed behavior. These children were enrolled in classes which were selected for participation in the study without revealing to the teacher the criterion for selection. The results of the study seemed to indicate that the teacher's judgments of emotional disturbance are very much like the judgment of clinicians. The implications of this study may suggest that the classroom teacher is capable of differentiating the emotionally disturbed children from other children in the classroom.

Nelson (1971) reported a study in which a direct observation technique was used to investigate differences between children classified as conduct disturbed or normal on the basis of ratings given by their regular classroom teachers. The results of this study agree with Bower's study that teachers are capable of identifying emotionally disturbed children in their classrooms with a high degree of accuracy. Nelson also points out that a teacher rating alone is not sufficient for identification of disturbed children, because the rating procedure may be based upon the individual teacher's standards of normal behavior. It is doubtful that all teachers could agree on normal behavior; there is, therefore, a possibility of an error in the rating assigned to a given child. The error, of course, as stated by Nelson could cause a child to be assigned a higher rating simply because he represented the upper end of the distribution of an unusually calm class.

A 1966 (Maes) report indicated that emotionally disturbed children in grades four, five, and six can be identified as effectively through use of a teacher rating scale and a group intelligence test as through use of these two sources of information plus arithmetic achievement, reading achievement, a modified sociometric technique (a class play), and a self-concept inventory. Maes continued by indicating that the teacher rating scale and group intelligence test results can be useful in making decisions relative to referrals to psychologists for individual diagnostic study, and that other information such as achievement, sociometric status, and self-concept has little predictive value, but may have value for understanding and meeting pupil needs in the educational setting.

Caplan (1964) reports that experts argue for early case findings on the premise that the earlier treatment starts, the more effective and brief secondary prevention will be. Kessler adds that early detection can be dangerous because without treatment, early detection may lead to a self-fulfilling prophecy. She also relates that by alerting parents or teachers to possible future difficulties their anxieties are increased, which will reduce their effectiveness unless they are given some directions. Therefore, she feels that without any promise of treatment, early diagnosis may only compound the problem and prove to be a curse in disguise. Methods of identification must be consistent with the knowledge that is available from the many different areas of human behavior. A teacher, psychologist, social worker, psychiatrist, child development specialist, or guidance counselor is not by himself equipped to make a conclusive report upon a child's emotional problems. Each person who is concerned with this child's emotional health, should be a contributing member of a team that suggests methods of identification and treatment. The authors have witnessed diagnoses of children by one professional that were blatantly in error, and these errors of judgment became visible only after there had been an evaluation review for a composite by different professional personnel. Evidence in theory and practice does not support the fact that one person has the singular professional skill to determine the life course of a particular child. Therefore, an assist from another person who may know something about the child's school, home, or community skills may be of great importance in determining whether a child is to be tested or treated for emotional disturbances.

Characteristics of the Emotionally Disturbed

Characteristics of emotional disturbances are so plentiful that one may nearly suffer anxiety by trying to tabulate all of them. Apparently, though, each behavioral scientist has his specific method of coding these children into distinct areas of behavior or disturbances. The authors will offer an overview of some of the current practices of characterizing disturbed children and hope that the reader will not conclude that it is an easy process to separate the disturbed from the nondisturbed child when both children possess the same or similar characteristics.

The authors offer brief descriptions of the following classifications in four different categories:

I. Psychoses
   A. Schizophrenia, withdrawn
   B. Manic-Depressive Illness, Depressed
   C. Paranoia
II. Neuroses
   A. Anxiety
   B. Hysterical-Psychosomatic
   C. Obsessive-Compulsive
   D. Depressive
III. Personality Disorders
   A. Antisocial
   B. Passive-Aggressive, Passive Type

IV. Transient Situational Disturbances
    A.   Adjustment Reaction of Childhood
    B.   Adjustment Reaction of Adolescence

Psychoses

    Schizophrenia withdrawn is marked by disturbances of thinking, mood, and behavior. Alterations in concept formation and the individual's misinterpretation of reality are common. Sometimes delusions and hallucinations will occur. Mood changes are ambivalent, constricted, and inappropriate. Loss of empathy with others is commonly found. The behavior of a schizophrenic individual is often characterized as withdrawn, regressive, and bizarre. Although mood disturbances are found within the category, schizophrenia is generally described as a thought disorder as distinguished from an affective or a mood disorder.

    In the category of schizophrenia withdrawn there are varying degrees of personality disorganization. The schizophrenic individual fails to test and evaluate correctly his external reality. He attends to too many aspects of a situation and is unable to filter out irrelevancies. This results in disturbances in his thought processes. Tasks demanding sustained attention and effort are futile. The disorder is also marked by disturbances in reality relationships, concept formations, and intellectual performance. Disorganization and disturbances in associations and thinking also occur. There do not appear to be any clear links between ideas or associations.

    Feelings or emotions appear inappropriate to the situation. The individual experiences ambivalent reactions as though he were being pulled in different directions. Disharmony between mood and thought is common. Emotional blunting marked by apathy and indifference also occurs.

    Autistic thinking is found in withdrawn schizophrenia. The individual's thinking and perceiving is regulated by personal wishes rather than by objective reality. In teaching this individual, concentration should be placed on relationships with others and with objective reality. Depersonalization or misidentification of self with others is characteristic of schizophrenia. Self-concept should be stressed along with expression of thoughts, feelings, and perceptions.

    Scattering, moving from word to word without filling in the gaps for the listener, and forming neologisms, or coining new words are typical of the thought disturbance patterns found in schizophrenia. Stress should be placed in the areas of continuity in thought and feeling, order and sequencing in words and events, and building re-sponse sets to aid the individual in relating to external reality.

Ullmann and Krasner (1969) cite a study done by Cameron and Margaret (1951) which describes factors resulting in disorganization in a schizophrenic individual.

1. Interruption of activity (frustration)
2. Environment change (alteration in previously supporting envi-ronment)
3. Preoccupation (single theme dominates, all else excluded)
4. Emotional excitement (anger or fear increases errors and muscu-lar tension; destroys fine coordination)
5. Ineffective role-taking (unable to see perspective of other per-son)
6. Situational complexity (new or conflicting demands)

Reactions to situations that are difficult and stressful produce defi-cits in effective role-taking, thought organization, and emotional functioning. Social withdrawal also occurs. Therefore, these situa-tions should be avoided.

Manic-Depressive, Depressed states are characterized by sad af-fect, psychomotor retardation which may progress to an acute stupor, isolation, withdrawal, and apathy. The individual experiences a loss of enthusiasm and feelings of hopelessness and helplessness. Hypochondriacal complaints may be expressed. Guilt over wrongdo-ings is often expressed. Agitation, restlessness, perplexity, and de-mands for attention are other characteristics.

This disorder is classified as a primary mood disorder. It differs from a psychotic-depressive reaction which is more easily attribut-able to stress. Illusions, hallucinations, and delusions, if present, are usually of guilt-laden, hypochondriacal, or paranoid ideas and attri-butable to the dominant mood disorder.

In working with this type of individual, the activity level should be increased so as to lower the level of apathy. A variety of activities should be offered so as to keep the individual busy in order that he not have time to think about his problems. Tasks should be brief as this individual may have difficulty in concentration over a longer span of time. This individual should be encouraged to relate with others, and placed in activities involving groups. He should be given tasks at which he can succeed in order to build his self-concept and ease his feelings of hopelessness and helplessness; and should be posi-tively reinforced for behaviors incompatible with those behaviors which are to be modified, while behaviors which reinforce the de-pression should be avoided.

Paranoia is the gradual development of an intricate, complex, and elaborate paranoid system based on and often proceeding from misinterpretation of an actual event. The individual considers himself endowed with unique and superior abilities. The paranoia is considered restricted in range and does not interfere with the rest of the individual's thinking and personality.

The range of paranoid reactions include adjectives such as sensitive, cautious, rigid adherence to rules, social isolation, overcriticism of others, self-righteousness, and sometimes delusions of persecution (people out to destroy him), grandiosity (individual is important), and reference (the individual gives personal meaning to events that do not apply to him; belief that others are paying special attention to him). Other characteristics of paranoia are suspicion, nontrusting of others, tenseness, insecurity, fearfulness, and a high level of anxiety.

The individual suffering from paranoia has difficulty confiding in others because he expects to be betrayed. This individual feels and acts hostile. He is characterized as exhibiting behavior which is reaction-sensitive. He reacts with defensive hostility to certain kinds of situations, personalities, and implied threats. He is overready to react with counteraggression to what he experiences as an assault upon his integrity threatened from without.

The paranoid individual relies heavily on the defense mechanisms of projection and denial as well as repression. In projecting, he attributes his own unacceptable traits to another person. Because he believes that he cannot trust others, he withdraws socially and emotionally. He has a tendency to deny responsibility for his failures and ascribes them to others. He also denies his own unmanageable hostility and projects it onto others.

Techniques which could be used in dealing with this type of individual would be to reduce the anxiety level by teaching newer, more appropriate methods of response. This type of individual should be confronted with his behavior and its consequences. From this point, emission of an alternative and more socially appropriate act can be developed. He should be provided with new experiences which are contrary to and incompatible with his prior belief system.

This individual experiences feelings of internal discomfort or anxiety. Through projective thinking, he mistakes internal discomfort for external pressure. This reflects the confusion and difficulty that this individual encounters in locating problems responsible for his discomfort.

Some psychotherapeutic techniques used are persuasion: attempting to convince the paranoid that his suspicions, hostility, and grandiosity are unwarranted or unnecessary; confrontation: suggestion or interpretation concerning the behavior exhibited. A rapport should be developed prior to confrontation so that the hostility and suspicion will be diminished and a nonthreatening relationship can be developed.

The individual dealing with a paranoid should be honest. He should avoid keeping secrets from the individual. Maintaining secrets with the paranoid individual should be avoided and recognized as attempts to manipulate and question the trust of the teacher or therapist.

In dealing with the paranoid, an individual must be dependable and consistent. Failure will give the paranoid an excuse to label the individual as untrustworthy. The teacher or therapist should appear nonthreatening to the paranoid individual. He should accept the paranoid's views without practicing deception. He should not argue about the delusions but simply state that he does not agree with them. Direct confrontation concerning the paranoid's behavior may serve to relieve tensions.

Neuroses

Anxiety neurosis seems to occur when an individual subjectively experiences uneasiness, apprehension, anticipation of danger, doom, and feelings of going to pieces or disintegration. The source of these feelings are unknown to the individual. He experiences an anxious over-concern which may extend to panic and which is frequently associated with somatic symptoms. Anxiety neurosis is distinguished from normal apprehension or fear which occur in a realistically dangerous situation. The anxiety is not restricted to definite situations or objects.

In his relationship with others, this individual expresses a compulsive need for dependency and symbiosis, aggression and domination, and detachment and isolation. He feels that he is driven rather than moved, that he is not an active force in his own life, and that he is utterly helpless.

Systematic desensitization is often used in dealing with anxiety neurotics. The individual needs to learn new ways by which he can effectively reduce his anxiety level. Assertion training in which the individual is taught to take the initiative of standing up for his own rights is used to instill confidence and reduce anxiety.

In working with this individual in a classroom, pressure should be kept at a minimum. Competition which would create an arousal of anxiety impairing his ability to function should be avoided. This individual would do well to learn to function in groups as well as to work independently. Control of his anxiety, as well as free choice of actions in situations, should be taught.

Hysterical-Psychosomatic neurosis is an involuntary psychogenic loss or disorder of functioning. The symptoms begin and end suddenly in emotionally charged situations and are symbolic of underlying conflicts. In psychoanalytic terms, the symptom formation in hysteria represents the unconscious solution, or attempted solution, of an emotional conflict. The symptoms are a protection against the perception of the anxiety and depression associated with the conflict. Often, the individual expresses *la belle indifference* with respect to his symptoms. He does not seem to be alarmed by the loss and welcomes the opportunity to talk about his symptoms.

In an hysterical-psychosomatic reaction, or a conversion reaction, the anxiety is not experienced consciously but is converted into bodily symptoms. There do not appear to be any physiological or anatomical reasons to explain the dysfunctions.

Precipitating factors which may evoke hysterical reactions are conflicts produced by changes in the individual's life situation. Therefore, the maintenance of a stable environment is essential. Possible resolutions to conflicts which may produce somatic symptoms are conscious assimilation resulting in a decisive action on the part of the individual, sublimation into a social activity, work, or some other means of compensation.

Discussions in which the individual talks about his symptoms or physical disabilities should be avoided as they tend to positively reinforce the illness. Possible techniques to use in modifying the behavior are aversive stimuli, with the objective of extinguishing the negative behavior; positive reinforcement for desired behavior; rewarding a positive behavior which is incompatible with the behavior to be extinguished; practicing the emission of the undesired behavior until a ceiling is reached to the end that the behavior will then decline in frequency; deprivation of a desired activity or reward if negative behavior is produced; and systematic desensitization—all are possible methods which can be used to shape the individual's behavior.

Obsessive-Compulsive neurosis occurs when an individual experiences persistent, unwanted thoughts or actions which he is unable to stop. Anxiety and distress is often present. Concern that he will be unable to control himself or unable to complete the act is often present.

The anxiety found in this disorder is associated with the persistence of unwanted ideas and of repetitive impulses to perform acts which may be considered morbid by the patient. The individual may consider his ideas and behavior as unreasonable, but feels compelled to carry out his rituals.

The compulsive individual displays excessive concern with adherence to standards of conscience and conformity; he may be over-inhibited, overconscientious, and have a great capacity for work; or may be characterized as rigid and lacking in relaxing, enjoyable pursuits. In modifying this individual's behavior, attempts must be directed at inconveniencing the individual for his undesired behavior to the point where reinforcements for attempts to change it can occur.

Depressive neurosis is an excessive reaction of depression because of an internal conflict, or due to an identifiable event such as loss of a love object or a cherished possession. Acute feelings of despondency and dysphoria of varying intensity and duration also occur. Foreboding about the future, apathy, and fatigue are other symptoms.

Depression is a disorder primarily characterized by symptoms, among which are a diminished level of activity, lowered self-assurance, apprehension, constricted interests, and loss of initiative. The reaction is frequently precipitated by a current situation involving a loss to the individual and associated with feelings of guilt for past failures or deeds. The symptoms of neurotic depression overlap those found in psychotic depression.

Operant and respondent conditioning is used in treating a depressed neurotic. Behavior which is antithetical to a depressed role should be reinforced. New response sets must also be taught. Supportive techniques to ease guilt feelings should be employed. Distractions such as books, movies, and television will aid the depressed individual in getting his mind off of his problems. Sleep is another very useful aid.

Personality Disorder

Antisocial personality is characterized by developmental defects or pathological trends in the personality structure, with minimal subjective anxiety and little or no sense of distress. It is seen as a lifelong pattern of action or behavior, rather than a disorder caused by mental or emotional symptoms.

Chronically antisocial individuals are always in trouble, profiting neither from experience nor punishment, and maintaining no real loyalties to any person, group, or code. They are frequently callous and hedonistic, showing marked emotional immaturity, with lack of a sense of responsibility, lack of judgment, and an ability to rationalize their behavior so that it appears warranted, reasonable, and justified.

Impulsivity, shortsightedness, and self-defeating acts mark the individual's behavior. The individual seems unaffected by stimuli that control the behavior of most other people in the society. Social conditioning is slow in that the individual must learn new response sets.

This individual has a pattern of being inconsistently rewarded for his acts. For example, if making amends in being charming is the behavior which is reinforced, this person called psychopathic learns well. He becomes very agile at using his charm to manipulate. However, the behavior which makes it necessary for this individual to manipulate is unaltered.

In working with this type of person, new response sets must be taught. Appropriate ways of social interaction need to be learned. Attention and care should be directed at which behaviors are reinforced. The individual modifying the behavior should be aware of manipulation attempts which are common among the personality disorders.

Passive-Aggressive. Passive type is characterized by behavioral patterns of pouting, obstructionism, procrastination, intentional inefficiency, and stubbornness. These behaviors are a reflection of the hostility that the individual feels he cannot express openly. Often the behavior is an expression of the individual's resentment at failing to find gratification in a relationship with an individual or institution upon which he is overly dependent.

Two other subtypes found under the passive-aggressive personality are passive-dependent which is characterized by helplessness, indecisiveness, and a tendency to cling to others as a "dependent child to a supporting parent." Irritable, resentful behavior marked by temper tantrums characterized the second subtype, aggressive.

In working with the passive type individual, attempts should be directed at discovering more appropriate modes of expressing hostile feelings. Control and expression of feelings should also be developed. New roles by which the individual can discover other forms of gratification in relationships should be explored.

Transient Situational Disturbances

Adjustment Reaction of Childhood is a habit or conduct disturbance which is generally a reaction to an event and is temporary in nature. It is marked by irrational, self-defeating behavior which is atypical of the way the individual usually acts or is expected to act. There is no underlying personality disturbance present. An adaptive capacity to return to normal functioning is present. Recession of symptoms occurs when the stress is diminished.

Special attention at a personal level should be given to help the individual work through his problems. Encouragement in the area of relating to others should be stressed. Success should be provided in all areas of work.

Adjustment Reaction of Adolescence is marked by irritability and depression associated with school failure and manifested by temper outbursts, brooding, and discouragement. This disorder is transitory. Emancipatory strivings, vacillation of impulses, and behavior which resembles personality or psychoneurotic disorders is generally found.

Attempts should be made to help this individual work through his problems independently. Solutions should be left up to the individual who should be encouraged to attempt more appropriate manners of responding to situations and events. Independent action should be stressed.

Chapman (1965) reports that psychoneurosis designates a group of emotional disorders in children which may be divided into different categories of behavior:

1. Phobias, which are abnormal fears of specific things or situations. Phobias constitute the most common psychoneurotic disturbance of childhood.
2. Anxiety Reactions, in which the child experiences much tension, varying from mild restlessness to sheer panic; they may be acute or chronic.
3. Obsessive and Compulsive Reactions, in obsessive reactions the patient is afflicted with persistent, distressing ideas of which he cannot rid himself, and in the compulsive states he feels strong urges to perform repeated physical acts to relieve tension.
4. Conversion and Dissociative Reactions, which include various disorders of sensation, movement and special sensory perception. The term conversion reaction is, in general, synonymous with the older term hysteria. The dissociative disorders are clinically related and are characterized by disturbances of awareness or memory, as in psychogenic amnesias.
5. Tics, which are discrete, repetitive, muscular movements caused by emotional tension. Because mild tics are common in children and have particular characteristics, we shall treat them as a

separate category, though tics in adults are often included under the conversion reactions.

Many symptoms may be characteristic within a "normal" behavior and these symptoms, even though present, do not cause any functional problems within the environment. The same symptoms exhibited within a disturbed child's repertoire may cause considerable distracted behavior. Such things as nail-biting to the "normal" child may not become an obstacle, but to the disturbed child this type of symptom may be the overlay of a very serious problem. Each nail-biting session is then a very anxiety provoking situation. Some disturbed children will not manifest characteristics such as bed-wetting, nail-biting, or thumb-sucking as distinct symptoms of anxious behavior. They will, instead of, invest themselves into a personality structure that causes difficulties in their total interpersonal relationships. Chapman has divided what he refers to as interpersonal and personality functioning behavior into three general areas:

1. Personality-pattern disturbances, in which the emotional troubles of the child produce problems in his personality structure. This category includes the depressed child, the passive child, the aggressive child, the compulsive child, and the emotionally insecure child.
2. Acting-out behavior disorders, in which the child acts out hostile feelings in antisocial ways. Examples are running away, stealing, lying, school truancy, fire-setting, use of alcohol and illicit drugs.
3. Disorders of sexual behavior, in which emotional turmoil produces disturbances of sexual behavior, as in homosexuality and tranvestism.

Disorders of the learning and training processes of children may cause maladjustment in the acquisition of the necessary skills for communication, social, and academic proficiency. Children are somewhat characterized by their experiential framework. Therefore, if the child's world has been infested with socially inappropriate behaviors he will probably gravitate to these behaviors and appear to be a helpless, paralyzed, dependent, noncommunicative child. Chapman (1965) has approached a three-section division of disorders in training, learning, and speech as possible characteristics of emotionally disturbed children:

1. Adjustment disorders of habit training, in which a socially necessary type of training is not developed, as in enuresis and

encopresis. This group also includes thumb-sucking, hair-pulling, and sleep disturbance.

2. Adjustment disorders of learning, which include difficulties in mastering the skills of scholastic learning, all of which involve the use of symbols. Examples are reading problems and general learning inhibitions.

3. Adjustment disorders of speech, which include delayed speech, stuttering, and disorders of speech articulation.

Chapman also divides psychosomatic illnesses into categories characteristic of some emotionally disturbed children. The authors contend that there really isn't much need to sort out the psychosomatic illnesses into distinct areas of illnesses, because the concern should not be for a child's specific malingering illness, but should instead be for the fact that he is ill. The specific kind of illness manifested—asthma, ulcers, hyperventilation, acne, headaches, abdominal pains, chest pains, back aches, etc.—are not as important characteristically as is the fact that the child consistently manifests these illnesses and symptoms when no apparent organistic cause can be determined. The physician will quite likely impress medical treatment upon the child in the same manner as he would with other children. It is interesting to note, though, that disturbed children will manifest varying kinds and degrees of severity of their psychosomatic illnesses, and placebo or medication application will have relatively little effect upon his aches and pains for any significant period of time. Therefore, one should note the frequency and tenure of the child's illness and the child's response to his illnesses.

Many characteristics of emotionally disturbed children should be evident to the classroom teacher. These characteristics may clearly present obstacles in the way of the child's progress or they may remain somewhat subtle. The teacher is exposed to the child for the second largest number of hours in each day, and the child probably is in a position at school to exhibit his problems even more obviously than he would in many home situations. Therefore, a considerable number of different kinds of characteristics of behavior should be visible to the teacher. Bower (1969) has indicated five different areas from which a teacher could observe visible signs of trouble:

1. An inability to learn which cannot be explained by intellectual, sensory, or health factors.

2. An inability to build or maintain satisfactory interpersonal relationships with peers and teachers.

3. Inappropriate types of behavior or feelings under normal conditions.

4. A general, pervasive mood of unhappiness or depression.
5. A tendency to develop physical symptoms, pains, or fears associated with personal or school problems.

In a study conducted in California, Bower (1969) noted that the emotionally disturbed child differed from other children in the following ways: He scored significantly lower on group I.Q. tests. He scored significantly lower on reading and arithmetic achievement tests. Other children tended to select him for hostile, inadequate, or negative, rather than positive, roles in class activities.

Quay, Morse, and Cutler (1966) subjected the Peterson Problem Behavior Rating Scale to a factor analysis on a variety of populations, and these studies indicated that three independent dimensions account for about two-thirds of the variance of the interrelationships among problem behaviors. These three dimensions, of course, possess activity that may be characteristic of emotionally disturbed children. The first dimension listed aggressive, hostile, and contentious behaviors which also are referred to as conduct disorders, unsocialized aggressions, or psychopathologies. The second dimension included the anxious, withdrawn, introvertive kinds of behavior, which also have been labeled personality problems or neuroticism. The third dimension considered preoccupation, lack of interest, sluggishness, laziness, daydreaming, and passivity. The third dimension generally seems to have accounted for much less of a variance than the first two dimensions.

Children's strange behaviors are many times the emission of and hopefully the detection of their problems. The child will express himself possibly in many different avenues of behavior and he will undoubtedly defend his actions as being acceptable. Unknown to himself and many times to those around him the child is expressing a need for help through his unacceptable behavior. Morse (1969) points out the importance of being able to detect the symptoms of the emotionally disturbed child. His reasoning is that most disturbed children are still in regular classrooms, and probably will continue to be there until more and better provisions are made for them. Therefore, he sees the need for the teacher to be able to recognize a child's symptoms which indicate that he is having a problem, and is calling for help.

If teachers and professionals are able to discover the cry for help from a disturbed child, they should consider many questions relevant to a particular child's behavior and background. It should be noted, though, that a child does not necessarily emit all the characteristics that are listed below. These different behaviors are possible characteristics possessed in large numbers by some children, and possessed in small quantities by others. The authors have had experiences with a number of disturbed children, who emitted excessive unacceptable behavior through expression of the different characteristics that are listed below. This list of characteristics is not conclusive, but it does contain a number of important considerations for those who are concerned about identifying emotionally disturbed children.

1. Does the child express excessive anger?
2. Does the child appear hostile?
3. Does the child have significant academic deficiencies?
4. Does the child appear to maintain acceptable physical hygiene?
5. Does he appear to receive adequate sleep?
6. Is he sleepy and bored with school?
7. Does he appear negative?
8. Is he exceptionally hyperactive?
9. Is he significantly withdrawn from his peers?
10. Does his I.Q. score appear to be compatible with his functioning level?
11. Does he participate in extracurricular activities?
12. Is he destructive to property?
13. Does he have temper tantrums in school or at home?
14. Is he truant or tardy consistently?
15. Does he appear to be depressed or exhibit suicidal tendencies?
16. Is he suspicious of the teacher and his peers?
17. Does he appear to have hallucinations or delusions?
18. Does he complain of physical illnesses?
19. Do his moods vascillate from pleasant to unpleasant?
20. Is there indication of sexual preoccupation?
21. Is there indication of stealing, fire-setting, or enuretic behavior?
22. Does he exhibit sudden emotional outbursts?
23. Is his self-image depreciatory?
24. Is he accident prone?
25. Does he exhibit regressive forms of behavior?
26. Is he a perfectionist and succeeds academically?
27. Does he appear to be a daydreamer?
28. Has he attended special classes?
29. Has he had a migrant education program (moved alot)?
30. Has he repeated grades in school?
31. Does he reject all authority figures—school, home, police?
32. Does he defy structure and school rules?

33. What is the sociological culture of his home?
34. Does he live in a broken home situation?
35. Does he appear to be a parentally neglected child?

These are only a few of the characteristics that may be manifested by a child who is having emotional problems. These characteristics should not be considered in sequence, nor should a child have to possess a certain number of characteristics in order to be disturbed. A determination of his functioning level must be related to the seriousness of his actions, the frequency of his behavior, and whether the behavior lasts over a period of time that appears to be excessive.

Narcotics

Many youngsters who are manifesting emotional problems will turn to illegal drugs, stimulants, and narcotics to enable themselves to achieve a diminution of their problems. Drugs without proper medical supervision will only magnify the disturbed person's internal problems. Therefore, the authors offer the following information from table 3 as a guide to understanding some of the more common symptoms associated with improper drug usage.

Services Available

Presently there appears to be a lack of proper or adequate facilities for emotionally disturbed children. Different states have provisions which include self-contained classrooms, resource rooms, general special education classes, hospital classes (both inpatient and outpatient), and itinerant teachers, but generally the overall provisions for emotionally disturbed children are quite deficient throughout the United States. Schultz, Hirshoren, Manton, and Henderson (1971) point out that education programs for emotionally and socially maladjusted children have existed within a few public school systems, primarily in large cities, for over fifty years. It has only been recently, though, that Emotionally Disturbed programs have developed in small school districts with help from the Office of Education Federal Funds. Schultz, et al. also indicated an approximate twenty-year growth of classes from a 1948 total of ninety public school programs serving 15,300 children, to a 1966 total of 875 school programs serving approximately 32,000 emotionally disturbed children. It should be interesting to note the improvement over the twenty year period of the number of children being served by ninety

Table 3

NAME OF NARCOTIC	POSSIBLE BEHAVIOR SYMPTOMS	MATERIAL EVIDENCE	PHYSICAL-EMOTIONAL CONSEQUENCES
Glue Sniffing	Violence, appearance of drunkenness, dreamy or blank expression	Tubes of glue, glue smears, large paper bags or handkerchiefs	Lung/brain/liver damage. Death through suffocation or choking, anemia
Heroin (H., Horse, Scat, Junk, Snow, Stuff, Harry, Joy Powder) *Morphine* (White stuff, Miss Emma, M., Dreamer) *Codeine* (Schoolboy)	Stupor/drowsiness, needle marks on body, watery eyes, loss of appetite, blood stain on shirt sleeve, running nose	Needle or hypodermic syringe, cotton, tourniquet string, rope, belt, burnt bottle, caps or spoons, glassine envelopes	Death from overdose. Mental deterioration, destruction of brain and liver, hepatitis, embolisms
Cough Medicine containing Codeine and Opium	Appearance of drunkenness, lack of coordination, confusion, excessive itching	Empty bottles of cough medicine	Causes addiction
Marijuana (Pot, Grass, Locoweed, Mary Jane, Hashish, Tea, Gage, Reefers)	Sleepiness, wandering mind, enlarged eye pupils, lack of coordination, craving for sweets, increased appetite	Strong odor of burnt leaves, small seeds in pocket lining, cigarette paper, discolored fingers	Inducement to take *stronger* narcotics
LSD (Acid, Sugar, Big D, Cubes, Trips) *DMT* (Businessman's High) *STP*	Severe hallucinations, feelings of detachment, incoherent speech, cold hands and feet, vomiting, laughing and crying	Cube sugar with discoloration in center. Strong body odor. Small tube of liquid	Suicidal tendencies, unpredictable behavior, chronic exposure causes brain damage. LSD causes chromosomal breakdown
Amphetamines (Bennies, Dexies, Co-Pilots, Wake-Ups, Lid Poppers, Hearts, Pep Pills) *Methamphetamines* (Speed, Dynamite)	Aggressive behavior, giggling, silliness, rapid speech, confused thinking, no appetite, extreme fatigue, dry mouth, shakiness	Jars of pills of varying colors, chain smoking	Death from overdose. Hallucinations. Methamphetamines sometimes causes temporary psychosis
Barbiturates (Barbs, Blue Devils, Candy, Yellow Jackets, Phennies, Peanuts, Blue Heavens, Goof balls, Downs)	Drowsiness, stupor, dullness, slurred speech, appearance of drunkenness, vomiting	Pills of varying colors	Death from overdose or causes addiction, convulsions and death as a result of withdrawal.

Ref: I. Taxel, Woodmere, N.Y. 1970

schools compared to the number of children served by 875 schools. Evidently, there was a tremendous change in the teacher-pupil ratio.

Presently, it would be somewhat difficult to arrive at the exact number of services available to emotionally disturbed children, because of the many deceptive means of placing these children in school situations. Some children will be hidden in regular classes; some children will be in mentally retarded classes; some children will be in learning disability classes; and many children will be school dropouts. A conservative estimate of public and private school and institutional placement would be for approximately two hundred thousand children. This estimate, though, represents the number of children who are probably receiving adequate treatment, and it does not include the children who are misplaced in other service or categorical areas.

The availability of services is considerably deficient compared to the needs for placement of emotionally disturbed children. A recent report by the National Institute of Mental Health (1970) indicates that surveys conducted through school systems imply that 2 to 3 percent of the children are in need of psychiatric care and an additional 7 percent are in need of emotional help. A total estimate of all children in need of special programs for emotional problems is conservatively placed at 1,200,000 children. Therefore, it is quite obvious that the services for emotionally disturbed children are drastically insufficient.

The authors of this text do not advocate any particular service need, because different children may be served under various kinds of programs. The need for all kinds of services exist, rather than a need for one specific kind of facility or program. Schultz, et al. sought information about educational services for emotionally disturbed children and discovered twelve specific kinds of services existed: special class programs, resource room programs, crisis intervention, itinerant teacher program, academic tutoring, home-bound instruction, guidance counselor, school social worker, psychotherapy by school psychologist, psychiatric consultation, public school transportation to nonschool agency, and payment by public school for private school. Hopefully each school system would be able to provide at least one of the above stated services, but realistic observation at the present time indicates that these services are not available to the majority of the disturbed children in public schools. Until states adopt mandatory special education laws, the schools will probably fail to provide the necessary services for emotionally disturbed children. Schultz, et al. found a general profile in the United States to indicate that the majority of programs for emotionally disturbed children were on a permissive basis. They discovered that special classes were the most often mentioned service (47 states), and re- source room programs (40 states), and home-bound instruction (38 states) were the next most common programs. They also noted that more than half of the states permitted the twelve services previously stated, and that some states prohibited services (specifically, pay- ment to private schools) that other states mandated.

Number of Students Per Class

Many states have laws or state education department require- ments on the maximum and minimum number of students permitted in each class or unit of instruction. Generally throughout the United States it appears that approximately ten students seem to be the maximum load for an individual class. Five as the minimum number of students necessary for a class appears to be a fairly consistent figure in many states. Although, a range from a minimum of five to a maximum of fifteen is indicated in various school systems. The maxi- mum or minimum number of students also may be somewhat depen- dent upon the age and severity of the children's problems. Without question, a teacher should be able to work more effectively with five older students who have already acquired some academic skills than with five very young disturbed children who have not achieved any academic success.

Schultz et al. also discovered that there were considerable dif- ferences among the states relative to the number of students assigned to a particular staff member. They received information from fifty states which indicated an extremely heavy load in some states for resource teachers—60 students; for crisis interveners—75 students; for social workers—250 students; and for psychologists—700 students. In other states they found extremely small case loads for teaching pro- fessionals.

There isn't any magical number of students per class that will ameliorate the problems of working with disturbed children. Logic does dictate, though, that a professional can achieve only limited success if he overloads; therefore, a reasonable student-teacher or student-professional ratio must be maintained. What is reasonable will have to be determined by the professional and teacher-possessed skills, and by the age and severity of the students' problems.

Eligibility for Special Class Services

Provisions for special class placement is generally the function of the state department of education. States have different criteria for placement of children into special classes. These criteria are usually consistent with the particular categorical definitions as described by each different state. Therefore, the child's eligibility to receive special school services are determined by his meeting the guidelines established by his state's department of special education. These procedures for admission are not compatible among the different states. Some states may require a psychiatric examination for admission to an emotionally disturbed class, while other states may place the child in a special class merely on the advice or recommendation of the school's administration.

Eligibility for admission should dictate that the program is special, and that it is not a program that becomes a convenient means for the teachers or administrators to sidetrack their problem children. Guidelines for admission should be strict enough to keep children *out* of the class as well as permit them into the class. A standard procedure for referral, evaluation, and placement should exist within each state. The procedure need not be common among the states, but it should be procedurally sound if the class or program is to maintain its identity and serve a specific function for emotionally disturbed children.

Many times teachers will refer children who they think need psychological services, but it may be the teacher's particular problems that become evident; and the child has been the result of that teacher's inability to function. Therefore, the next step should be an evaluative process that determines the child's emotional level of functioning. After adequate evaluation the child may then be placed in a special class or returned to the regular program. The recommendation should *not* be made on the basis of the initial referral whether it came from a teacher, a parent, an administrator, or even a psychologist; unless the report has been reviewed thoroughly with other school or professional personnel.

Educational Planning

The child has received a good evaluation. He has been referred to the special class program. Now, what are his chances of succeeding and returning to the mainstream of school and life? If this child is to succeed, he must have the advantage of sound educational, social, and intellectual planning. The child cannot be discarded into a special class to vegetate and deteriorate. He must receive the benefits of experienced personnel, who have reasonable objectives for remediation of social, emotional, and academic problems. The child will, hopefully, be placed in a situation that will best meet his needs, whether it is a contained room, a resource room, or whatever. After he has been placed, a plan should be developed which is concerned with this particular child's growth. Wood (1968) has expressed the need for a therapeutic educational plan that should be considered generally for all children who are placed in special programs, but noting that the details of the plan will vary with each situation. His suggested plan is as follows:

1. What is the child's educational problem? If the assumption is made that all children should be kept as closely integrated into the regular educational stream as possible, this becomes a question of which of the child's special needs can be met by adjustments within the regular classroom and which require special programming outside the regular class. Perhaps a special placement should be coordinated with part-time placement in a regular class.
2. Are any special conditions of placement necessary for exconcurrent psychotherapy, or medication? Who will be responsible for seeing that these conditions will be met?
3. What educational and management procedures are the regular or special class teacher to use with the child?
4. What period of time is to elapse before the success of the placement is to be evaluated? Who is responsible for making this evaluation and communicating it to the members of the team?

Wood's plan is a general guideline that could be followed with the placement of each child in an emotionally disturbed class, but the plan cannot be effective if the individual consideration for each different child is not exemplified.

Bullock and Whelan (1971) completed a study relative to teacher competencies which indicates that teachers for emotionally disturbed classes must be characterized through adequate training and affectually sound models. Their study produced the following information:

A competency committee, selected by the national advisory committee, was given the task of defining the specific competencies needed by teachers of emotionally disturbed and socially maladjusted children. This committee made the following recommendations regarding the personal qualities of teachers:

They should be people of good judgment, possess a sense of humor, have the ability to place people and events in proper perspective, have adaptability and flexibility of mind, be conscious of their own limitations and idiosyncrasies, and have a normal range of human contacts outside the daily task of working with problem children.

After a careful analysis of the opinions of the competency committee and those expressed by teachers themselves, several suggestions for teacher training programs were postulated. Rabinow's program relies heavily on psychiatry, psychology, sociology, and communications and education. Schwartz proposed the training of a clinical teacher—one proficient in the diagnosis and remediation of learning and behavioral disorders. Hewett has a hierarchial framework—(a) objectivity, (b) flexibility, (c) structure, (d) resourcefulness, (e) social reinforcement, (f) curriculum expertise, and (g) intellectual model—which he believes to be vital for the teacher of emotionally disturbed children. Mackie, Kvaraceur, and William's program contained the above characteristics also.

Bullock and Whelan drew a comparison between two different groups of teachers of the emotionally disturbed—how each group viewed the competencies which a special study staff chose as important. The participants in the Bullock and Whelan investigation (a) did not view the competencies as being as important as did the original group; (b) viewed themselves as being more proficient in the competencies than did the original group; (c) tended to rank the items similarly to the original group on importance and on proficiency; (d) saw themselves as being less proficient in the items that they rated as being less important; and (e) tended to view themselves as being proficient in the items which they viewed as important.

It is apparent that continued and more intensive research must be undertaken to determine the most important competencies needed by teachers of emotionally disturbed and socially maladjusted children. Without this research, teacher preparation institutions lack scientific data to substantiate their existing programs and serve as guidelines for program development and expansion.

It is suggested that preparation programs for teachers of emotionally disturbed and socially maladjusted children need to place renewed emphasis on individualized and sequential programing techniques in order to ensure school success for these children. Such an approach calls for teachers with a comprehensive overview of both regular and special curriculum materials for all grade levels. Since a large proportion of these children are below grade level academically, it seems imperative that teachers also have a thorough knowledge of remediation procedures, particularly in the areas of reading and arithmetic. Teachers also need thorough knowledge and understanding of behavioral principles as they apply to the management of these children. Since a multidisciplinary approach is also desirable; teachers need to become aware of other professional personnel and work with them as a team.

During the process of training persons to become teachers of emotionally disturbed children, it has been most difficult to assess an evaluation of these teachers' performances. The national picture of programs for training teachers of emotionally disturbed children reflects program training in terms of numbers of courses in common, and of hours spent in practicum and classes. Haring and Fargo (1969) believe further training is necessary. They indicate that the evaluation of a teacher's skills cannot be measured by the courses listed on his college transcript or by the total number of course-hours completed, but rather by the effectiveness of his teaching of children.

To accomplish this goal, the techniques required are continuous structured evaluation of teacher performance, and clear statements of behavioral objectives. The behavioral objectives recommended by Haring and Fargo have been summarized as follows: (1) to establish procedures of observing, recording, and analyzing behaviors systematically; (2) to assess child performance in four areas—academic, verbal, social, and physical; (3) to assess the child's academic placement and the skill areas which need emphasis while also recognizing preference of activities which are most motivational; (4) to develop systematic procedures for initiation and maintenance of work in specific skills; (5) to demonstrate that the above-mentioned skills can be used with individuals and groups of children.

These criteria for evaluating the teacher were made by the cooperating classroom teacher and by the teacher's self-evaluation. This self-evaluation was enhanced by use of videotapes so that the teacher could get the full effect of the job done, and reflect and review methods he had used. Use of videotape as a method of assisting in evaluation is highly recommended.

Evaluation, which in the past has tended to be a general, nonmeasurable entity, can be specific and more effectively done. Through means of observation and evaluation of the teacher's effect on the end result—the child and his performance—a true and accurate evaluation of the effectiveness of a teacher may be obtained.

Parental Considerations

Many years' experience in the field of special education has impressed upon the authors the realization that parents of exceptional children are generally sophisticated relative to the specific problem area of their child. The majority of parents seem to have genuine concern about their child's problems. Therefore, if an emotionally disturbed child is present within the home, the parents are usually quick to learn all they can about emotional disturbances. They are aware of the child's different behaviors, and they probably are not content to live with them; consequently, when they do seek help they are willing to involve themselves within a therapeutic program.

McKinnon (1970) reported a study in which parent and pupil perceptions of special class placement were assessed. His study involved two urban communities where special classes for emotionally disturbed children had been in operation for several years. Consequently, it is somewhat obvious that the program was an accepted part of the school system. This study involved 88 children and their parents. The students had been in special class elementary schools for an average of seventeen months and had an average age of fourteen. At the time of the study the students had terminated attendance in classes for an average period of three years. Even though the perceptions were in retrospect, his study indicated the parents were able to recall experiences and they generally expressed positive views about the special classes. The parents indicated too that the teachers were positive also and had a stabilizing effect upon the parents and their children. The parents also reported relief when their child was taken from the failing regular class situation and was placed in the special class.

McKinnon's study indicated furthermore that pupil perceptions reflected a pleasant and positive experience. Some of the questions that he asked the students seemed to reflect answers that expressed an understanding of, or an awareness of their problem behaviors. An example would be the response most frequently received from students when they were asked to give reasons for entering the special class. These responses were reflections upon themselves for having tempers and the ways they acted. The second most frequent response was a recognition that they were unable to do the work in the regular classes.

Parents' realistic perceptions of problem behaviors may be the turning event which dictates other constructive behaviors within the child. It should be an interesting experience to be able to note whether the child's behavior has actually changed or whether the parents' perception of the same behavior has changed. Many times parents obviously see what they want to see; and even though the child possesses demonic qualities, the parents may still perceive him as a little angel child. Another parent may have a child who functions within a normal curve and they perceive his behavior as considerably deviate. Proper or improper behavior may lie in the eyes of the beholder.

Children Considerations

Apparently the largest majority of children who have experienced a special class setting have realized the advantages of which they may avail themselves. McKinnon reported that generally the children were positive about their feelings toward academic and craft work in the special classroom. They enjoyed both nonacademic and academic areas where assistance and success were possible. He also reported that a high percentage of the pupils did not like other students in the classes, because they exhibited explosive, unpredictable, or "nutty" behavior. The authors agree with McKinnon that this pupil perception could be an individual student's projection of his own "nutty" behavior.

Students sometimes seem to have intellectual understanding of their problems, but they are unable many times, to benefit from an emotional or affective investment. The students are able to tell the teacher of their problems, and sometimes identify those elements of their behaviors that create obstacles for them; but they are unable to present a feeling-level of understanding. If a student were able to integrate his intellectual and affective involvement in problem behavior he should then be able to master his problems with relatively little assistance. Generally, though, the student will manifest intellectual conversations that say, "Yes, I know I do not behave. I know that I cause my parents and teachers problems, but I don't know why." Therefore, the child will continue his emission of poor behavior possibly because he knows of no other way to say, "Please, help me. I need help."

This child needs the structure, supervision, and assistance that is available to him only in special programs. He will not receive the affective kinds of understanding that he so desperately needs from a traditional education program. Consequently, it should not be difficult to understand why these children, even in retrospect, perceive their experiences in special classes as enjoyable and foundationally sound growth periods of their lives. The time spent in special programs has enabled many of these students to be involved in the first successful academic and social experiences that they have ever had.

Residential Treatment

The National Institute of Mental Health (1969-1970) reported that in 1969 there were 261 facilities classified as residential treatment centers. The majority of these treatment centers were small, privately owned institutions, which were primarily located in the Northeast Central, Pacific, and Middle Atlantic areas. Approximately two-thirds of these residential treatment centers included special education as a part of their treatment programs. Also, approximately one-third of the facilities placed no diagnostic restrictions on their admission requirements. Those centers that had restrictions tended to mention most frequently that mental retardates were not eligible for admission. The National Institute also indicated that nearly twenty-one thousand patients were under care in residential treatment centers during 1969. That number of patients is small compared to the total needs of children throughout the United States. Therefore, it is quite obvious that residential settings do not possess sufficient means to handle the emotionally disturbing problems for the general population. Quite likely the majority of the patients seeking care from residential centers were either those people who were financially able or those who qualified for public assistance.

Treatment in residential centers may primarily be involved with those patients who are too disturbed to be under treatment in a less intensive environment. Children who manifest behaviors that are destructive to themselves or to others would not normally be handled in a community or school project; therefore, a number of these children will be placed in residential settings. The authors are not suggesting that there should be a general flow of child admissions to residential settings. Instead, it is suggested that children should be in their home environments if at all possible. Children do not get functionally well if they are confined to a sick environment. They must be exposed and integrated into a "normal" milieu, which provides them with contacts of realistic life conditions.

Institutional settings many times will separate the children from their families, which in some situations is quite therapeutic; but this separation will also deny the facility the opportunity to work with the parents due to geographic barriers. Consequently, the residential center must concentrate its treatment procedures with the child, and hopefully reconstruct and remediate his problems to such a degree that he can return home and tolerate his parents' child-rearing deficiencies. The parents are requested by some facilities to seek treatment for themselves in their own communities. Home visits by the child or institutional visits by the parents would then offer observations to determine the growth of both parents and children.

The authors have worked with some children who seem to offer evidence that the further the geographic separation the quicker the child responds to treatment. If the child and parents arrange a visitation either at home or at the residential setting there seems to be a level of anxiety indigestion which causes the child to regress. It has also been observed that if children are allowed to have telephone contact with their parents for longer than two to three minutes, disagreements and arguments usually follow.

A practical suggestion for parent and child contact may be that the child should not be forced to call or write to his parents. The parental contact should be made by the child only if he wishes to do so, and the parents should not have the opportunity to phone or visit their child unless it is recommended by the staff as therapeutic. If the parents contact the child and they have not modified their own parental problems they will very likely resort to their usual child-rearing, provoking attitudes which possibly caused the child's residential placement initially.

Heiting (1971) points out that the practice of maintaining close family relationships while the child is placed in a residential treatment program is advantageous for the following reasons:

1. It helps offset the child's fear of being abandoned and his feeling that he was sent away because he is bad.
2. It helps keep alive the anxiety the parents have developed from feelings of guilt and failure in having placed their child away from home—anxiety that can be used in the treatment process to stimulate the parents to find new and more effective ways of interacting with their children.
3. It keeps the conflicts between parents and child active and provides the treatment staff with specific types of behavior on which to focus in helping the child and parent effect change.
4. It forces the detached, neglectful parent to acknowledge his responsibilities to the child, or, failing that, opens the way for steps to provide a substitute family for the child.

A residential setting may be the answer for some children, but not for others. Parents and professionals should examine closely the particular needs for that child before he is placed. Parents should also be aware before they waste time seeking information about residential treatment, that it is generally a very expensive program.

Care Responsibilities

Bower expresses a concern that the care of the emotionally disturbed child is a community-centered problem, not just a school problem. He indicates that the school should cooperate with other civic agencies and campaign actively for complementary programs such as foster homes, detention homes, day-care centers, and residential settings. Kessler suggests the new social concepts and patterns of comprehensive care offer good potential, but she sees a danger in that the needs of children may be slighted in favor of those of the adults.

The National Institute of Mental Health points out that the community mental health center should provide comprehensive services that are particular to the communities' needs, and services should be provided by the specific community's resources. NIMH suggests that a community center should provide at least five essential services:

1. *Inpatient care* offers treatment to patients who need 24-hour hospitalization.
2. *Outpatient care* offers patients individual, group, or family therapy, while permitting them to live at home and go about their daily activities.
3. *Partial hospitalization* offers either day care for patients able to return home evenings, or night care for patients able to work but in need of further care and who are usually without suitable home arrangements. It may include both day and night care and/or weekend care.
4. *Emergency care* offers emergency psychiatric services at any hour around-the-clock, in one of the three units mentioned above.
5. *Consultation and Education* is made available by the center staff to community agencies and professional personnel.

NIMH also suggests that a community center should offer the following services in addition to the basic five in order to maintain a full comprehensive program.

1. *Diagnostic services* provide diagnostic evaluation and may include recommendations for appropriate care.

2. *Rehabilitative services* include both social and vocational rehabilitation. For example: vocational testing, guidance, counseling or job placement.
3. *Precare* and *aftercare* provide screening of patients prior to hospital admission, home visiting before and after hospitalization, and may make available follow-up services for patients at outpatient clinics, in partial hospitalization programs, in foster homes, nursing homes, or halfway houses.
4. *Training* programs may be provided for all types of mental health personnel who serve the center's patients.
5. *Research* and *evaluation* may be undertaken by the center to evaluate the effectiveness of its program and to analyze the needs of the area it serves.

Care responsibilities should involve many different agencies within a community setting. The public schools will have a major portion of the responsibility simply because they are exposed to almost all of the children in a community, but the schools can only be as effective as is their willingness to share their problems and constructively involve other community resources.

METHODS AND MATERIALS FOR EMOTIONALLY DISTURBED CHILDREN

There are no method or material panaceas available to teachers. If there is a panacea in teaching it has to come from within values and expertise of the teacher. Unquestionably the teacher has a tremendous effect upon the child's cognitive and affective world, and the traditional application of educational procedures will not enable the child to reach his potential growth. The teacher must discover those materials which will apply to the problem area of the child, and then those materials must be structured and regulated to an aspirational level that is compatible with the level of growth of the child. Therefore, materials are not necessarily the answer to the child's problem; it is instead, the teacher's ability to integrate methods and materials through his own flexible affective tones.

Aspects of the different behavioral theories are somewhat applicable to the teaching and academic setting of the emotionally disturbed child. Professional education and behavioralists should not restrict themselves to one rigid scheme of treatment. One should screen all systems, and approach the parts of the different systems that may be applicable to a particular child. A brief overview of some of the different systems or theories of behavior reflect resemblances of Freud's original concepts of personality development. The theories which are in action today, even though they possess flashbacks to the Freudian concepts, emphasize that their basic principles have application in the emotionally disturbed child's classroom.

Analytic Theory

The analytic theories suggest that the permissiveness and acceptance that are expressed in a client-centered environment could be advantageously applied in a teacher-child relationship. Naturally, the teacher should not expect a continuous positive therapeutic transference, because there will be times of regression in the child which may exemplify severe negative transference of feeling. The general principles of psychotherapy do, though, have distinct applicable qualities for the classroom setting. The child, hopefully, would be able to reduce the conflicts between himself and his environment when through acceptance, respect for his teacher, and the setting-of-limits, he is enabled to discover the need to want to be included into the community. Changes in the student's adaptive behavior may occur when he effects changes with his environment or changes within himself. The student may change as a result of the psychophysical (relation between mental action and physical phenomena) reduction of the psyche and somatic conflicts which previously had caused him to be involved in a hypochondriacal symptomatic state of asthenia. Also, adaption to a functional level may happen as a result of the student's choice of a new environment which contributes to his functioning level, rather than restricting it. Sometimes the environment causes the child to appear abnormal, when in reality he could function properly in a different environment; therefore, the child's changing of his environment may enable him to be an acceptable individual.

Behavioral Theories

Pavlov and Skinner to some extent started the present behavior modification trend that appears to be rapidly spreading throughout the United States. Even though their primary work was years ago and was involved in laboratory settings, they created the basic techniques that have enabled behavior management methods to reach the classroom in the public schools. Behavior modification is discussed in another chapter in this book, but some examples of successful modification methods will follow:

Axelrod (1971) reports a study by Gallagher, Sulzbacher, and

Shores with a group contingency procedure to reduce disruptive classroom behaviors of five boys ranging in age from approximately seven to eleven. The study hypothesized that more deviant behaviors existed when a member of the class was not seated. Therefore, the goal was to eliminate out-of-seat behavior, which in turn should reduce the other deviant behaviors. The students were offered a 24-minute coke break at the end of the day if they did not leave their seats without permission. A chart in the room indicated two-minute segments from 24 to 0, and each child's name was marked by a different color of chalk. Therefore, when a child left his seat without permission the teacher would mark off two minutes from the entire class's coke time. The color coding would, of course, designate which student left his seat. The results of the study indicated a reduction in out-of-seat behavior from 69.5 to 1.0 times per day, and a significant decline in disruptive behaviors.

Glavin, Quay, and Werry No 6. (1971) conducted a two-year research study with conduct problem children who exhibited severe difficulties in the public school. These children were placed in an experimental special class situation, and the first year (1967) the program emphasized the elimination of the grossly deviant behaviors and the acquisition of attending behaviors that were preliminary to academic success. The second year (1968) the emphasis was placing of rewards for academic performance. Attractive reinforcers were given for appropriate performance on academic tasks. Various intangibles may have had influence on the results, but a comparison between the 1965 and 1968 data seems to favor the 1968 program as the primary contributing factor for improved academic and behavior performances.

Behavior modification programs are not the total answer to the remediation of children's problem behaviors, but they provide a functional method that can be systematically applied. Management techniques should never be without the affective levels of warm, human interaction; and behavior techniques must be void of rigid, cold, and mechanical application.

Ecological System

The ecological theory appears to encompass the individual and the environment into a single concept. The individual is not separate from his environment; therefore, the problems of the individual become the property of the community and the problems are not dealt with as a single attribute of the child. Consequently, if there are disturbances within the community the individual will be affected by the ecology.

A psychologist who visits a home, classroom, community living space, or the total school and community environment can distinguish behaviors contributive to the child's deviations. The child is also contributing to the system's deficient pattern, but possibly he should not be identified as the primary etiology of the disturbed environment. The ecological system presents a pattern or reciprocity which says, "You hurt me, and I'll hurt you."

Lewis (1970) writes that ecological planning offers fresh insight into ways of helping children with behavior problems. He indicates that ecology tells us that children need more than a good educational program, because ecological planning suggests an enlarged scope to include the child's total environment, which includes the people with whom he lives and interacts regularly. The general program goals in the ecological system would be to remediate the child's behavioral and/or academic problems. Remediation enables the child to interact appropriately with his environment, which would then cause his environment to interact appropriately with the child.

Sociological Theory

Society appears to be a collection of structures which dictate the needs of individuals. Personal needs seem to have no limitations, but the individual is commanded to contain himself within certain norms of behavior that are determined by the majority of society. Consequently, the more limited a particular society's structure becomes, the more obvious the individual's deviation will be. An example of limited structure could be found within the confines of a church setting where an individual is to act with certain dignities. If this person were to use profanity, the deviation would be very obvious; but if he were a sailor on ship and used profanity the deviation would not be so obvious. Therefore, obviously the controls of society can cause a child to be categorized as a disturbed child. Movies which exhibit pornography may be within the mores in some communities while in other communities a person may be labeled a sex deviate if he were to attend such movies.

Drugs for Treatment of Emotionally Disturbed Children

Few topics of discussion generate more heat and less light than the proper role of drugs in the treatment of emotionally disturbed children. At one extreme are those who argue that meaningful treatment is possible only by using the insights provided by psychotherapy and that drugs, if they function as more than placebos, do so only as chemical straightjackets for troublesome children.

At the other extreme there are those who consider drugs to be the agents of choice because they attack the disturbed function at the physiologic level; the place they believe the ultimate pathology lies. This controversy engages the passions of psychologists, social workers, parents, and teachers. But for the empiricists, however, the relevant question is, "What are the facts?"

Historically, the search for drugs to influence behavior or learning, or to induce a feeling of inner calm and contentment, extends far beyond modern pharmacology. Many natural substances such as opium, alcohol, and mescaline have been used to calm, soothe, and increase acceptance of a poor situation or simply cause partial oblivion or sensory dullness.

These "cures" are often worse than the illness. Adverse effects of these drugs include habituation, addiction, and loss of personal control.

These natural drugs in "raw" form do not meet the necessary requirements of an effective "tranquilizer." The effective tranquilizer should produce rapid therapeutic responses in a majority of cases, without inducing tolerance or addiction. It should have low incidences of toxic effects and side effects. Hopefully, it would not dull the senses or decrease perception, or interfere with mental alertness, to any extent (Cruickshank 1969).

The first major group of synthetic drugs to be used in this way were the barbiturates. They offered considerable advantage over the natural drugs, but had one major shortcoming. They dull the senses and blunt mental response because they are sedatives rather than tranquilizers (Wilson 1964).

Early in the 1940s some favorable responses to the administration of amphetamines were observed. These drugs were known for their stimulating effect on the central nervous system. These compounds were better known commercially as Benzedrine and Dexidrine.

There was little additional work completed until the 1950s when Chlorpromazine was introduced by French investigators. Since that time, the literature dealing with drugs that affect behavior has grown at an incredible rate. Numerous compounds have been developed and some have emerged without careful study. Unfortunately, to this day there are few well-designed and controlled scientific studies to assess the psychological state of the patient and the relationship to agents under study (Conners 1971).

Therefore, the decision to initiate drug therapy for children with behavior problems is still a very controversial issue, now complicated by the climate of the times. The psychostimulant drugs do have a place in treatment, but the high rate of placebo effect, the reaction of the public against drug therapy in general, a lack of knowledge concerning long-term effects of these agents, and the possibility of drug abuse are all factors to be considered in the initiation of any drug therapy (Solomans 1971).

Tranquilizers

Tranquilizers are drugs which are used to control anxiety, psychomotor agitation and related symptoms. They consist of two clinical groups: (1) the major tranquilizers and (2) the minor tranquilizers. The major tranquilizers can be divided into the phenothiazines and Rauwolfia derivatives, and the minor tranquilizers can be divided into diolcarbamates, the diphenylmethanes, and a miscellaneous group.

Additional groups are becoming necessary as new compounds appear. Although this classification is incomplete and tentative, it currently offers a useful guide. After this general introduction, a presentation of the therapeutic properties of the major and minor groups is possible:

1. A diminution of emotional tension and a reduction of mental activity and agitation.
2. An absence of depression of any aspect of cognition.
3. A suppression of psychomotor activity and excitement.
4. An alleviation or abolition of delusions and hallucinations.
5. The reduction or dispersal of mental confusion in psychosis (Benson and Schiele 1962).

Pharmacologically, there are distinctions among the tranquilizers; although many similarities do exist in the action of representative drugs from each group, there are also considerable differences.

The major tranquilizers exert greater autonomic effects (on the nervous system) and, in addition, are prone to induce tremors. The most significant action is their ability to depress the hypothalamus (controls basic drives) without depressing the cortex (senses). The minor tranquilizers differ among themselves in that autonomic blocking activity is more characteristic of the diphenylmethanes while the muscle relaxant action is a prominent effect of the diolcarbamate drugs.

Chlorpromazine (Thorazine) was the first major tranquilizing drug introduced which was used to modify behavior. The most remarkable action of Chlorpromazine (Thorazine) is its ability to reduce the frequency of aggressive agitated outbursts in seriously ill psychotics with relatively less ataxia, skeletal muscle incoordination, and drowsiness associated with bromides and barbiturates. The primary site of action of Chlorpromazine (Thorazine) is the central nervous system (Benson and Schiele).

The other major tranquilizers are characterized by one or more of the following:

1. Produces a type of emotional calmness with relatively little sedation.
2. Is capable of producing the reversible extra-pyramidal syndrome (outer limbs) characterized by tremors, rigidity, and drooling.
3. The incidence of annoying side reactions is relatively high with the use of this and other major tranquilizers, and serious dangers do exist to some extent.
4. They produce little, if any, dependency or habituation.

Trifluoperazine (Stelazine) is at least twice as active as chlorpromazine, but otherwise is similar in its spectrum of action. It produces no drowsiness, but on the contrary has been said to have an awakening effect.

Fluphenazine (Prolixin) is, in terms of miligrams potency, the most active compound available at the present time. It is considered to be more than twenty times as potent as Chlorpromazine (Benson and Schiele). The authors have worked with students who were administered Prolixin and it has a cramping effect if additional dosages of Congentin are not administered; therefore, it is used to control behavior by withholding Congentin.

One caution should be added at this point. The dosage should be made according to the individual patient—with small dosages in the beginning, to be increased only after evaluation by the physician. In the major tranquilizers there reside the danger of toxicity and harmful side effects. These two facets of the drug should be evaluated before they are prescribed for any patient.

The minor tranquilizers are very widely used and are the preferred drugs in common nervous illness. In many cases, their calming action is sufficient to help the patient attain relief during the acute phase of his disorder.

In spite of the widespread use and great popularity of the minor tranquilizers, much less is known about them than is known of the major tranquilizers.

Neprobamate (Equanil) has a mild sedative action with muscle relaxing and some anticonvulsive activity. It is the most widely used of all tranquilizers. Although it is a safe compound compared with the major drugs, habituation, ataxis, and skin reactions occur occasionally.

Chlordiazepoxide (Librium) is a potent central muscle relaxant which has sedative and tranquilizing action. It is closely related to the maprobamate in activity, but is much more potent (Benson and Schiele).

The Antidepressive Drugs

The antidepressive drugs are useful in the treatment of psychiatric depressions. Depression varies as much as pain, and like pain is one of man's most common ailments.

The use of amphetamines to alleviate behavioral disorders in children was originally advocated in 1937. In 1958, methylphenidate was first used on children with behavioral disorders, and eventually became even more popular than the amphetamines. When the era of tranquilizers and other psychoactive drugs erupted in the 1950s, a milieu was created in which dependency on the need for effective drug therapy produced many studies, which lacked control and scientific validation (Solomans).

Today, the main problem is the lack of an operational definition of minimal brain dysfunction, learning problems, or deviant or hyperactive behavior. This automatically produces confusion in the choice of medication and the evaluation of its efficiency.

The site and mechanism of the psychostimulant drugs have not been definitely established. They do, however, have a paradoxical effect on many children, especially those with hyperkinetic behavior. Logically, the hyperkinetic behavior should increase with amphetamine. Connors and Rothchild (1968) state that the drug action in the hyperkinetic child is not a pharmacologically true paradoxical effect, but rather a direct stimulating effect of the amphetamines which cause an increase in general alertness and excitation along with an increase in the ability to focus attention. Responses to interfering stimuli are then decreased, resulting in the child being more receptive to positive reinforcement from parents and teachers (Solomans).

With emotionally disturbed, underachieving boys, methylphenidate (Ritilan) significantly increased correct responding, decreased reaction time, and hyperactivity; and in the classroom significantly increased attention and cooperation behavior (Sprague et al. 1970). This was a well-controlled study using laboratory as well as clinical procedures (Solomans).

Side Effects and Addiction. Admittedly, no psychotrophic drug is a panacea. None of these agents attack the etiologic factors which are sometimes unknown, uncertain, or unresponsive and few bring permanent symptomatic relief.

While most are safe in competent hands, many drugs carry undesired reactions and the fear of these side effects frequently acts as a deterrent to the use of both tranquilizers and antidepressants. On this point, psychiatrists with extensive experience have commented, "Irreversible side effects are virtually unknown" (Remmen 1962). "Weighted against the stress of mental disturbance, the inconvenience of most side effects is inconsiderable (Uhr 1960).

In general, there is one major drawback in the group of major tranquilizers; extrapyramidal reactions or Parkinson syndrome. The symptoms of the Parkinson syndrome include deficiency of will power (abulia), poverty of movement (akinesia), stiffness of muscles (rigidity), masklike expressions, and in nearly every case, tremor, which may be like a fine tremor of the fingers of a violent, coarse trembling (Burke and Hornykiewicz 1969). Although these reactions are not serious, they may be frightening for the patient. They may be controlled by dosage reduction or the use of antiparkinsonian drugs such as benztropine (Cogentin).

Most authorities in this field consider the extrapyramidal syndromes as part of the normal drug action. Their occurrence is an indication that the drug is affecting the deeper brain centers, where much of the drugs' effective antipsychotic activity presumably takes place. Other side effects may be photosensitivity, drowsiness, or fatigue. These also would be a sign that brain functions are being altered by the medication.

The minor tranquilizers, when given in therapeutic doses up to the maximum dosage, have rarely shown the extrapyramidal reactions. Also, serious toxic effects are almost unknown and photosensitivity does not occur. There have been no cases of jaundice or severe dermatitis reported (Benson and Schiele). In children, however, overdosage leads to a very marked central nervous system, depression, and prolonged hypotension (Burke and Hornykiewicz).

Another concern is *addiction.* Addiction is a complex and little understood problem in humans. The definition of drug addiction, according to the World Health Organization, emphasizes damage to the individual and society. The person who is habituated will readily self-administer the drug if it is available, but he has little tendency to increase dosage and exhibits no physical abstinence syndrome on withdrawal of the drug. Another term applied to this category of drug dependence is psychic dependence. This term suggests that the process is mental as opposed to physical and therefore not measurable (Shuster 1968).

A degree of habituation to the phenothiazines may occur. Patients, who after administration of large doses cannot get up without suffering anorthostatic collapse, are able to do so during the course of continuing treatment. The sudden termination of prolonged treatment with large doses of phenothiazines usually leads to exacerbation of the basic disease. Many authors believe this to be a sign of withdrawal whereas Domino (1962) states that there is no reason to assume that Phenothiazines induce true addiction (Burke et al. 1969). There were many differing accounts in the literature in regard to the compulsive use of and physical dependence on minor tranquilizers.

In the final analysis the use of tranquilizers and antidepressants depends on correct and therefore appropriate use of the drugs which are prescribed, and the practitioners' knowledge in this area. The various groups of drugs themselves counteract specific types of symptoms rather than a specific illness. From the point of view of treatment, it is frequently the quantity, not the quality of specific action that renders the drug of therapeutic value (Uhr 1960).

Antidepressants and Stimulants. Dr. Burack, physician and author of "The New Handbook of Prescription Drugs," says that Ritilan was first developed in an effort to find a substance with the "mood elevating" effects of amphetamines, minus its drawbacks; but, the drug has been a disappointment. It begins to appear that Ritilan may not achieve full separation of amphetamine's desirable and undesirable effects, and amphetamine abusers are beginning to ask for it. The U.S. Food and Drug Administration has urged physicians to exercise extreme caution in prescribing the drug, because of the danger of addiction (*Washington Post*). In the dosage used for children, the question of toxicity, noted in the stimulant abuser, is not a critical issue. Unwanted physical and mental effects rarely appear in children when there is cessation or adjustment of dosage. Physicians who care for children treated with stimulants have noted that they do not experience the pleasurable subjective effects that would encourage misuse. They observe that most often the child is willing to stop the therapy, which he views as "medicine." These drugs are usually not given to children after age 11 or 12, when actual risks of experimentation or misuse might become significant (*Education Digest* February 1972).

Summary Listing of Drugs

The use of medication with emotionally disturbed children is a very controversial issue, even though studies have shown that there is a place for medication as part of their treatment. These studies have shown that when the medication is effective the child can organize his activities in the direction he wishes. Hopefully, other secondary consequences will also appear. These can be better peer relationships, improved self-image, and pleasures from achieving success.

Dosage may require shifting to minimize unwanted side effects, such as loss of appetite and insomina or the Parkinson syndrome. It cannot be emphasized too strongly that the use of drugs is only one aspect of the total treatment of the emotionally disturbed. Drug administration can improve the symptoms from which the patient suffers, but drugs are not a solution to the environmental problems or mental maladjustment which cause the problem. The child who benefits from the use of psychotherapeutic medications should not be stigmatized. His situation is no different from that of the child who benefits from glasses. And finally, drug treatment should and need not be indefinite, and is usually stopped after age 11 or 12.

The most important aspect of drug treatment is correct diagnosis and careful administration of the medication. When the drugs are used correctly, they will help most children achieve their desired goals. Some of the improvement is a result of the placebo affect. Oftentimes, just the expectation of a beneficial effect is sufficient to cause a striking improvement, or many times reports of behavior reflect a change in attitude of the observer.

Some drugs recently discovered are especially effective with children who are quite anxious, depressed, or hyperactive. The physician is the key member of the team whenever medication is involved with any child. He should make all such decisions. Other team members—the school nurse, psychologist, teacher, counselor, and parent must work together for more effective results.

Some general conclusions can be drawn about the use of psychotherapeutic drugs. First, improvement in emotional stability and general behavior may occur but there will be no change in intellectual ability. There are no pills to make children smarter, but pills may alter behavior characteristics. Secondly, behavior changes that do occur are generally more in the terms of degree than of kind. And thirdly, any drugs capable of marked psychotherapeutic action should, of course, be employed with caution, under the supervision and control of the physician who has known the child awhile and can prescribe wisely in the case (Crawford 1966).

A teacher should be aware of the type of medication used by the children in her classroom, along with the normal daily dosage and possible reactions to such medication. If a child is being administered a drug with which the teacher is unfamiliar, it would be wise to contact the child's physician to become aware of any possible side effects. To help the teacher become more familiar with drugs, the following list containing only a few of the more commonly used forms of medication has been provided. (Van Osdol, Van Osdol, Shane 1973).

Atarax: (Roerig) 50-100 mg daily. Used in management of anxiety and tension and psychomotor agitation in conditions of emotional stress.

Side Effects: Rare adverse reactions, occasional drowsiness, dry mouth, tremor.

Aventyl: (Lilly) Children 10-75 mg daily, Adults 20-100 mg daily. Used in treatment of mental depression, anxiety, tension states. Symptomatic reactions of childhood enuresis, passive-aggressive personality, obsessive compulsive reactions, psychophysiological gastro-intestinal reactions.

Side Effects: Dryness of mouth, drowsiness, tremor, dizziness, blurred vision, restlessness, etc.

Benadryl Hydrochloride: (Parke, Davis) Children 20-80 mg daily, Adults up to 250 mg daily. Antihistaminic action. Used to quiet hyperactive emotionally disturbed child.

Side Effects: Drowsiness, dizziness, dryness of mouth, nausea, nervousness, etc.

Benzedrine: (Smith, Line and French) 5-10 mg daily. To control appetite; stimulatory effect helps restore optimism and dispel fatigue; to control narcolepsy and childhood behavior problems.

Side Effects: Restlessness, insomnia, over-stimulation, tremor, headache, sweating.

Deaner: (Riker) 100-300 mg daily. For learning problems, reading difficulties, shortened attention span. Behavior problems, hyperkinetic behavior, perseveration, distractibility, impaired motor coordination, etc.

Side Effects: Mild headache, insomnia, transient rash, constipation, tenseness in the neck.

Dexedrine: (Smith, Kline and French) Spansule, 30-50 mg, Elizer 2½-5 mg (3 to 4 times daily). Control of appetite, childhood neurotic behavior disorders, narcolepsy, mood evaluation.

Side Effects: Undue restlessness, insomnia, gastro-intestinal disturbances, palpitation, headache.

Dilantin: (Park-Davis) .2-.6 gms daily. Used in treatment of gran mal and other convulsive states. Controls seizure without hypnotic effects of many anticonvulsant drugs.

Side Effects: Gastric distress, nausea, weight loss, sleeplessness, gingival hypertrophy, excessive motor activity.

Equanil (See Meprobamate)

Librium: (Roche) 15-40 mg daily. Used for relief of anxiety, tension and apprehension.

Side Effects: Ataxis, drowsiness, confusion, etc.

Mellaril: (Sandoz) Children 20-75 mg daily. Adults up to 100 mg daily. Reduces excitement, hypermotility, agitation, apprehension, anxiety, behavioral disorders.

Side Effects: Drowsiness, nocturnal confusion, dry mouth, headaches, nasal stuffiness.

Meprobamate Tablets: (Rexall) Children 300-600 mg daily, Adults 1200-1600 mg daily. Also: *Equanil* (Wyeth) and *Miltown* (Wallace). Used in management of anxiety or tension by tranquilizing action. May help spastic conditions secondary to neurological disorders. Relaxes skeletal muscles.

Side Effects: Drowsiness, rash, occasional visual disturbances.

Prolixin: (Squibb) Children 1-3 mg daily. Adults up to 10 mg daily. Reduces anxiety and tension, severe mental disorders, behavioral problems in children. Behavior modifier with sustained and prolonged action. Should be used with caution in patients with history of convulsive disorder.

Side Effects: Jaundice, blood disorders, soreness of mouth and gums. Dystonia (impairment of muscle tone), dyskinesia (pain on movement), oculogyric (movement of eyes).

Ritalin Hydrochloride: (Ciba) 20-30 mg daily. Mild stimulant and antidepressant, brightens mood and improves performance. Indicated in chronic fatigue, drug-induced lethargy, psychoneurosis, withdrawn behavior, functional behavior problems in children (hyperactivity, stuttering, etc.).

Stelazine: (Smith, Kline and French) Children 1-15 mg daily. Adults 4-20 mg daily. May be used with Thorazine. Relieves symptoms of anxiety whether expressed as tension or apathy.

Side Effects: Drowsiness, dizziness, skin reaction, dry mouth, insomnia.

Thorazine: (Smith, Kline and French) 40-75 mg daily. May be used with Stelazine. For agitation, tension, apprehension or anxiety. Behavior disorders.

Side Effects: Drowsiness, dry mouth, nasal congestion.

Tofranil: (Geigy) 30-150 mg daily. Used as an antidepressant, may help in "target symptoms" as lack of interest, feelings of inferiority, psychomotor retardation and inhibition.

Side Effects: Tremor, dizziness, weight gain, dry mouth. Some of these symptoms may show at first and then disappear with continued use.

Valium: (Roche) 5-15 mg daily. Used in deal with anxiety reactions stemming from stressful circumstances whenever somatic complaints are concomitants of emotional factors.

Side Effects: Fatigue, drowsiness, ataxia, mild nausea, dizziness, headache, diplopia, tremor, etc.

OVERVIEW

The total program for emotionally disturbed children is one that may glean aspects of treatment from many different theories of personality and methods of teaching. There are no static techniques or methods that would solve the problems for all teachers. There are some definite affective considerations of which the special class teacher should be aware. The emotionally charged behaviors of children can many times manifest distorted perceptions from the teachers. The teachers should not expect a profile of an emotionally disturbed child to reflect abnormal behavior throughout his daily routine. The children may have functionally sound periods of time in which they exhibit no profound behaviors. The teacher should not be quick to judge a child as a well individual and rush him back to the regular class. A good look at the child's total environment level of functioning is required. Some children may become academic whiz kids and pass all subjects with little effort, but they may still be very sick children. The child's resources are thrust into the avenue which presents less obstacles; therefore if the academic area is easy for a child, he may place all of his energy in his studies and he then has nothing left for the rest of his environment. That level of functioning, even though comfortable for the teacher, is not a manifestation of good mental health. The teacher should remain somewhat suspect of the children. It is not reasonable to believe that a teacher can befriend a child, buy him a coke, and believe that suddenly his problems will disappear. As a teacher, you will have to prove again and again that you are trying to help the child, because he will test your tolerance of him repeatedly until he really feels that you are on his side. A teacher should want to be able to like the children, but don't assume that a display of love and affection will relieve the child of his problems. He may be a child who cannot afford to be loved, and he will reject all your efforts to get close to him, because he has many times experienced the same reaction; when he loves someone, he gets hurt. Therefore, love to this particular child may represent pain. The teacher should expect to receive the aggressive behaviors from the children. These aggressions may be displaced, or they may be deliberately aimed at the teacher authority figure; but either way they are, again, the means for the child to test the teacher's response to him.

Generally, one of the best approaches to any teaching situation is to use just plain good common sense. There are no magical cures, and people were raising children long before Freud and the other behavioral scientists were visible in this world, and many parents and teachers developed some good products. Maybe Billy the Kid's mother missed, but so have a lot of other parents and teachers in this contemporary world even with professional help.

Bibliography

Axelrod, Saul. "Token Reinforcement Programs in Special Classes."*Exceptional Children* 137, no. 5 (1971).

Benson, Wilbur, Ph.D., and Burtrum, Schiele, M.D.*Tranquilizing and Antidepressant Drugs.* Springfield, Ill.: Charles C. Thomas, Publisher, 1962.

Bower, Eli M. *Early Identification of Emotionally Handicapped Children in School.* Springfield, Ill,: Charles C. Thomas, Publisher, 1969.

Braun, Samuel J.; Holzman, Mathilda S.; and Lasher, Miriam G., "Teachers of Disturbed Pre-School Children: An Analysis of Teaching Styles." *American Journal of Orthopsychiatry* 39, no. 4 (1969).

Burke, F., and Hornykiewicz, O. *The Pharmacology of Psychotherapeutic Drugs.* Heidelberg: Springer-Verlag, 1969.

Buhler, C.; Smitter F.; and Richardson, S. In *Conflict in the Classroom,* edited by N.J. Long, W.C. Morse, and R.G. Newman. Belmont, Calif.: Wadsworth Publishing Co. Inc., 1965.

Bullock, Lyndal M., and Whelan, Richard J. "Competencies Needed by Teachers of the Emotionally Disturbed and Socially Maladjusted: A Comparison." *Exceptional Children* 37, no. 7 (March 1971).

Caplan, Gerald. "Patterns of Parental Response to the Crisis of Premature Birth: A Preliminary Approach to Modifying Mental Health Outcome." In *Principles of Preventive Psychiatry.* New York: Basic Books, Inc., 1964.

Chapman, A.H. *Management of Emotional Problems of Children and Adolescents.* Philadelphia: J.B. Lippincott Company, 1965.

Connors, Keith C., Ph.D. "Recent Drug Studies with Hyperkinetic Children." *Journal of Learning Disability* 4 (November 1971): 471.

Crawford, John E. *Children with Subtle Perceptual Motor Difficulties.* Pittsburg, Pa.: Stanwix House, Inc., 1966.

Cruickshank, William M., ed. *The Teacher of the Brain Injured Children.* Syracuse: Syracuse University Press, 1969.

Dupont, Henry, ed. *Educating Emotionally Disturbed Children.* New York: Holt, Rinehart and Winston, Inc., 1969.

Eisenberg, Leon. *Educating Emotionally Disturbed Children.* New York: USA: Holt, Rinehart and Winston, Inc., 1969.

Glavin, John P.; Quay, Herbert C.; and Werry, John S. "Behavioral and Academic Gains of Conduct Problem Children in Different Classroom Settings." *Exceptional Children* 37, no. 6 (1971).

Glavin, John P.; Quay, Herbert C.; Annesley, Frederick R.; and Werry, John S. "An Experimental Resource Room for Behavior Problem Children." *Exceptional Children* 38, no. 2 (1971).

Haring, Norris G., and Fargo, George A. "Evaluating Programs for Preparing Teachers of Emotionally Disturbed Children." *Exceptional Children,* 36, no. 3 (1969).

Heiting, Kenneth H. "Involving Parents in Residential Treatment of Children." *Children* 18, no. 5 (1971).

Jones, Edward V. "A Public Health Approach to Emotional Handicap in the Schools." *The Journal of School Health* 39, no. 9 (1969).

Kessler, Jane W. *Psychopathology of Childhood.* Englewood Cliffs, N.J.: Prentice-Hall, Inc., 1966.

Lewis, Wilbert W. "Ecological Planning for Disturbed Children."*Childhood Education* 46, no. 6 (1970).

Maes, Wayne. "The Identification of Emotionally Disturbed Children." *Exceptional Children* 32, no. 9 (1966).

McCaffrey, Isabel, and Cumming, John. In *Educating Emotionally Disturbed Children,* ed. Henry Dupont. New York: Holt, Rinehart and Winston, Inc., 1969.

McKinnon, Archie J. "Parent and Pupil Perceptions of Special Classes for Emotionally Disturbed Children." *Exceptional Children* 37, no. 4 (1970).

Morse, William C. "Disturbed Youngsters in the Classroom." *Today's Education* 58, no. 4 (1969).

National Institute of Mental Health. Mental Health Statistics, series A., no. 6. National Clearing House for Mental Health Information. Residential Treatment Centers for Emotionally Disturbed Children, 1969-70.

Nelson, Michael C. "Techniques for Screening Conduct Disturbed Children." *Exceptional Children* 37, no. 7 (1971).

Quay, Herbert C.; Morse, William C.; and Cutler, Richard L. "Personality Patterns of Pupils in Special Classes for the Emotionally Disturbed." *Exceptional Children* 32, no. 5 (1966).

Remmen, Edmund, M.D. et al. *Psychochemotherapy.* Los Angeles: Western Medical Publications, 1962.

Rubin, Eli Z.; Simson, Clyde B.; and Betwee, Marcus C. *Emotionally Handicapped Children and the Elementary School.* Detroit: Wayne State University Press, 1966.

Schultz, Edward W.; Hirshoren, Alfred; Manton, Anne B.; and Henderson, Robert A. "Special Education for the Emotionally Disturbed." *Exceptional Children* 38, no. 4 (1971).

Shuster, Charles R. *Behavioral Pharmacology.* Englewood Cliffs, N.J.: Prentice-Hall, Inc., 1968.

Solomans, Gerald, M.D. "Guidelines on the Use and Medical Effects of Psychostimulant Drugs in Therapy." *Journal of Learning Disability* 4 (November 1971): 471.

Telford, Charles W. *The Exceptional Individual.* Englewood Cliffs, N.J.: Prentice-Hall, Inc., 1972.

Uhr, Leonard, M.D. *Drugs and Behavior.* New York: J. Wiley & Sons, 1960.

Ullman, Leonard P., and Krasner, L. *A Psychological Approach to Abnormal Behavior.* Englewood Cliffs, N.J.: Prentice-Hall, Inc., 1969.

"Use of Stimulant Drugs for Behaviorally Disturbed Children: Report of a 1971 Conference." *Education Digest,* February 1972 pp. 51-54.

Van Osdol, B.; Van Osdol, William R.; and Shane, Don. *Learning Disabilities K-12 Manual.* Idaho Research Foundation, Inc., Moscow, Idaho: Idaho University, 1973.

Washington Post, June 29, 1970.

Wilson, John R. *The Mind.* New York: Time Inc., 1964.

Wood, Frank H. "The Educator's Role in Team Planning of Therapeutic Educational Placements for Children with Adjustment and Learning Problems." *Exceptional Children* 34, no. 5 (1968).

EMOTIONALLY DISTURBED CHILDREN
Study Sheet #1

1. Define the emotionally disturbed child and cite the complete reference data which you have used.

2. How do you personally assume that public schools should provide for emotionally disturbed children?

EMOTIONALLY DISTURBED CHILDREN
Study Sheet #2

1. Describe the type of training which should be required of a teacher who is planning to teach emotionally disturbed children.

EMOTIONALLY DISTURBED CHILDREN
Study Sheet #3

1. Compare the paradoxical similarities and distinct differences between learning disabled and emotionally disturbed children.

'We, both, learn by doing.'

9

Practicum—An Integral Part of Special Education

INTRODUCTION

College students who are entering the field of Special Education should have some awareness of the type of training they are about to enter. Although the college catalog can be read and a student can see that practicum experiences are included as a part of a training program, specific information related to this particular area is most pertinent.

The authors decided to include a chapter on practicum within this textbook for several reasons. First, this experience is an essential feature of a comprehensive training program in the field of Special Education. A training program for future teachers of exceptional children which does not require practicum experiences will not "arm" the students with sufficient information to be able to perform adequately on the job upon completion of training.

Secondly, information related to the experience of practicum is also important because this is another way in which special services can be provided for exceptional children. Special projects can be prepared by the college student for implementation in a practicum setting and these projects may bring about the provision of services which would not otherwise be available.

Thirdly, the inclusion of practicum courses for special education teachers indicates the experiential direction in which many college training programs are being developed. No longer does the college training program provide lecture courses which fail to include any application of the skills which are supposedly learned. Many training programs are moving toward the establishment of procedures which will evaluate the future teacher through his performance in working with exceptional children. The important point in this respect is that a college student may be able to progress successfully through the training program as far as theory courses are concerned;

however, he may not be able to work effectively with children in a classroom or other settings. By providing many experiences in practicum situations, the staff within the special education training program can meaningfully observe and evaluate a college student's ability to work with children in a real life setting. The implementation of practicum experiences within university special education training programs is rapidly becoming referred to as a performance based training program.

Most universities and colleges which offer training in the field of Special Education are now providing programs which emphasize the involvement of students in a variety of practicum settings. The inclusion of practicum in addition to student teaching within a training program in Special Education has become essential in order to prepare well-trained professional personnel; and has been the most practical method universities and colleges have had for bridging the gap from the university classroom to the "real" world. Practicum has also added an additional aspect to the training program which is above and beyond the more traditional approach of providing only student teaching experiences.

Although the literature on the subject of practicum for the training of special education personnel is rather limited, several reports regarding these efforts have been published. The primary purpose of this chapter is to synthesize some of these reports and discuss the wide range of purposes and implications regarding meaningful student practicum experiences.

Purposes of Practicum

In several universities and colleges, theory, practicum, and student teaching for the special education major are not easy to establish nor are colleges able to provide continuous experiences throughout the student's college training program. Detailed descriptions of practicum are discussed by Shane (April, 1970), Anderson and Little (1968), and Shane and Manley (Fall, 1971). Although programs such as these are essential for the adequate training of special education personnel; a more sequential and comprehensive practicum based program is required.

One of the first reasons practicum is essential in today's college and university training programs is to provide a meaningful method of permitting the student to become a part of the selection process. In the past, special education personnel have attempted to recruit students from the high schools into the fields of Special Education;

and, once recruited, these students were not seen in the training program until their junior year. Practicum provided as early as the Freshman or Sophomore year is an absolute necessity if the potential Special Educator is to have an appropriate information base from which to make a decision regarding his future. For example, as a freshman, a student may be assigned a practicum with the type of exceptional child he desires to work with, and this should enable the student to realize the extent to which he can or cannot be effective in providing services to a particular type of exceptional child. Practicum early in the college student's career may help him to decide if he has chosen the right professional field; or, even in more detail, if he has chosen the type of exceptional child with whom he can be the most effective.

In addition to providing an effective means of recruitment, the practicum should and can be offered as an elective to students from throughout the campus. By providing college students actual contact with exceptional children, with special education teachers, and with other personnel, and a seminar for discussions of the practicum a more appropriate awareness of exceptional children is thus given those students who plan to enter other professional fields. They can also become more effective members of the interdisciplinary approach to solving the problems of exceptional children which have often been stressed. These college students can enhance the total approach to the education and training of the exceptional child by contributing knowledge from their own fields of preparation, and help to make future special education professionals more aware of potential contributions from other professional personnel.

The purposes described above are certainly sufficient if one is attempting to justify the reasons why practicum should be offered within the university or college training program in the field of Special Education. However, this is only one small aspect for justification. Perhaps just as important is the way in which the university practicum experience in special education can implement more of a noncategorical approach to the training of future teachers, counselors, supervisors, administrators, diagnosticians, and other supportive personnel. When one enters the professional field of Special Education, he seldom has a "neat" categorical group of children in his program. Anyone who has taught exceptional children or worked with these children in capacities other than teaching, knows that many exceptional children have more problems than just the primary problem for which they were placed in the special education setting. Many graduates are employed in positions other than that for which they were specifically prepared on the college level. Therefore a variety of practicum experiences, individual studies, and student teaching will and can provide to future special education professionals some introductory experiences with a cross-section of exceptional children. This variety of practicum experiences can be further enhanced by requiring a seminar once a week in order to give students the opportunity to discuss their experiences openly with their college supervisors.

Another purpose of practicum throughout the college students' careers is to provide experiences with exceptional children which call for actual involvement with those children. Becoming involved with exceptional children through individual tutoring, counseling, or just individual contact will better prepare the college student for his student teaching as well as his professional career. If a college student in Special Education enters his student teaching with a background of three or four practicum experiences; he is more familiar with materials and methods which have been effective with different children, and has increased his own knowledge with respect to skills which he can now apply more easily and more confidently.

Although more purposes could be mentioned, the last purpose to be discussed in this chapter with respect to practicum is that of implementing a means by which the college or university training program can join theory and practice in a more meaningful way.

A minimum of four hours' credit in practicum for the undergraduate and the graduate students should be required. This requirement definitely helps to join theory and practice and provides a more practical approach in the total training program. For example, if a freshman student declares Special Education as his major, he is encouraged to enroll in a practicum with children of his choice at least by his third or fourth semester. As the student progresses through his course work in the field of Special Education, he should take a practicum that is directly related to a Special Education course in which he is currently enrolled. If the student is taking the introductory course in mental retardation, a practicum with mentally retarded children is appropriate. Then, if he later takes a course in the area of Learning Disabilities, his practicum should be with children who have learning disabilities. Therefore, he has the opportunity to see the children who are being discussed in the course, the Special Education teachers in operation, and the instructional materials which are being used as well. This approach adds to the noncategorical emphasis described earlier and also offers a compatible integration of theory and practice.

Graduate students should have a wide variety of practicum throughout their programs. They should be required to complete four credit hours of practicum—one credit hour of practicum should require three hours per week or sixty-four hours per semester of field work—and may receive additional experiences by requesting a practicum assignment through an individual study. As university programs in Special Education continue to progress, graduate students should have greater flexibility with respect to choosing a practicum assignment. Plans could be developed to assign graduate students to rural school systems in nearby metropolitan areas in order to provide a training program that exposes the students to children from rural areas in addition to the metropolitan area to which they may generally be assigned.

Services Provided Through Practicum

It is a well-known fact that there continues to be a shortage of qualified personnel in the field of Special Education. Part of the emphasis in practicum is, therefore, to provide the potential manpower among student groups to the population of exceptional children. Although not completely trained, or certified, the undergraduate students within any program are certainly capable of providing services on an equal basis with voluntary aides who are used widely in some areas. Many graduate students have had teaching experience prior to entering a training program and are well qualified to provide services to exceptional children.

A training program in Special Education at the university level should tend to help the university become more service oriented to the local communities by providing services to public schools, private clinics, psychiatric wards, guidance clinics, and to other special programs. Recognizing the fact that students must have a period of observation prior to working with an individual or a small group of children within a special setting, the majority of students do become "involved" in providing services during their assignments. As a continuous program within a total training program, this aspect of the program should tend to provide many services of a supplementary nature to exceptional children.

Assignments of graduate students to rural school systems, as mentioned above, could be an attempt to provide screening services for students who are having learning or adjustment difficulties and an attempt to help personnel of the rural school systems discuss, consider, and hopefully plan cooperative agreements with each other in order to provide programs, nonexistent at the time, for exceptional children.

Upon completion of their theory, practicum, and student teaching programs, students should certainly be somewhat proficiently trained. They will have had ample time to apply their skills, and receive supervision from a university staff during their assignments.

Implications of Practicum

The reader should readily see many implications through the provision of a variety of practicum settings for undergraduates and graduates in the field of Special Education. In general, courses which are intended to get the student "involved" with children during his college training provides implications that many more personnel may choose Special Education as a major field. With proper supervision, students who may not have the potential, the desirable attitudes, or the good personality adjustment will be eliminated from the program prior to the time at which it may be too late for the student to choose a different major field. The indication could well be, in this instance, that the field of Special Education may obtain more personnel who are really interested and capable of working with exceptional children in a variety of settings.

In our modern day programs of teacher training, students also have a very strong desire to become involved—involved not only in working with children, but also in the program of training. The type of practicum offered, plus the continuity of the practicum experiences, should certainly keep students involved. Students should be involved with staff members in small group discussions regarding a wide variety of programs in order for the training program to move one step closer to meeting the needs of individual college students.

Through practicum, students have opportunities to apply the skills which they have learned and to "test" a variety of approaches about which they have studied. Therefore, a training program becomes more of a "testing" experience for the student in self-evaluation.

Implementation of Practicum

Practicum may be implemented in a variety of ways. Several university training programs have courses which are titled "Practicum." In other situations one may have to be more specific in a course title such as "Introductory Experiences in Special Education." One may also use practicum as individual study or as an internship; and, in a few cases, one hour of a three hour required course could be used as an assignment in practicum. The main point is that practicum can, through some existing means, be implemented as an integral part of the total training program.

Conclusion

The inclusion of practicum as an integral part of Special Education training programs is essential in the training of future teachers and other professional personnel. It is, in all probability, the most effective means available to provide a practical orientation in teacher training.

An advantage in practicum is the flexibility which it offers by assigning students to different settings which provide services to different types of exceptional children. Students, therefore, can have very meaningful experiences in gaining first hand knowledge regarding the wide variances in personality and learning characteristics of exceptional children. As knowledge of practicum increases, and as more community services are initiated, training programs will continue to improve in the basic and fundamental training which are required for the professional person.

References

Anderson, R.M. and Little, H.A. "A Practicum Oriented Teacher Education Program." *Education and Training of the Mentally Retarded.* (1968).

Shane, Don G. "Introductory Experiences With Handicapped Children." *Education and Training of the Mentally Retarded.* (1970).

Shane, Don G., and Manley, Max W. "Undergraduate Practicum Experiences in Special Education." The Council for Exceptional Children. *The Teacher Education Division Newsletter* 8, no. 1 (Fall 1971).

'We can help many children
when we work together.'

10

Special Education Teachers, Administration, and Parents

INTRODUCTION

A discussion of the varied school personnel essential to providing educational services for exceptional children should include the new emphasis on accountability. Accountability certainly applies to the special education teacher and the teacher education program which has been responsible for his training. Although accountability is still an evolving concept, and probably should remain so, the emphasis seems to be increasing and the abilities and characteristics of special education teachers seem to be related directly to this concept. For study and comparative purposes, the new special education teacher may also benefit from a discussion of the abilities and characteristics of practicing special education teachers. A few suggestions regarding accountability of special education programs may serve as guidelines for the individual special education teacher in his efforts to develop effective instructional programs for exceptional children.

The role and responsibilities of the special education teacher seem to be changing. Although, the special education teacher may be the primary person in the school setting who influences the personal, social, and vocational development of exceptional children, he certainly cannot provide the required services in isolation. The special education teacher is no longer viewed as a self-contained classroom teacher. He must be prepared to assume the responsibilities of a diagnostic teacher, a resource teacher, a crisis teacher, or some other related capacities. In addition to the various roles to which a special education teacher may be assigned, the comprehensive planning and programming which is necessary for exceptional children requires the services of other school personnel and the support of the children's parents.

Accountability

The term accountability is not a new word to people in education. Administrators, school boards, and the entire educational community have not been able to escape the concept of accountability. Accountability is a management concept. It involves agreeing upon objectives, deciding upon the input to achieve the objectives, and measuring the output to determine the degree to which the objectives have been met. The application of accountability to all aspects of the educational system is increasing and this will certainly require thorough study in order for the concept of accountability to be meaningful, not only to educators, but also to the children who are directly involved.

Accountability can be viewed as an administrative concept, or a branch of technology through which one can make education more effective. Education can use this technique constructively with careful planning; however, a haphazard approach in its use could apply too much pressure on everyone concerned. Accountability may be viewed as a process which can provide feedback regarding the extent to which a particular procedure or program has been effective.

Other terms are arising from the concept of accountability. Terms such as merit pay, performance contract, turnkey approach (a type of performance contract), educational auditors, voucher systems, and Project Yardstick are emerging for the purpose of increasing accountability (Hyer 1971).

Accountability is becoming the "in" word of higher education. The call for accountability has come from the President of the United States, Congress, agencies of the federal government, school boards, teacher training institutions, from the taxpayers, and the classroom. Theodore A. Dolmatch, president of the Pitman Publishing Corporation said, "Asking for accountability is a legitimate response of government which wants to know how efficiently its money is being spent" (Stocker and Wilson 1971).

The new emphasis on accountability has implications for teacher training institutions with special education programs and also for the teacher of exceptional children. Although answers will not be given to this new area of concern, the purpose of this chapter is to concentrate on the implications of accountability for colleges and universities and special education teachers in the public schools.

Implications for Teacher Training Institutions with
Special Education Programs

Special education training programs throughout the country have become increasingly aware of their responsibilities for producing better teachers. Special education programs have developed in all fifty states to attempt to meet the needs of educating more than 7 million handicapped children. Special education must be included as a part of the total educational program if it is to be an effective procedure (Bulletin of Special Education 1971).

Special education programs in college and university settings have received federal funds since 1959 for the purpose of teacher training and program development. The present trend nationwide is to hold these special education programs accountable for implementing new program designs and providing teacher training programs which are relevant to the needs of the state in which the program is located. In essence, the trend toward accountability for college and university special education programs necessitates the planning and implementing of effective evaluation systems.

Financial assistance for special education programs is received from the Department of Health, Education, and Welfare. More specifically, federal assistance comes from the Office of Education, Division of Training Programs, a branch of the Department of Health, Education, and Welfare (Scholarship Program 1971).

The funds which are received by the special education programs on the college or university level must be expended according to guidelines which are established by the Department of Health, Education, and Welfare. Adhering to the guidelines is the responsibility of the university special education program and, in this manner, the local university program is accountable for the way in which the funds are expended. The amount of monies received is not the essential feature of an accountability program. The most pertinent questions to be asked are: How effectively are the personnel of the special education program spending the monies received? Is the money being spent to benefit the education of exceptional children? Is the teacher training program producing quantity or quality in the persons who are admitted to and who are completing the program? In what ways can the special education program be held accountable for the expenditure of funds?

The accountability of university special education programs to the federal government is usually handled through the university business office which knows the guidelines for the expenditure of funds. This is certainly a valid procedure since no one would want to authorize a departmental staff complete freedom in the expenditure of public funds. The monies are consumed in several major areas: (1) staffing of the program, (2) structuring and program content, (3) purchasing appropriate supplies and equipment, and (4) providing student traineeships at the undergraduate and graduate levels in the fields of emotional disturbance, learning disabilities, mental retardation and others. University special education programs are also encouraged to develop teacher training programs which will prepare individuals to teach the more severely handicapped such as the trainable mentally retarded or the severely emotionally disturbed child. In addition, encouragement is given a special education program to develop meaningful programs in vocational training and physical education training of exceptional children.

Each program establishes its own objectives and areas of concentration in training with respect to the needs of the state. There is a general agreement among personnel of special education programs that staffing is of vital importance for the simple reason that these persons will be training prospective teachers, speech therapists, counselors, educational diagnosticians, and other professional personnel in the skills and methods of the various specialized areas. The professional staff members of a program must have a variety of competencies and skills as well as experience in teaching children within their own specialized field of training. Each program is accountable for developing a staff which is well-trained and experienced since these are the individuals who instill quality into the total training program.

Besides using federal money as a supplement to acquire competent staff members; the structuring of the training program with respect to content and sequence may be enhanced through the use of these monies. Although guidelines for program development are suggested by the Department of Health, Education, and Welfare, each special education program on the university or college level must develop its own program in accordance with the laws of the state and the rules and regulations of the university. The program may or may not cover a variety of exceptionalities. The extent of the services offered through the special education training program will depend, of course, upon the number and competencies of the department staff. A special education program may cover the area of learning disabilities or it may be more comprehensive and cover areas such as slow learner, physical handicaps, speech handicaps, mental retardation, emotional disturbance, and learning disability. There is no requirement from the federal government with respect to the areas which are included in the overall training program since this factor must be left up to an individual training program. The recent trend, however, has been for the Division of Training Programs to encourage a university or college special education program to develop programs which place less emphasis on labels and more emphasis on the learning difficulties of exceptional children. This encouragement is not a mandate since the university program is still permitted to maintain and improve a structured categorical field of training which allows the students on the college level to receive training across fields or categories. The primary question, with respect to accountability of the training received by a student in a university or college special education program, is: Does the content of the program provide for a competent output? The program as developed by the department staff may be enhanced through federal funds by acquiring the services of experts who are consultants in such areas as neurology, psychological testing, physical therapy, group therapy, and parent counseling. The program may also be supplemented by using the funds to purchase or rent films, video tapes or other types of media which will strengthen training provided for students.

Although staffing of a department, structuring the program, and the content of training are vitally important to the concern of accountability, financial assistance to students in the form of traineeships and assistantships are the most difficult form of accountability to be faced by the personnel of a special education department. Many pertinent questions arise in the screening and selection of students who have applied for financial assistance to be trained in a specific area of special education. The personnel of a special education department have generally been awarded a specific amount of monies, within the total grant, which must be used in awarding traineeships to students in different areas of exceptionalities. This assistance is received on the basis of program structure, program content, and the objectives and goals of the teacher education institution. The funding source (Division of Training, Office of Education) reviews these specific details, which have been submitted to them in the form of a proposal, and awards a specific grant to the institution. A specific amount of the grant is usually earmarked for areas of training as requested by a special education department and approved by the Division. The reader should be aware that a special education program does not necessarily receive all the funds which it has requested nor is it always permitted to spend the monies received in the manner which was specified in the program proposal. Through this financial assistance, a special education program has funds for a specific number of traineeships which are to be awarded on an academic year basis to selected students who have applied for the grant. To fulfill the objectives and goals of the program, the first implication for accountability for a special education program is the screening and selection of students who will be awarded the traineeships. Several questions must be considered by the personnel in the selection process. For instance: What competencies in students are expected? On what basis are students selected who will receive awards? Is the primary question one of financial need, or of competencies, including past experiences and grade point average; one of personality to meet the established goals and objectives, or a combination of all these factors? The decision must be made by the personnel of a department with respect to the best qualified and the most deserving students. This process is by no means an easy task to accomplish.

The personnel of a special education department have to determine if the supplementary funds received from the Division of Training are to be directed toward quantity or quality. For instance: How many teachers can be trained with the allowed funds? Although a specific number of traineeships are usually awarded to the university for training of future special education teachers, the personnel of the program may decide to take one traineeship, which might consist of an award of $300.00, and award it to two students by awarding each one a total of $150.00. The question the staff must answer is: which procedure will produce the best product for serving handicapped children?

Besides determining the amount of awards or traineeships, another question the personnel of a department must ask is: Does a student who is receiving financial support graduate as a more qualified teacher of exceptional children than a student who has completed the same program without a traineeship? Should a student who receives a traineeship have the same training program which is required of a student who does not receive a traineeship? There are several considerations in these problems. The trend toward accountability of special education training programs necessitates that answers be sought with respect to the above questions.

Awarding traineeships to students seems to imply that a student attending the university on a grant will be a more outstanding teacher of exceptional children than the nonsupported student. At the present time, there seems to be no effective system which can be implemented to assess the strength of this assumption. Again numerous questions exist for which there are no appropriate answers. One may assume that the financially supported student should have more time available for library work, practicum assignments, field trips, and have opportunities for interactions on a one-to-one basis with the college professors of a program. The problem is whether or not the financially supported student takes advantage of the opportunities afforded him since he may not have to be employed during his training. Of course, another problem may be whether or not the financially supported student is given the opportunity to become involved in interaction with the college staff, involved in doing library research, or given additional opportunities for practicum assignments.

The financially supported student is, hypothetically speaking, a more outstanding teacher because of his extracurricular activities. Which person or persons will represent a special education department in extracurricular activities, such as attending conventions and meetings? The representatives to these functions will be the choice students and frequently choice students are viewed as those who have been selected to receive traineeships. Based upon the above information, the financially supported student should have more time to be involved with relevant activities during his training program. If he does get involved and participate to a greater extent, in all of the opportunities afforded him, will this added feature of his preparation tend to result in a better prepared teacher? Are there any adequate and reliable means of measuring these factors of input with respect to their product? Will any system devised which attempts to measure the product of these variables be objective, or will the system resort to the use of subjective measures which are present?

Many professional individuals within the field of special education are taking it for granted that the various factors of a student's training program are contributing to his overall effectiveness as a classroom teacher of exceptional children. Are the factors which are included in most training programs, such as those discussed above, contributing to a more meaningful and appropriate learning situation? Are these experiences, such as interactions with college staff members and attending conferences, valuable experiences or simply additional status symbols achieved in a materialistic society?

The objectives of special education training programs for meeting accountability criteria imply that traineeship students enter the professional field of special education after graduation. Implications are also made that the students enter the areas of special education for which they have been trained. If they do enter the professional field of special education, do these financially supported students remain in the field for longer or shorter periods of time than do the nonsupported student? Do more of the financially supported students pursue and obtain an advanced degree in the field of special education or a related field of study than do the nonsubsidized students? In comparison to students who do not receive financial support, do the financially supported students have a greater or a lesser tendency to become leaders in the field of special education, such as serving as supervisors or directors of special education? Are these types of questions relevant to the question of accountability and have programs attempted to ascertain the results of their training programs?

The federal government has appropriated supplementary funds for college and university special education programs for several reasons. The basic reason for awarding funds to these programs, which have been involved in training teachers of exceptional children, has been to attempt to alleviate the shortage of teachers in the different areas of exceptionalities. The federal government was prompted to provide funds in order to implement the development of programs which could train competent teachers of children who are mentally retarded, emotionally disturbed, physically handicapped, deaf, or learning disabled. Of course, the gap between supply and demand has not closed, so the Division of Training, Office of Education, has been encouraging training programs to implement new program designs in an attempt to provide competent teachers for all handicapped children.

Answers to the questions of accountability of special education training programs are not known at the present time. The purpose of this discussion has been to present a few questions which must be considered in the further operation of training programs in the field of special education. As appropriate evaluation systems evolve through research and reevaluation, perhaps more information will be available to college personnel who are most interested in the continuous improvement of the teacher training programs.

Implications for the Teacher of Exceptional Children

The special education teacher is accountable for specific areas of education. Among these specific areas the following are included: academic preparation and continuing professional growth, concern and knowledge about exceptional children, effective communication with other school personnel and parents, involvement in community activities, and provision of an environment which maximizes opportunities for each individual in learning to his capacity. Special education teachers are accountable to themselves, their students, the teaching profession, and the public (Stocker and Wilson).

Teacher Abilities and Characteristics

In order to accomplish his desired level of accountability, a special education teacher should have certain characteristics. The ability to mobilize and sustain a high level of energy is one specific characteristic. A high energy level is considered important because to provide an individualized program for six to ten children is a difficult task. When these children are exhibiting a variety of learning and/or behavioral problems, the assigned task is even more difficult. The management of a classroom can be extremely exhausting to any teacher but even more so to a teacher with little energy (Reger, Schroeder, and Uschold 1968).

A special education teacher must be alert and responsive. These characteristics are important because teachers must continuously be aware of each event in the classroom and be able to respond quickly and appropriately. A teacher who does not attend to disruptive behavior in the initial stage will expend more effort to correct the behavior as it increases. It is more economical, on the part of all individuals, to stop disturbances as soon as possible. The ability of a special education teacher to observe systematically the children within his classroom is essential in controlling discipline as well as instructional planning. Without skilled observation, the special education teacher will have serious difficulties in appropriately planning for the type of learning environment needed by the majority of exceptional children.

Personal stability and self-control are also essential for a teacher of exceptional children. These characteristics are mentioned because of the naive misconception that a teacher of exceptional children appears to enjoy wallowing in problems of emotional, brain damage, or physical defects.

A special education teacher should develop an orientation toward being a teacher, and to develop this orientation a special education teacher should achieve an emphasis on such concepts as educational therapy, so relevant to teachers of children with problems. This type of teacher will develop a sound educational philosophy and be interested in individualized instruction. Behavioral change is the main concern of a special education teacher and this factor can be a teacher's answer to accountability. Teachers are agents who assist in behavioral change—and behavioral change results in learning (Reger, Schroeder, and Uschold).

Although the positive characteristics are important for the attainment of accountability, a teacher of exceptional children should be aware of negative traits. The following characteristics of a teacher are considered to be unfavorable: developing attitudes of being sentimental toward the exceptional child; believing in permissiveness in that he allows exceptional children complete freedom in self-expression; to seek frequent counsel of other professionals for help in planning the daily instructional program; becoming easily upset over insignificant events, and having little understanding of the relationship which should exist between children and the curriculum (Bulletin of Special Education 1971). The less accountable teachers think of working with exceptional children as a glamorous opportunity to sacrifice themselves to society.

Besides having positive general characteristics and knowing negative traits, a teacher should demonstrate the following positive characteristics on the job. A teacher must work toward developing a meaningful understanding of children. Learning to form a working relationship with children, and describing them verbally is essential for the purpose of providing an appropriate instructional program (Bulletin of Special Education 1971). A demonstration of a grasp of the relationship between children's needs and the curriculum is an important ability of an accountable teacher of exceptional children. An inexperienced teacher may choose one reading series or method, but the experienced teacher has a grasp of individualized instruction and chooses many materials and approaches. He will observe each student's needs and search for materials or techniques to meet these needs. The accountable teacher is knowledgeable of materials such as those described in *Instructional Materials and Resource Materials Available to Teachers of Exceptional Children and Youth* (1969) which has over 460 pages of resource materials.

Besides having these abilities and characteristics, a special education teacher should have the ability to communicate with parents about their children in a descriptive, basically informative language. Discussions with parents should be in a language which parents can understand. For example, if a child is having a reading problem, a teacher should not tell the parents why the child cannot read but rather what he is doing to help the child's reading. The ability of teachers to communicate in a direct understandable language with parents and meaningfully discuss children is a complicated but necessary asset for accountability (Reger, Schroeder, and Uschold 1968).

A teacher who is not accountable will not effectively manage children and will often resort to the use of labels or technical terms in an effort to explain behaviors of children. He will also place too much emphasis on the use of hardware or other novel devices with no understanding about the degree to which these tools are pertinent to the needs of children. The teacher who has not become accountable will, in addition, hesitate to upgrade his teaching skills through inservice training or supervisory activities (Reger, Schroeder, and Uschold 1968).

If a special education teacher does not have these positive characteristics, he should be capable of acquiring them. Teachers are usually well prepared at the teacher training institutions for positive characteristics and there are seldom any major problems. Where teacher training institutions have not prepared teachers in developing positive characteristics, this can be a problem especially in the area of accountability (Reger Schroeder, and Uschold).

Behavioral Objectives

A special education teacher, like a regular classroom teacher, is searching for means through which he can adequately be accountable to his peers, the public, his students, and to himself. Demands from the public are requesting more concrete evidence of the teaching-learning process (Scholarship Program 1971). In order to meet the challenge, teachers, as well as administrators, curriculum planners, members of boards of education, and researchers are beginning to implement the use of behavioral objectives.

"Behavioral objectives are statements which describe what students will be able to do after completing a prescribed unit of instruction" (Kibler, Barker, and Miles). For example, a behavioral objective for an exceptional child for a unit in arithmetic might be as follows: The emotionally disturbed child will be able to work correctly at least five out of eight long division problems with four digits in five minutes. Behavioral objectives serve two functions, one of which is allowing teachers to design and evaluate their instruction. Secondly, they communicate the goals of the instruction to students and those persons who are responsible for evaluating their teaching.

In the preparation of behavioral objectives, a special education teacher needs to consider four factors: (a) selection, (b) classification, (c) analysis, and (d) specification (Kibler, Barker, and Miles). A teacher determines what a student is able to do before selecting his objectives, which are based upon what the student should be able to do after accomplishing the assigned unit and after completing his education.

After the selection of behavioral objectives, a teacher must classify his selected objectives. The classification may focus on a desired behavior such as the acquisition of knowledge, comprehension of knowledge, or analyzing and evaluating information (Kibler, Barker, and Miles).

Once the objectives have been selected and classified, a special education instructor must determine what each student will be expected to do. This step needs to be accomplished in order to match objectives to individual students and to demonstrate the achievement of objectives. In an analysis of selected objectives, a teacher chooses important stimuli to which a student responds positively. He will note the responses made and measure these responses in an attempt to determine to what extent each has met the behavioral objectives (Kibler, Barker, and Miles).

The type, the conditions, and the criterion of behavioral objectives will be specified by a teacher and a description of the type of observable behavior must be stated. For instance, a teacher will decide if a student is to demonstrate a mastery of writing, solving, identifying, or describing. He must specify under what conditions a student will demonstrate the objectives and what criteria will be implemented. This will involve questions such as: How many problems must be correctly solved? How many principles will be applied or in what length of time a task will be correctly completed? (Kibler, Barker, and Miles).

A special education teacher can discover individual needs through using behavioral objectives. By using these objectives, a teacher can have a well-structured class and not a class program which is rigid and stale. Also of value, a pretest and posttest can be compared to illustrate to what extent learning has taken place. The greatest value of using behavioral objectives is that a teacher can evaluate each student individually in comparision to his own objectives. This eliminates evaluating each student on the basis of competitive student performances or subjective information.

There are several controversial issues regarding behavioral objectives about which special education teachers should be acquainted. In using objectives, it is difficult to prespecify the objectives for a unit which the teacher has not previously taught or for a group of children whom he has never seen. Even though difficult to plan and implement, behavioral objectives can still serve as a means toward developing appropriate instructional programs for exceptional children. A special education teacher plans his objectives to meet individual needs, rather than attempting to limit teaching to specific academic course content. If he finds that his objectives are inappropriate, he must evaluate his entire plan and make decisions which will enhance the child's progress. This entails a study of the behavioral objectives to determine if the steps for a student's learning are improperly sequenced, too advanced, or too easy. Continuous evaluation is essential if the use of behavioral objectives is going to be helpful in the area of establishing a system of appropriate accountability.

Critics of behavioral objectives say that a teacher may decide that all students should be required to achieve the same objectives. Special education programs should orient their students toward individuality and thus avoid requiring the same achievement of all students.

Critics also hesitate to implement behavioral objectives because a teacher has a choice of deciding whether all students should be required to achieve the same level of mastery for each objective. The well-trained special education teacher is aware of Frank Hewett's developmental sequence of goals including attention, response, order, exploratory, social, mastery, and achievement levels. A teacher of emotionally disturbed children, as well as teachers of mentally retarded, and learning disabled children, should incorporate this methodology into his educational program. Through the use of this approach, a special education teacher should be aware of the individualized performances of each student (Hewett 1968). If teachers of exceptional children are accountable they will implement and rely on the use of behavioral objectives.

The incorporation of accountability in all phases of educational programs should result in improved instruction and services for exceptional children. As suggested by Vergason (1973), accountability would not only improve education but would provide a means whereby parents could legally demand appropriate educational services for their child. In addition, parents could also be required to accept adequate educational services for their child.

If accountability is to require improved planning by teachers by the insistence upon the production of data to support pupil progress, then school administrators will also be required to provide appropriate means for the teacher to accomplish the specified objectives. In short, Vergason's discussion provides many implications for teacher training institutions, administrators, practicing teachers, parents, and publishing companies with respect to the increasing development and application of accountability.

Guidelines in the Evaluation of Teacher Training Programs and Instructional Programs for Special Education Teachers

Evaluation is an involved, complex, and ongoing process. Through evaluation, various facts about a system or program are accumulated which must be integrated and interpreted. Evaluation, as used in this chapter, is a procedure used in determining the effectiveness of teacher training programs and the instructional programs for special education teachers. Evaluation is a system or a process of examining information relevant to a particular program for the purpose of making meaningful decisions about that program. If used appropriately, evaluation should be a major factor in the achievement of planned changes rather than change which is based solely upon opinion (Guba 1968).

A group serving as an evaluation team must focus on several aspects of a training or instructional program. The team will have to decide upon factors which may be described as the context of the program, factors which may be considered as input, processes which are used in the operation of the program, and the product or output of the program (Guba). Each of these factors is related to all the others, and the evaluation of one factor must lead to the evaluation of all factors if information relative to possible needed changes is to be meaningful.

This is a comprehensive approach to evaluation but planned changes of training or instructional programs, which are in existence for the purpose of benefitting exceptional children, must be based upon a comprehensive approach. Obviously, an evaluation of only the input into a program would be entirely insufficient because the results of input must be measured by the extent to which a program meets its objectives. In essence, therefore this type of evaluation should attempt to ascertain the importance of factors such as the staff, the training of the staff, cost factors, the scope and depth of the curriculum, supportive systems through supervisory or consultant personnel, practical activities such as field trips or practicum experiences and the degree to which program objectives (output) are met. A partial evaluation may, on the other hand, result in premature changes and changes which are not warranted.

Implementing an effective evaluation system for teacher training programs and the instructional program of special education teachers would imply that changes are needed. With change in mind, the evaluation team must first identify areas where change is needed and focus attention on those selected units. Once a need or problem has been identified, a response is called for. For instance, what can be done about a curriculum program? Has anyone else done anything about effective curriculum programming? Does anyone have any ideas? Is there any research on curriculum programs? After it is determined that a change is needed, one needs to decide what change should be attempted (Guba). This information is the first step the evaluation team must take, but the team must also continuously use self-evaluation. For example, the team must be careful to avoid implementing changes because they would like to see certain types of alterations in a program. To what extent is a change warranted at this time? That is the primary question the team must ask itself. Abraham Kaplan (1964) once said, "Give a small boy a hammer and he will find that everything he encounters needs pounding."

The administrative team must also study all aspects of its recommendations for changes before submitting them to an appropriate board or group for implementation. For example, if a certain type of change is recommended, are the monies required for it currently available? Are those certain types of professional persons who may be recommended for employment, available at this time? The final analysis of any recommendations for change must be evaluated in an attempt to determine if the program personnel being evaluated can implement the recommendations. A critical series of statements which suggest changes that are currently beyond the ability of the personnel involved will accomplish nothing other than frustration and discouragement. The implementation of gradual improvements which are presently feasible seems to be a much better approach than one which would demand sweeping changes which, for the most part, would be impossible to incorporate.

Evaluation of teacher training programs and instructional programs of special education teachers ultimately brings the subject of behavioral objectives into focus. Only worthy evaluation will trace everything back to improved student performances. It is assumed that proper methodology of evaluation is the methodology of research. Evaluations should be designed the same as experiments are designed in that data is collected and interpreted the way research is collected and interpreted. However, research and evaluation differ with respect to their objectives. For instance, research is concerned with universal true knowledge, and controls must be carefully observed. Evaluation will do none of this (Guba).

A few types of evaluation methods have already been mentioned. A closer examination of these methods is needed for a more thorough understanding. "Context evaluation is concerned with providing information about the context or setting within which the educational activity is taking place" (Guba). In this case, the context of the special education department and the classroom for exceptional children will be the context evaluation. The evaluation team, obviously, must have a starting point. To illustrate: At what level of achievement is Jimmy presently functioning? After determining this factor, the evaluation team should establish limits, choose subareas or topics to explore and gather the desired information.

Secondly, "Input evaluation has to do with decision alternatives, their delineation, and their relative worth" (Guba). Input evaluation is making a decision about the problem. In doing this, the administrative team will have developed certain specifications based on context evaluation. The team is to assess each specification and decide which one will have the highest payoff potential. There will be several specifications which the evaluation team must explore if the evaluation is to be comprehensive.

Process evaluation is a type of guidance system in that it signals whenever the program is off course and provides a mechanism of protection. It is also the stage where further refinement and extension of the problem is handled.

"Product evaluation is concerned with final outcomes. The decision here is whether or not the item being evaluated should be retained, eliminated, or altered in some way" (Guba). In this case, the item being evaluated should be altered instead of eliminated. In the final analysis, an evaluation should be evaluated for the purposes described above. The general criteria are as follows:

1. Internal validity
2. External validity
3. Reliability
4. Objectivity
5. Relevance
6. Significance
7. Scope
8. Credibility
9. Timeliness
10. Pervasiveness (Guba)

In the near future, an administrative evaluation will become a part of every ongoing program in the field of special education. If professional educators approach this area with specific concerns regarding the learning and adjustment of handicapped children, then perhaps the evaluation systems which are to be devised will be effective. If there is anxiety regarding teaching positions or other professional positions in the use of an effective evaluation system, then the product of the ongoing evaluation will not bring about the changes which are and will be required for the development of appropriate instructional programs for exceptional children.

Personnel in Programs for Exceptional Children

Educators in the field of special education have advocated that many persons are needed in order to deliver appropriate and comprehensive services to exceptional or handicapped children. The special education teacher cannot continue to function in isolation and accomplish all the tasks which are required to habilitate or rehabilitate handicapped children. In recent years there has been a trend to recognize that professional personnel must be trained to work with handicapped children in settings other than the classroom. This has come about because the needs of handicapped children have been identified through research and practical experiences. More handicapped children have also been identified, and where children are recognized as having learning or adjustment problems, then additional supplementary services are indicated.

Special Education Counselor

The position of Special Education Counselor within the organization of the public schools is a recent concept. This additional position will greatly enhance services which are provided handicapped children, in as much as the increase in the number of counselors in public schools has failed to keep pace with the demand for counseling services. Most counseling training programs for school counselors have not emphasized the inclusion of information which is pertinent in working with disabled students; therefore, counseling of exceptional children is usually provided by the special education class teacher (Fine 1969).

The training of regular school counselors seldom prepares the counselor to provide services for exceptional children. With a lack of information and training, such as a practicum experience with exceptional children, the school counselor hesitates to work with this group of the school population (Patterson 1969). A review of the professional literature over the past decade indicated that there were only sixteen instances relative to school counselors who had provided some type of counseling for exceptional children (Cormany 1970).

The student who is placed in a special education class needs professional counseling services for a variety of reasons. He may have experienced frustration and failure prior to his placement in special education to the extent that his self-concept has been seriously damaged. His parents may have feelings of guilt or place too much or too little emphasis on the child's problems and, therefore, inadvertently create more frustration for the child (Fine). These problems may have existed for one or more years and the child will need long term counseling services to help him adjust and improve his functioning. As the exceptional child grows older he may be confronted with experiences which add to his frustration and his adjustment, and, as a result, need counseling services to help him confront the "new" situations.

A recognition of the counseling needs of exceptional children may place the regular school counselor in a difficult position. He may agree that children who have learning, adjustment, or physical problems are in need of continuous counseling services, but typically this group of children would constitute approximately 5 to 10 percent of his total student population. Therefore, the counselor is faced with the problem of deciding whether he should expend most of his time and energies with a small group for whom he has usually been inadequately trained to provide service, or whether he should attempt to serve all of his school population. For these and other reasons, the need for a special education counselor is slowly being recognized.

The state of Texas has recently created the new position of Special Education Counselor. This position is described as follows: "To provide educational and vocational guidance to students with limited personal guidance. Philosophically the intent of this position is described as liaison between pupil, parent, and teacher and between home, school and community" (Hansen 1971). In addition, the person who becomes a Special Education Counselor would be trained to provide counseling services for parents in order to help them make an adjustment in their feelings and their treatment of their disabled child. Training would also focus on the development of counseling techniques which would help the exceptional child in his personal and vocational adjustment (Hansen).

Special Education Counselors should also be trained in the area of group counseling. Group counseling of exceptional youngsters has been an effective procedure and, of course, is quite time saving on the part of the counselor. The use of group counseling can also serve to bring to the fore indications of children who may need more intensive individual counseling services and accomplish more than one objective.

To be effective in bringing about changes in a child's adjustment to his environment and his classroom, peer groups may be used to supplement the services of the counselor. Children may react more positively to counseling services if supplemented by peer interaction. The use of peers as helpers in group counseling sessions was successful in providing services to a group of children who had adjustment problems and the initial training of the peer helpers only involved three hours. The investigation was conducted over a period of nine weeks, during which the peer helpers received additional training once a week, and the findings indicated that the peer helpers were successful in supplementing the services of the counselor (Kern and Kirby 1971). Additional research of this nature should provide more insight regarding the effectiveness of group counseling and the use of peer groups in counseling. Implications could also be discovered which would lead toward more effective training of school counselors or special education counselors in the area of group counseling and factors which are essential in the training of peer groups to supplement group counseling.

If the training of peer groups is not feasible within a school program, then the training of volunteer groups to assist in the provision of counseling services may be another approach to consider. A program was initiated in Auburn, Maine, in 1968, to incorporate community volunteers into a school guidance program to assist exceptional children. This program was developed because of the number of children who needed additional services which the school system was not able to provide through existing professional staff. Pamphlets describing the program and emphasizing the need for volunteers were distributed throughout the community. During the first year of the program 32 adults, of whom 29 remained for a second year, provided additional services for children. The program emphasized the development of a relationship between an adult and a child and did not merely attempt to train the volunteers as tutors or teacher aids. From this program came a description of general characteristics which adults should possess to be the most effective in counseling sessions: (1) a sincere desire to be a part of the program and to be of service to a child, (2) a sense of humor, (3) understanding and acceptance of children, (4) enthusiasm, (5) flexibility, and (6) a well-balanced personality (Muro 1970).

As the recognition for the need of special education counselors continues, the factors mentioned above should become a part of the integral training program for the individual pursuing this particular type of position. School systems will have to make decisions regarding the number of exceptional students who can be effectively served by a special education counselor. This may entail considering a special education counselor as an itinerant resource person in that he may have to serve more than one school building. A special education counselor should also be well trained to assist the special education and regular classroom teacher in providing classroom counseling services.

Diagnostic Teachers

Diagnostic teachers are essential if the use of resource centers, learning laboratories, or precision teaching, which were described earlier, are going to be effective with exceptional children. An individual who is trained as a diagnostic teacher must be able to integrate diagnostic information to the extent that an appropriate instructional program may be developed for a particular child. A diagnostic teacher must be able to systematically evaluate the effects of an instructional program and be willing to make changes in his program which will benefit the learning characteristics of the individual child. Training of a diagnostic teacher must also include the careful planning, sequencing, and development of teacher-made materials. In addition, a diagnostic teacher will serve as a liaison person to the classroom teacher and must be able to communicate with others in the school program regarding procedures and materials which are effective in ameliorating the learning problems of children. Because of the short period of time a diagnostic teacher may have with individual children, a person in this position should also be afforded the time and opportunity to conduct follow-up services with his former students. Follow-up services will be essential for the reevaluation of the child's progress and the effectiveness of the home-base teacher in implementing the prescribed instructional program which the diagnostic teacher has prepared.

The lack of trained special education teachers is a primary reason for developing the position of a diagnostic teacher. If children with learning and adjustment problems are going to be served adequately, it will require more than one model, such as the self-contained classroom with a qualified special educator. The growing demand for classroom space is, of course, another reason why the services of a diagnostic teacher may be an effective procedure. To provide effective and economical services, two or more school systems may want to explore the possibility of a cooperative school agreement similar to that developed by three communities in Virginia. These communities wanted to improve existing services offered exceptional children and also provide a program which would serve a greater number of exceptional children. After studying their problem, feasible plans, financing, and available professional staff, these communities applied for and were awarded a grant through Title III of the Elementary and Secondary Education Act of 1965 to implement the models of the diagnostic-prescriptive teacher and the crisis-resource teacher (Tenorio and Raimist 1971).

Diagnostic-Prescriptive Teacher

A diagnostic-prescriptive teacher must be a trained observer of children's behavior. When a classroom teacher requests the services of a diagnostic-prescriptive teacher, the first phase of the referral process involves an observation of a child's behavior in his classroom setting. Observing a child in his assigned classroom setting will provide a realistic basis for initially collecting data regarding the child. A diagnostic-prescriptive teacher will also obtain personal information regarding the child during the initial phase of observation. This may include factors such as his age, sex, grade, recent achievement test scores, and his primary learning difficulties.

A diagnostic-prescriptive teacher first decides if he can help the classroom teacher modify his approach or materials. If this procedure is not feasible or does not help the child, then the child is temporarily assigned to the diagnostic classroom.

While in the diagnostic classroom, the diagnostic-prescriptive teacher will, through experimentation, decide what approaches and materials are appropriate for a child, formulate a prescription, and in conference with the classroom teacher discuss the implementation of the prescription. Periodic follow-up contacts are made with the classroom teacher to effect any changes which may be needed to meet the child's existing and changing needs (Tenorio and Raimist).

Crisis-Resource Teacher

A crisis-resource teacher provides services similar to those provided by a diagnostic-prescriptive teacher. A primary difference in the roles of these two positions seems to be that the crisis-resource teacher must be immediately available. The needs of a teacher or a child would be of a critical nature and the crisis-resource teacher would have to be constantly "on call." A person in this capacity may be needed immediately by a teacher or a child; therefore, he would have to be available at all times. Based upon the immediacy of the situation, a crisis-resource teacher would have to be a very skilled person in order to make appropriate decisions. The decision may involve counseling, changing environmental consequences of the classroom, or helping the teacher to select and use an appropriate technique (Tenorio and Raimist).

It seems, from the description of the crisis-resource teacher, as given by Tenorio and Raimist, that every elementary and secondary school would have to be assigned a person who would fulfill this function. Otherwise, situations which would require immediate action could not be appropriately met. Perhaps a school system could establish target schools to which the assignment of a crisis-resource teacher would seem most feasible. This could be accomplished by surveying all schools within the district in order to obtain pertinent and current information relative to the problems of teachers and children. A crisis-resource teacher could also be assigned full-time to one school building for a specified period of time, (i.e., nine weeks) and serve approximately four schools during the school year. Granted, this would not be as effective as having one crisis-resource teacher for every school building, the availability of personnel who could function in this position and the funding of these positions, or its limitations, might necessitate an adaptation or compromise of the approach as recommended by Tenorio and Raimist. Flexibility would be absolutely necessary for any school system desiring to implement the effective use of a person in the crisis-resource teacher position.

Consulting Teachers

The use of a consulting teacher is not as recent as other trends in special education. A consulting teacher is also referred to as a helping teacher or supervising teacher. This position often requires additional certification requirements beyond those of a classroom teacher; however, some states have no criteria established for the qualifications of a consulting teacher. In states without certification requirements, a local school system generally promotes a classroom teacher based upon his performance and years of experience in the classroom.

Efforts to determine the number of teachers with whom a consulting teacher can work effectively have not been too successful. One would not usually find specific information relative to this situation in the job description of a consulting teacher. Questions which are proposed in attempts to solve this problem involve such factors as follows: How often should a consulting teacher visit a classroom teacher? How many schools should a consulting teacher serve? Is a consulting teacher a resource person to whom children can be referred for evaluation or reevaluation? Should a consulting teacher expend the majority of his time visiting classroom teachers, or in developing in-service training programs? To what extent should a consulting teacher be assigned administrative duties? Solutions to these questions may determine how effective a consulting teacher can be in helping to improve the instructional program which is probably the primary task which he must confront.

A program organized in Vermont is an example of one in which consulting teachers served as resource persons for classroom teachers. The University of Vermont, the Vermont State Department of Education, and five school districts near the university trained a number of elementary teachers as specialists in behavior modification and its application to exceptional children. Elementary teachers were trained over a two-year period in the many facets of behavior modification, including training to help the classroom teacher apply principles of behavior modification in the classroom. The program also included the assignment of the consulting teachers to the University for the purpose of training future and present teachers in the area of behavior modification (McKenzie 1970). Specific training of consulting teachers is a different approach in an attempt to aid the classroom teacher in implementing appropriate uses of techniques.

Paraprofessionals

As the need for qualified staff in the field of special education has not kept pace with the identification of children who are in need of special services, school systems have begun to train and use paraprofessionals to assist classroom teachers in delivering services to handicapped children. Paraprofessionals may be parents, volunteer adults, high school youths or college students. A school system may provide long term training for paraprofessionals or may provide on-the-job training depending upon the extent to which it is deemed desirable for these persons to become involved in working with exceptional children. A few school systems have provided for an additional paraprofessional in special education and regular education classrooms through developing the position of teacher aid.

A person working in the capacity of a paraprofessional may be required to provide a variety of services. A handicapped child may need special tutoring in one area which the classroom teacher cannot consistently provide. Here the paraprofessional can be quite helpful—relieving the teacher of a special responsibility. A paraprofessional may also develop and present special projects which focus on the development of manipulative skills, physical education programs, art projects, or language skills. With very little supervision from the classroom teacher, the paraprofessional can conduct activities such as those mentioned above and be quite successful in appropriately contributing to the instructional program.

Karnes, Hodgins, and Teska (1970) conducted a three-year experiment to compare the performance of professional teachers to that of adult and teenage paraprofessionals in teaching preschool-age children from economically and educationally deprived families. The adult paraprofessionals were Negro mothers with no previous teaching experience and the teenage paraprofessionals were girls who were members of a high school work-study program. The emphasis in the content of the lessons was on language development as exemplified in the Illinois Test of Psycholinguistic Abilities. All of the paraprofessionals were trained and their effectiveness, as compared to that of the teachers, was based upon the children's performances on standardized tests. The results indicated that there were no significant differences between the progress of the three groups of children; however, the teenage paraprofessionals were considered to be less satisfied with their experiences.

Mothers have been trained as paraprofessionals with their own preschool-age children. The training was conducted by a demonstrator who went to the home and demonstrated play activities with the child in the presence of the mother. The play activities centered around verbal interaction with the child and the ultimate objective was to increase intellectual functioning. Since the beginning of the program in 1965, follow-up studies have been conducted with the children. These studies have indicated increases in cognitive functioning through gains in I.Q. points and achievement test scores which were up to grade level during the first year of school (Levenstein 1971).

Another interesting project using parents to help young children increase their learning skills was developed by the Far West Regional Laboratory in 1970. The concept of a toy library was established through this project. Parents were trained in the selection and use of toys with their children and could then go to the toy library and borrow educational toys. From this program, parents began to see their children and the educational process differently. Other materials could be provided in the library and these could be loaned to parents to use with their children at home. These libraries could be established in the public schools and parents would have relatively easy access to the materials and the training in the use of the materials (McDonald 1971).

Programs involving parents as paraprofessionals, similar to those programs described above, could have a tremendous impact on special education programs. Children from families with limited incomes and limited resources could be helped to overcome some of their learning deficits prior to entering school and thus be better prepared for the new environment of the school. Parental attitudes toward their children could also be modified to such an extent that the children would develop attitudes as participants in the learning process.

Paraprofessionals have also been used extensively in institutional settings for the mentally retarded. Institutional or residential facilities for the mentally retarded, and for all exceptional children, are usually understaffed. Projects which require one-to-one activities or even small group activities have been difficult if not impossible to organize because of low ratio of staff as compared to that of the residents.

Paraprofessionals in the residential facility must be trained at the facility to be cognizant of the tasks with which they will be confronted. A project involving training language specialists for institutionalized mentally retarded children who were functioning at a low level was successful in training and using the paraprofessionals and also in increasing the skills of the children (Guess, Smith, and Ensminger 1971).

Considering all of the trends regarding programs and personnel which have been discussed in this chapter, the special educator can no longer complain about a lack of programs or a lack of personnel. The programs or personnel may not presently exist in a particular area which is attempting to provide services to exceptional children, but as discussed in this chapter, there are ways to implement ideas for the provision of services which are within the grasp of a community with respect to both finances and manpower. This chapter has by no means attempted to present all of the unique ideas which can be developed for the purpose of increasing and improving services for exceptional children, but perhaps the reader has gained insight into the problems and ways in which the solving of these problems can become meaningful programs.

Administration of Programs for Exceptional Children

The School Principal.

The administration of programs for exceptional children is the responsibility of all local, state, and federal governmental agencies which are related to the development and implementation of such programs. A closer examination of the administration of programs for exceptional children would probably reveal that it is the school principal who is the primary school person involved in promoting adequate programs for the exceptional child. The school principal is considered to be the person who determines the attitude and sets the tempo for the total educational program established within the building to which he is assigned. The principal is the educator who encourages flexibility, innovations, and the use of appropriate techniques to improve all education services particularly those offered exceptional children.

In order to effectively implement procedures and more flexible approaches in meeting the needs of exceptional children the educational leader, one must agree, should have some basic information regarding exceptional children. The principal needs information regarding exceptional children if he is to work effectively with his teachers and the parents. If one were to conduct a survey of school principals, he would probably find that only a very few have completed any course work pertaining to the exceptional child. In fact, such a survey was conducted by Bullock (1970) in which he showed that of 92 principals only 12 percent had taken more than one course in special education and 65 percent had elected no courses in special education.

The principal may be the key person; however, the total program requires a coordinated effort on the part of the entire administration—the teachers, the parents, and appropriate community agencies (Melcher 1972). The emphasis must be on developing a program which is child-centered and not merely based on administrative decisions. The special education teacher operating a program in isolation may still be in existence today, but this type of a program is not comprehensive and lacks the variety to meet the needs of exceptional children. In other words, operating programs for exceptional children without support and cooperative efforts of school personnel, parents, and community agencies severely limits the possible effects of the program. All teachers and children can benefit from cooperative efforts and cooperative sharing of procedures and skills which are effective in the educational process.

Cost factors and other related aspects. Of course, the provision of special services for exceptional children will always add to the cost factors of a school system. Many school boards and/or school administrators hesitate to develop or expand services for exceptional children because of the "excess" cost factors, and these actions may be based on the realistic fact that there is a lack of monies to support programs. Frohreich (1973) compiled data regarding variables such as administration, teachers, supplies, counseling, transportation, etc., which increase the costs of providing services for all types of exceptional children. His information was based on surveys conducted in school systems which were selected as providing exemplary programs, and may well serve as a guide to beginning or expanding programs. All school administrators, directors of special education, and special education teachers should study this report in detail for developing their own decisions regarding programs.

In addition to cost factors and variables which are pertinent in establishing good programs, the acceptance of exceptional children in the schools should be emphasized. Programs for exceptional children are required in order to prevent the possible total or partial loss of an individual's potential, and also to prevent the costly factors which are created when programs are not provided. The exceptional child, regardless of his abilities or difficulties, is a worthwhile human being and if he requires specialized teaching, counseling and/or equipment, programs of quality offering these services and materials should be provided for him. Developing human resources or at least preventing their loss should be a mandate for all educational programs.

An important factor in providing exemplary programs for exceptional children is the selection of the best teacher available for a particular group of children. Again, the role of the principal is paramount in making this decision. A well trained special education teacher can provide a more meaningful and realistic instructional program, and also serve in the capacity of a resource person to the other teachers in the building. If the instructional programs and other supportive areas of special education programs for exceptional children are to be improved, then the special education teacher must have the training which is essential for making worthwhile contributions to these differences. If the program is not different from that of the regular class program; then the effects of the programs cannot differ.

The administration of special education programs and the role of the administrator may not appear to be very meaningful to the college student preparing to enter the field of special education. These aspects are, however, of utmost importance when the practicing special education teacher seeks support from the administration and doesn't receive it, or when he asks for additional monies for supplies and equipment and is refused. It can be most discouraging to the new special education teacher to discover that the children with whom he is working are devalued and merely tolerated within the school program—and even slight deference is due to external pressures.

Directors of Special Education.

The position of director of special education is certainly not a new one. Special education has had directors of programs on the state level for several years, and as special class programs in the public schools have grown the position of director has been added to the school staff.

School systems will continue to have a need for qualified and well-trained directors of special education as legislation provides for the establishment of additional classroom teachers and resource persons for exceptional children. The development of sound procedures for referring and evaluating children with exceptional abilities or disabilities; the hiring of competent staff to provide services for exceptional children; involving the staff in seeking appropriate federal and state funding for special projects in special education—will require a specialist who can function as a director of special education.

The director of special education is responsible to the teachers of exceptional children for promoting and developing ongoing in-service education programs and special workshops. He should assist teachers in the appropriate referral and use of community agencies, and in the development of curricular materials. The director may be of considerable value in interpreting the program for exceptional children to all school personnel, parents, and the general public. He is responsible for building a sequential, comprehensive program for all exceptional children, and also for the development of a good professional library for the staff.

In addition, the director of special education has the responsibility of keeping the school administration informed of the needs for personnel, classrooms, transportation, diagnostic and evaluation procedures, and methods for the evaluation of the total program.

With such a variety of responsibilities, the person selected as director of special education must be well trained and have a good experiential background with exceptional children. An example from one state regarding the specifications applicable to the director of special education is presented below.

Legislation in the state of Ohio has recently provided for the position of director of special education. This provision includes the requirements for certification and has described the primary functions of the director of special education as that of leadership and supervision. Specific duties listed are as follows: (1) Planning and program development, (2) Administration and program coordination, (3) Staff selection and development, (4) Budgeting and fiscal control, and (5) Program evaluation and reporting (Kern and Mayer 1971).

A majority of special education programs have developed certification requirements for a director of special education. A recent survey in all fifty states concluded that an educational program for directors of special education should include courses in administration, education foundations, psychology, guidance, and research. The training should also include a practicum or internship in special education administration, certification in a teaching field, and a master's degree with emphasis in the field of special education (Kern and Mayer).

Parents of Exceptional Children

Aspects regarding parents have been discussed previously in the chapters relative to the specific types of exceptional children and will not be repeated. However, the parents of exceptional children are a very important link in the provision of educational services, and further delineation regarding parents is worthy of consideration. Parents are influential in the diagnosis and evaluation of their children, and their support of programs is essential. Supplementary services which parents may provide in the home or through a community agency are extremely beneficial to their children's education and training.

Recognition and Acceptance.

The recognition and acceptance of exceptional children in families may be difficult whether the children are gifted or severely mentally retarded. In many situations educators should realize that parents may not be aware that their children are exceptional. The factor of recognition is, of course, the first step toward acceptance and this aspect alone may determine whether or not parents are willing to support the provision of program modifications. In other situations, parents may have no problems in recognizing that their children are different yet have not reached the stages where they are willing to accept all of the implications of the children's abilities or disabilities.

Family Problems and Counseling.

School administrators, counselors, therapists, and teachers must be cognizant of the wide variety of problems which families may have regarding their exceptional children. These problems vary from difficulties within the family unit to difficulties which derive from external attitudes or pressures. Knowledge regarding family problems has to be directed to the specific individual family; however, a discussion of possible difficulties may serve to set up guidelines in providing counseling services. Space does not permit a comprehensive study of the families of exceptional children; consequently, the reader should pursue this type of study with reference to his particular area of concern within the field of special education.

If children are gifted and their precociousness continually thwarts the parents and siblings; then severe adjustment problems may develop. The attitudes, whether covert or overt, of other family members or friends and neighbors can be very distressing to the parents and may result in the implementation of family restrictions in social activities, travel, or participation in community programs. The effects of the families' self-images, or of externally imposed restrictions on exceptional children, will vary considerably. For example, if families become hostile toward their children as a result of the restrictions; the children may be rejected and neglected. If the restrictions are imposed for a long duration; the children may develop deficiencies in peer relationships, become fearful of persons outside the family, or become deficient in the development of curiosity or socialization skills. There is no doubt that family restrictions may seriously affect the development of exceptional children, and counseling would be required.

Parents may be overwhelmed at the extra financial needs which are necessary for exceptional children. The financial needs can include special tutoring services which may be essential for gifted children or for children with learning disabilities. The cost of medication, hospitalization, and other medical services may seriously lessen the monies which are available for other family expenditures.

Educators cannot directly lessen the financial strain of parents of exceptional children in the majority of cases. However, educators should be aware of appropriate community resources which may be able to provide assistance to the parents. An educator should know to what agency or agencies parents can be referred, and make every effort to insure that the parents follow through on the recommendations, and also insure that the parents are not sent on a fruitless and time-consuming shopping spree. Many parents may not have adequate transportation or financial resources to follow up referrals from one agency to another. Therefore, if parents find no temporary solutions or resources to help them, due to a lack of appropriate referrals, the relationship between home and school can be severely and irreparably damaged.

The counseling of parents regarding their exceptional children is one of the responsibilities of school administrators, counselors, and/ or teachers. In providing this service, educators should not assume that counseling is a single offering. For example, a school principal, counselor, and/or teacher may call upon parents to discuss possible placement of their children in some type of modified educational program, and assume that one contact will suffice for the parents. Repeated contact may be absolutely necessary if the parents are to accept the placement, and become knowledgeable regarding the type of program which has been recommended.

Many other contacts with parents will be made by school personnel by way of parent-teacher conferences; for example. School personnel should inform parents of children's positive growth and accomplishments, and not just contact parents when the children are having some types of learning or adjustment problems. A very important consideration is for school personnel to be able to recognize when they are not adequately trained to provide counseling for severe problems in the family unit. Again, appropriate referral should be made for those situations which are beyond the training and abilities of school personnel.

Parents and Residential Centers.

Many parents of exceptional children may be confronted with the possibility of placing their children in a residential center—a center for the emotionally disturbed child, a center for the deaf child, a center for the blind child, or a center for the mentally retarded child. The placement may be necessary because of a lack of appropriate programs in the community, or because of the severity of the child's difficulties. Consideration of this type of placement should never be a routine suggestion, but should be the last resource to which one refers parents. The community or a nearby community should be thoroughly explored regarding possible services before one recommends that parents seek placement in residential facilities for their children.

Avoiding residential placement of exceptional children is not a direct criticism of residential centers, because many of these centers have excellent programs. The factors of primary importance are to keep the children with their families and within their communities if at all possible. If the severity of the children's problems, or the insufficiency of family and community resources are such as to warrant residential placement, then the best and nearest program (geographically) should be sought. For accurate and detailed information regarding any residential center, the parents should be encouraged to visit, or at least communicate with the facility prior to making any formal application. Suggesting this type of placement for exceptional children may also result in the need for professional counseling services for the parents.

Parents As Teachers.

The previous discussion of paraprofessionals includes information pertaining to parents as teachers. School personnel should always consider the possibility of requesting parents to work as paraprofessionals or as teacher aides. In addition to this possibility, school personnel may ask parents to provide supplementary or extended educational services for their children in their own homes. Requesting parents to be a specific part of the educational process must include an evaluation with respect to the possible effectiveness of this procedure. For example, the parents may place undue pressure on their children to perform, and so cause more difficulties. This reference to parents merely indicates the fact that many parents cannot be very objective when working with their own children. Instead of involving parents in assisting their children academically, parents may be requested to take their children to places in the community which would strengthen the children's awarenesses and knowledge of their environments. It is also appropriate to ask parents to provide their children with the time, and any suitable place in their homes where they can pursue school-related activities with some degree of privacy and quiet. Perhaps just helping the parents accept their children's exceptionalities and recognizing the children as unique persons may alleviate some of the parents' frustrations regarding these children.

In short, school personnel have tremendous responsibilities in the development of the relationship between home and school. Every effort should be made to help the family with their exceptional children to the extent that the parents and other family members can contribute in a positive manner to the children's total growth and development.

SUMMARY.

Considering all of the programs and persons that have been discussed in this chapter; the special educator can no longer complain about a lack of programs or a lack of personnel. The programs or personnel may not presently exist in a particular area which is attempting to provide services to exceptional children, but, as discussed, there are ways to implement ideas for the provision of services which are within the grasp of a community with respect to finances and manpower. This chapter has by no means attempted to present all of the unique ideas which can be developed for the purpose of increasing and improving services for exceptional children, but perhaps the reader has gained insight into the problems and ways in which the solving of these problems can become meaningful programs.

Bibliography

"A Program of Education for Exceptional Children in Oklahoma," *Bulletin of Special Education.* Division of Special Education, 1973.

Bullock, Lyndal M."An Inquiry into the Special Education Training of Elementary School Administrators" *Exceptional Children* 36, no. 10 (Summer 1970).

Cormany, R.B. "Returning Special Education Students to Regular Classes." *Personnel and Guidance Journal* 48, no. 8 (April 1970).

Fine, M.J. "Counseling with the Educable Mentally Retarded." *The Training School Bulletin* 66, no. 3 (November 1969).

Frohreich, Lloyd E. "Costing Programs for Exceptional Children: Dimensions and Indices." *Exceptional Children* 39, no. 7 (April 1973).

Guba, Egon G. *Evaluation and Change in Education,* Bloomington, Ind.: National Institute for the Study of Educational Change, May 1968.

Guess, D.; Smith, J.O.; and Ensminger, E.E. "The Role of Non-professional Persons in Teaching Language Skills to Mentally Retarded Children," *Exceptional Children* 37, no. 6 (February 1971).

Hansen, C.E. "The Special Education Counselor: A New Role." *Exceptional Children* 38, no. 1 (September, 1971).

Hewett, Frank. *The Emotionally Disturbed Child in the Classroom.* Boston: Allyn and Bacon, Inc., 1968.

Hyer, Anna L. "From Gold Stars to Green Stamps." *Audiovisual Instruction,* 16, no. 5 (May 1971).

Instructional Materials and Resource Materials Available to Teachers of Exceptional Children and Youth, The University of Texas at Austin, July 1969 and July 1972.

Kaplan, Abraham. *The Conduct of Inquiry: Methodology for Behavioral Science.* San Francisco: Chandler Publishing Co., 1964.

Karnes, M.B.; Teska, J.; and Hodgins, A.S. "The Successful Implementation of a Highly Specific Preschool Instructional Program by Paraprofessional Teachers." Journal of Special Education 4, no. 1 (Winter-Spring 1970).

Kern, R.; and Kirby, J.H. "Utilizing Peer Helper Influence in Group Counseling." *Elementary School Guidance and Counseling* 6, no. 2 (December 1971).

Kern, W.H., and Mayer, J.B. "Certification of Directors of Special Education Programs: The Results of a National Survey." *Contemporary Education* 42 no. 3 (January 1971).

Kibler, Robert J.; Barker, Larry R.; and Miles, David T. *Behavioral Objectives and Instruction.* Boston: Allyn and Bacon, Inc., 1970.

Levenstein, P. "Learning Through (and From) Mothers." *Childhood Education* 48, no. 3 (December 1971).

McDonald, P. "Cross Currents: Parents, A New Resource." *Teaching Exceptional Children* 3, no. 3 (Winter 1971).

McKenzie, Hugh S.; Egnar, Ann N.; Knight, Martha F.; Perelman, Phyllis F.; Schneider, Betsy M.; and Garvin, Jean S. "Training Consulting Teachers to Assist Elementary Teachers in the Management and Education of Handicapped Children." *Exceptional Children 37,* no. 2 (October, 1970).

Melcher, John W. "Some Questions from a School Administrator." *Exceptional Children* 38, no. 7 (March 1972).

Muro, J.J. "Community Volunteers: A New Thrust for Guidance." *The Personnel and Guidance Journal* 49, no. 2 (October 1970).

Patterson, C.H. *Rehabilitation Counseling: Collected Papers,* Champaign, Ill.: Stipes Publishing Co., 1969.

Reger, Roger; Schroeder, Wendy; and Uschold, Kathie. *Special Education: Children With Learning Problems.* New York: Oxford University Press, 1968.

Scholarship Program, U. S. Department of Health, Education, and Welfare, 1971.

Stocker, Joseph, and Wilson, Donald F. "Accountability and the Classroom Teacher." *Today's Education* 60 no. 3 (March 1971).

Tenorio, S.C., and Raimist, L.I. "A Noncategorical Consortium Program." *Exceptional Children* 38, no. 4 (December 1971).

Vergason, Glenn A. "Accountability in Special Education." *Exceptional Children* 39, no. 5 (February 1973).

**Prescriptive
Teaching**

Diagnostic Teaching

Reintegration

**Preschool
Programs**

*'There may be a way
for each of us to learn!'*

Motor Training

**Resource
Centers**

Physical Education

**Behavior
Modification**

Trends in the Field
of Special Education

INTRODUCTION

The objective of this chapter is to acquaint the reader with recent trends in the field of special education. Approved methods of education which have been effective in teaching exceptional children include the resource center, precision teaching, behavior modification, and physical education. Emphasis is also being placed on the reintegration of exceptional children into regular classes, preschools for handicapped children, and the teacher's position in diagnostic-remedial activity.

Many model programs and methods are currently in operation and have proven effective in improving programs for exceptional children. There is also evidence that the ability to gain community understanding and participation in special education programs can greatly benefit our exceptional children. A goal, therefore, should be to implement these techniques and incorporate these needed paraprofessionals into the field of special education.

DIAGNOSTIC-PRESCRIPTIVE METHODS

The development and implementation of diagnostic-prescriptive methods is a relatively new endeavor in the field of special education. These methods are not static or rigid in the way in which they have been developed or implemented, as witness the fact that one may find differences in the application of one approach being used within the same school system or perhaps even in the same school building. Hopefully, this type of experimentation and modification will continue if the needs of exceptional children are to be met appropriately.

Flexibility should be paramount in the development and use of diagnostic-prescriptive methods. Without flexibility, programs can become stale, enthusiasm lost, and needs of children neglected. Certainly the use of diagnostic-prescriptive methods is not "the answer" in providing programs for exceptional children, but such approaches can definitely enrich instructional programs for exceptional children as well as teacher training programs.

Perhaps through learning about diagnostic-prescriptive methods, educators are also discovering more about the many factors involved in developing individualized instructional programs and even more important are the discoveries about the many facets through which children learn.

Resource Centers

One of the approaches in the area of diagnostic-prescriptive methods is the use of a resource center. A resource center may be located (1) within a single school building to serve the children from that school, children from a particular section of a metropolitan area, or all of the children within a small school system or, (2) within a single building to serve teachers from one school system, one state, or a regional area. The purpose of the center will, of course, determine the size of the center and the group of children or teachers whom it may serve.

One type of resource center which has many implications for teachers of exceptional children is the regional resource center for handicapped children which is intended to serve teachers who are having difficulty teaching their handicapped children. These centers were authorized by Title VI of the Elementary and Secondary Education Act of 1965 as amended. The program which is offered through the center may help the teacher to select instructional materials and appropriate methods in order to attempt to meet the current needs of the child as described by the diagnosis and prescription (Moss 1971).

The personnel of a resource center, which is designed to help teachers become more effective with handicapped children, may conduct a variety of services. Handicapped children may be referred to the center for a more thorough educational diagnosis and may even remain at the center so that a well-planned teaching approach that will match the diagnosis-prescription may be designed for him. Teachers may also go to the center to see the instructional program in operation with a particular child. In addition, the teacher's instructional program can be evaluated by the staff of the center in order to determine if changes are warranted. If a child needs more intensive services, the center staff can prepare an experimental teaching program for him, teach his homebased teacher how to implement the program and, after a short period of time, return the child to his own school. If any aspect of the program is not effective in helping the handicapped child begin to learn and make progress, the child or the planned instructional program can be reevaluated (Moss).

Of course, as proposed by Moss, such a center would require the services of many professional personnel who have been trained in providing programs to handicapped children. Such a center would utilize the team-approach concept in planning and developing the instructional programs for handicapped children and, in addition, specialists would be required to conduct comprehensive diagnostic evaluations. Liaison personnel would also be needed to make contact with the public schools and to communicate with them regarding the total services which were being offered. Evaluators of the center program would also be needed as a means whereby the effectiveness of the center program could be disseminated to professionals in the field.

From the authors' personal experiences, a similar approach has been developed in the state of Texas through the organization of regional educational service centers. These centers are not as directly involved in preparing instructional programs for handicapped children as the centers proposed by Moss; however, they do serve teachers of many exceptional children in a variety of ways. The centers in Texas serve approximately twenty counties and provide expert consultant services by conducting in-service training sessions at the center or by taking the in-service training program to the school. Many of these centers also have an instructional materials center from which the teacher may borrow materials for a period of approximately two weeks. For school systems which cannot provide diagnostic services, the center provides personnel to the school system for the purpose of conducting evaluations and writing prescriptions for the teachers to use. In addition, many of the centers provide films, filmstrips, videotapes, and records on a loan basis for the schools. School systems help to provide the centers by paying for the services through a formula which requires payments based upon the enrollment of the school system. These centers have been very effective in bringing programs and services to teachers in regions of the state of Texas where such programs may otherwise be very limited, if not impossible.

Diagnostic Procedures in the Classroom

The classroom teacher of exceptional children must become actively involved in the diagnostic-prescriptive program. It should be clearly understood that, at the present time, every teacher cannot expect to receive consistent services from a resource center such as those described above. Therefore, to enhance the learning of exceptional children, the teacher is obligated to learn everything he can about classroom techniques for diagnosis and designing effective instructional programs. These procedures are by no means easy to learn or implement and the special education teacher will find that his energies and talents are even in more demand in order to develop more appropriate individualized programs.

Smith (1969) has developed an approach which is intended to help the special education teacher understand his role in the problems of diagnosing and teaching the exceptional child. He has developed five levels of diagnostic-remedial activity the teacher can follow for identifying the nature of educational disorders in children. The first step involves assessing the child at a very early age to determine if there are any difficulties such as physical problems, etc., which are interfering with the learning process. After the child has been evaluated through step one, then he should be evaluated to determine what learning problems he may be having. If any weaknesses in learning are indicated through the use of achievement tests, then the teacher needs to probe further to determine if the weaknesses are actually evident in the child's classroom performances and if so, to what extent. Questions of particular importance in this step involve such areas as how the child approaches a particular learning task and what skills he may be using to accomplish the task. The next important step is to analyze what may be the reasons for the child's learning problems. Do they involve difficulties the child may have in perceiving or in assimilating material? Is the instructional program properly sequenced? Conclusions reached from this analysis will be tentative but will provide an objective means for the teacher to use in planning the steps which are necessary to effect an appropriate program for the child. The last step involves the testing of the tentative conclusions which were reached through step four. Of course, the plan as proposed by Smith is not intended to be a means of finalizing any instructional program provided for a child. The five steps require a consistent approach to evaluation and ongoing reevaluation of the instructional program. Through such a plan, the teacher can be the initial diagnostician and possibly the remediator of many of his children's problems.

Precision Teaching

A third trend in special education in the field of diagnostic-prescriptive work is precision teaching. Ogden R. Lindsley, Professor of Education at the University of Kansas, shaped and developed the idea in response to the needs of exceptional children as reported to him by their teachers.

In 1965, at the University of Kansas, he began the practice of collecting daily frequency records of students' performances to see if this information would be of help in monitoring instruction, evaluating curriculum or teaching in special and regular classes. Based upon experiences in using precision teaching, Lindsley's group discovered that the frequencies of the children's behaviors had to be recorded daily within the classroom setting. The recording of behaviors are placed on a standard chart which has a six cycle design for recording of an adequate range of behaviors which may occur once a day or as frequently as 1,000 times a minute. The use of a standard chart makes the recording of behaviors more objective on the part of the teachers, facilitates the sharing of data with other teachers and administrators, and in addition gives an ever ready, ongoing report system to the parents (Lindsley 1971).

From the standard chart, through individualized planning, every child is given his own curriculum. This system provides a more meaningful program for each child which is intended to help him accomplish instructional objectives and improve his ability to function. In addition, the child is involved in the process of selecting instructional materials, and behaviors are objectively recorded for the purpose of efficiently planning programs according to current needs of children (Lindsley).

Inner behaviors as well as outer behaviors are being recorded by the system of precision teaching. Attempts are being made to record such behaviors as success thoughts, anxiety feelings, joy, love and compassion. Although still in the experimental stages, the use of precision teaching to record inner behaviors could have many profound implications for programs for exceptional children as well as for other programs (Lindsley).

The standard charts used in precision teaching may also be used with gifted children who are not challenged by the instructional program. The gifted child may be making all A's in his program but the program may not be adequately designed to motivate the child to really put forth any effort in learning. The charts may be used to help determine special abilities of students in a single academic area and, therefore, help to plan a curriculum which is more appropriate to the child's abilities as well as his present needs. Further development of precision teaching could be instrumental in helping educators to plan appropriate instructional programs which, for all practical purposes, could make better use of the concept of nongraded programs (Lindsley).

Precision teaching can be learned easily by the classroom teacher and can serve as a supplement to the program which he is already offering. The use of precision teaching can also help the teacher to determine more objectively the extent to which a child is changing his behavior through observing the improvement in appropriate behaviors and the elimination of inappropriate behaviors. Thus, special educators have another means whereby they can efficiently supplement and attempt to consistently enhance teaching approaches and instructional materials (Lindsley).

Behavior Modification

Behavior modification is a relatively new approach which is becoming popular in classrooms for exceptional children. Although established as an effective process for changing behaviors of exceptional children, as well as normal children, many teachers are currently attempting to use behavior modification procedures without really understanding what they are doing and without using the objective techniques which are so much a part of this particular approach to working with children. One cannot study merely the surface aspects of behavior modification and then use the procedures with any real effective application. The use of behavior modification requires much study on the part of the teacher, or any other person, in order to insure that appropriate changes in the behaviors of children are being effected. If one does not grasp all of the factors of behavior modification, then one may, in fact, be rewarding inappropriate behaviors without realizing it. Just because one has done some reading with respect to the use of positive reinforcement for the purpose of accelerating appropriate behaviors does not mean that the individual has any "real" concept of the procedures and implications of the use of behavior modification.

According to Ullmann and Krasner (1965), "Behavior modification is the application of the results of learning theory and experimental psychology to the problem of altering maladaptive behavior." In essence, this definition refers to the planned and systematic control of human behavior for the purpose of helping the individual become more functional, better his academic achievements, improve his social relationships and his own control of his behavior, as a few examples. According to the behavior modifier, all behavior is learned and, therefore, through the application of consistent and systematic procedures, the old behavior may be unlearned and more appropriate behaviors learned.

The use of behavior modification requires that the practitioner be objective. The focus is on behaviors which are observable and not on behaviors which may be "internal" for the individual. One must objectively record a child's behavior, preferably with other observers also recording behavior in order to test for reliability, and then based upon the baseline record of the child's behavior decide upon the use of behavior modification. In other words the behavior to be modified must be chosen by objective methods and not by a random sampling technique. The appropriate selection of reinforcement techniques is also an area which requires some time and effort on the part of the teacher. An excellent description of selecting reinforcement techniques is presented by Birnbrauer, Burchard, and Burchard (1970) and this description can be easily followed by a classroom teacher.

The use of token reinforcement has become quite prevalent in the modification of children's behaviors. This system of reinforcement has gained in its acceptance because it saves the teacher time in the appropriate dispensing of rewards and is also effective in providing for immediate rewards and will additionally help young children to learn the process of delay of gratification. Several reports of the use of token reinforcement in behavior modification have been reported by Axelrod (1971).

An excellent review of studies which have involved the use of behavior modification procedures has been prepared by Axelrod. These studies have pertained to children who are severely mentally retarded, educable mentally retarded, emotionally disturbed, and learning disabled. The behaviors studied included academic and social behaviors, disruptive behaviors, and following instructions. For the reader who may desire a reference as a fairly comprehensive review of the current use and effectiveness of behavior modification, this is an excellent resource.

Behavior modification should not be viewed as a panacea for the learning problems of exceptional children. If used appropriately, this technique can definitely supplement the special education teacher's instructional program. The use of positive reinforcement for appropriate or desired behavior often has been interpreted as nothing more than using common sense. Certainly behavior modification is the use of common sense; however, if a teacher does not learn objectively how to observe, describe, record, measure, and shape behavior consistently and systematically, his efforts in using this approach will, in all probability, be totally ineffective.

Many concerns regarding the ethics of behavior modification have been expressed through the medium of the literature and also in person to the authors. Ethical considerations are important and must be taken into account when one is using this particular approach because the appropriate use of behavior modification can be and is a very powerful technique for controlling human behavior. In the field of special education, behavior modification procedures must be viewed as a technique which can be effective in implementing appropriate objectives for children. Rather than viewing this particular approach or technique as a method of indiscriminately controlling behavior, the special educator must view behavior modification as a technique which will aid him in helping children to develop or improve behaviors which are essential in the process of learning and becoming more functional in everyday living.

A text of this particular type cannot devote much space to the area of behavior modification; however, any person using this text in a teacher training course may certainly expand upon the material as presented here. A few years ago there were very few references in the professional literature regarding behavior modification. Today, one may find references in the professional journals dealing with exceptional children and a journal which is devoted exclusively to the field of behavior modification (*Journal of Applied Behavior Analysis*). These references as well as several books which are currently on the market will provide sufficient information for any interested student. Certainly this particular technique will continue to grow in emphasis and application.

Physical Education and Motor Development

There is a trend in special education to include physical education and motor development in the curriculum for all types of handicapped children. Perhaps these two areas should be presented as separate types of programs; the authors, however, decided to cover them together as related fields of development within the classroom program provided for handicapped children.

The increased emphasis in the area of physical education for the handicapped has been in existence for some time. The federal government has been responsible for encouraging the development of this critical area of emphasis by sponsoring workshops and programs which have demonstrated the use of particular techniques and also the designing of physical fitness programs for the exceptional child. In addition, several pamphlets have been published which focus on various aspects which are essential in the planning of a program. Although an increased emphasis in the area of physical education has been in existence, the majority of teacher training programs have not provided enough preparation in this area for the physical education teacher or for the special education teacher.

Musgrove (1971) says this problem can be solved by an inter-disciplinary approach involving the special education teacher and the physical education teacher. The teamwork approach would be employed in a public school setting by providing instruction in the special class and then an application of the skills learned through activities in the gymnasium.

Physical education activities are a must for the majority of exceptional children, many of whom have been overprotected at home for various reasons or have not had the opportunity to play and develop an interest in physical education. Children who have spent their formative years in the inner city, or the ghetto area are particularly less likely to have had meaningful experiences in play activities, or in activities which may be considered developmental physical education. These, among others, are the primary reasons why children who are mildly retarded, learning disabled, emotionally disturbed, or even physically disabled need physical education activities from the elementary school years through the secondary school years. Many of these children will also obtain employment during their young adulthood years and will need particular types of physical skills in order to be able to perform effectively. Teachers must, therefore, provide appropriate experiences in physical education for handicapped children through the development of team work (Musgrove).

Many attitudes can be enhanced through the involvement of exceptional children in physical education activities. Perhaps, for the first time, in some of their lives; these children may be taught concepts such as taking their turn, working cooperatively with others, learning the basic application of various rules and why rules are important in play activities. In addition, the use of physical education activities may enable some handicapped children to become actively involved in an experience which has concrete meaning. A teacher should also be able to analyze many different types of physical education activities and provide ways in which the "academic" program can come alive for the children. For example, many types of games readily lend themselves to the development and use of number skills and the use of sequencing with respect to the various activities in a classroom. Sequencing may be included as the teacher helps children to emphasize the first step, the second step, the third step and so on in the playing of a particular type of game. In some instances, the implementation of appropriate physical education activities can also supplement any activities which the teacher may plan for the development of rhythm and an enhancement of the child's body awareness. Many of these activities will help to promote appropriate attitudes for classroom behaviors and may even be extended to help the child develop appropriate behaviors for adult functioning (Musgrove).

During the past few years, the inclusion of physical education activities for exceptional children has become recognized as an essential feature of the total program. The special education teacher will often need help in planning and implementing these activities; however, the physical education instructor should not be expected to perform the function of providing the program by himself. The special education teacher should know his children well enough to be able to make decisions regarding activities which may be too demanding on the children either physically or mentally. For example, a game with too many rules or rules which are too complicated may be entirely above the mental abilities of the average mildly mentally retarded child. For the child with learning disabilities, the activity may require motor skills which are too detailed or too refined for the child in his present stage of development. Other examples could be given; however, emphasis in planning activities which are compatible with the children's present stage of development is the important point. It should be understood that the game or activity should not be so simple that the child is not motivated to participate, or unchallenged with the tasks; but certainly the inclusion of physical education activities for exceptional children should focus on activities in which the children can be successful. The academic program may have consistently presented nothing but frustration and failure for the exceptional child and one should not leave the impression that physical education would add to the learning problems or self-concept problems that the exceptional child may already have.

The area of motor skills is somewhat different from that of physical education activities. Both areas are instrumental in the development of skills of coordination, but they do differ because physical education activities may focus on gross motor coordination and motor skill training may involve fine motor coordination which includes a variety of areas.

Training in motor skills should never be viewed by the teacher as absolutely mandatory for every child. The teacher should also be aware that training in motor skills will not necessarily improve the child's functioning in any other area of development. Appropriate programs in the training of children to help them develop motor skills, or possibly improve some area of functioning such as visual perception, take considerable time on the part of the teacher in the planning process, as well as in the conducting of the program. On several occasions the authors have seen teachers attempting to use a motor skill training program with a group of thirty to forty children in one setting. There were so many children involved that the teacher could not possibly determine the extent to which the *individual child* was appropriately performing the task or learning from the experience. For a school administrator or a director of special education to issue an order for special education teachers to have motor development exercises as a daily part of the curriculum is also unnecessary. A mandate of this type may cause teachers to put together rapidly a motor development exercise lacking in the objectives or structure that would enable the children to benefit from the experience. In other words, a mandate to provide motor development training without insuring that the teachers have a foundation in the understanding of the importance of this area may lead to an activity which is no more than busy work and merely a time consuming project for the teacher as well as the children.

Educators should be cognizant of the extensive work of Kephart, Getman, Cratty, and others like them, who have prepared testing materials and appropriate types of motor development exercises for children. These professionals have also contributed much information to understanding the importance of movement and the development of body and motor awareness. A good example of the importance of motor development training is commented upon by Cratty who indicates that motor development exercises which do not require thought on the part of the child may help the child to increase his physical strength, but will not help him to develop an awareness of his body and how his body relates to space (Cratty 1967).

A good program in motor development will include such areas as visual-motor development, the development of body awareness, the systematic exploration of various concrete objects, movement of the body through a variety of situations, and orientation skills. As the classroom teacher begins to develop a program that is designed to help exceptional children develop motor skills, he must plan for specific objectives and match his activities to attempt to accomplish these objectives just as he does in the academic program. Motor development training must be taken seriously if educators are going to design and implement programs which will have significance for the children.

Reintegration of Exceptional Children

Placement of a child in a special education class should never, except in extreme cases such as the trainable mentally retarded, be considered a permanent decision. The majority of school systems have programs which, for all intents and purposes, are designed to prevent permanent placement in a special education class. This design is the inclusion of the requirement for retesting children within a period of one year, two years, or a maximum of three years after the child is first placed in the special education program. In practice, however, school personnel usually don't have the time or the additional manpower to carry out the provisions of the program design in this respect. In many situations, after the child is placed in the special education class, the door closes and no consideration is given for returning this child to regular classes even on a part-time basis. A recent report indicates that even though the psychological evaluation of students who were recommended for special education class placement suggested a one year follow-up for reconfirmation of the original diagnosis, a period of five years or more had elapsed without further evaluation (Cormany 1970). Conditions such as these contribute to the many questions which have arisen in recent years concerning the use of psychological testing and the labeling of children. In the authors' opinion, however, undue delay in the reevaluation of children is not always the fault of the psychometrist or psychologist. The classroom teacher has a very definite role in helping to schedule children for reevaluation as well as in evaluating children informally in the classroom in order to help clarify the original evaluation.

The development of class programs for children with learning disabilities has been most effective in helping educators to realize that all exceptional children do not necessarily need a self-contained class program in order to help them with their learning or adjustment problems. Part-time placement in learning laboratories and short-term placements in self-contained classrooms have helped many learning disabled children to successfully reenter the mainstream of education. This type of educational planning has begun to gain acceptance for other types of exceptional children. Special education classes should be considered as temporary placement for many types of children with learning problems and, as this practice gains wider acceptance, the role of many special education teachers will begin to change. By having fewer children in her room and having specialized training to work with specific types of learning problems, the special education teacher should be accepted as a resource person for the entire school building in which he is located. His instructional program should certainly not be considered a program for "those dummy children" or "those sick children," but a program designed specifically for helping children to work to their capacities, overcome some learning deficits, or learn to circumvent some learning problems. The child may then reach a level of functioning which is commensurate with his abilities.

Children who have been placed in special education classes need counseling and guidance when a decision is made to return them to the mainstream of education. This process should also, in the majority of cases, be a slow one in which the child is gradually programmed back into the regular classes. In other words, instead of just placing the child back into the regular mainstream of education, he needs to have an experience in one class in which he can be successful, and then gradually move into other classes in which he can function. To make an administrative decision to move a child from special education classes completely back into regular classes without counseling the child, or gradually providing him with successful experiences on his way to total return will undoubtedly result in failure and frustration on the part of the child.

Perhaps an example will clarify the concern one should have in the reintegration of exceptional children into regular classes. A child who is referred for special education placement often has been exposed to many failure situations prior to being assigned to a special class. The frequent exposure to frustrating failure experiences has damaged the child's self-concept to the extent that he may learn that it is safer to cease functioning rather than take the risk of failing again. In essence, this means the special education teacher, after the child is placed with him, must focus on learning problems and also focus on helping the child to regain his self-confidence. In other words, the learning problem is not the only problem the child may have upon placement in the special class, and his more serious problem of a negative self-concept must be alleviated before the special education teacher can begin to help the child to relearn. After a period of readjustment and relearning, the child may be ready for at least a partial return to the regular class program. Unless he is helped to view this experience as one that is not threatening and one in which he can function without a renewed threat to his self-concept; he may fail purposely in order to return to the security of the special class program. Therefore, in view of information of this type, the child's ability to function in a regular classroom program is only one of the factors we should consider when we are contemplating reintegration of handicapped children into regular education programs.

Cormany has reported on a successful approach to the problem of reintegration of exceptional children into the regular class. This program consisted of providing counseling services and role-play for one group of students, and a control group was reassigned to the regular class program with no preparation. The experimental group consisted of fifteen students, none of whom failed in the regular class program after preparation through counseling services. Over one-half of the control group of fifteen students failed in their reintegration experience and had to be returned to the special class program.

Yates (1973) has recently reported an in-service laboratory/ experiential approach for preparing regular classroom teachers for the reintegration of exceptional children into regular education. Actual experiences in working with specific exceptional children improved the acceptance of the regular classroom teachers in comparison to a control group of teachers who received no practical experiences. Thus, if the program, as suggested by Yates were to be implemented in more schools, perhaps empirical evidence would be provided with respect to the type of exceptional child who may be successfully reintegrated into regular education.

The reintegration of exceptional children into the regular education program is not going to be an easy process and should never be considered as merely an administrative matter. If educators expect exceptional children to be successful and function in the mainstream of educational programs, then efforts such as those by Cormany and his group will have to be extended. As professional persons, the paramount consideration must be upon what is happening to children in advocating their return to regular classes, and not upon how palatable special class placement may be for the teachers.

The Talented Among Minority Children

Rather than automatically and erroneously assume that children of disadvantaged or minority groups have limited learning potentials, there is a trend toward discovering and implementing techniques which would identify minority group children who are talented.

Much of this effort is focused on obtaining more positive information regarding cultural aspects of minority groups and making adaptations or modifications of teaching and curricular approaches.

Compensatory education programs have been in existence for some time and the results have been most promising from many of these programs. Educators and researchers have come up with positive information regarding the learning styles of disadvantaged or minority children; and, in many cases, techniques and/or approaches have been developed which enhance the learning of these children. According to White (1971) a few of these techniques include the following: providing concrete applications of material learned, using listening centers, the use of many audiovisual materials, and colorful presentations. The primary consideration, which White mentions, is that this is the beginning of the teaching approach which should progress gradually to more abstract learning such as problem solving. Although many programs within the total Head Start, Follow Through, and other compensatory education programs have been successful, relatively few educational modifications have actually been implemented which capitalize on the learning strengths and potential talents of minority or disadvantaged children.

A review of studies which focus on searching for the talented among minority groups of children indicates that the majority of programs for these children are remedial. However, this review also presents pertinent information from many researchers such as B.S. Bloom, E. Paul Torrance, Catherine Bruch, A.H. Passow, and others which indicates that the primary deficiency in schools which serve minority groups is in the areas of teaching and curricular modifications (Renzulli 1973).

Renzulli discusses several assessment procedures which have been developed for the purposes of exploring talents other than academic talent. These instruments are appropriate for use with minority or disadvantaged children and include such instruments as the *Torrance Tests of Creative Thinking* (Torrance 1966) and the *Sub-Cultural Indices of Academic Potential* (Grant and Renzulli 1971). Through the use of such instruments, as well as others mentioned by Renzulli, educators may become more aware of the talents of disadvantaged or minority children and, as a result, begin to plan and implement more effective teaching and curricular modifications.

In conclusion, it seems very appropriate to give further consideration to this area, which should become a primary focus on many educators, by discussing preschool programs for handicapped children. Early education programs are essential for the majority of disadvantaged or minority children and through the continued development of preschool programs which include parent involvement and training, and a search for talent among these children, the status of disadvantaged or minority children may be improved considerably.

Preschool Programs for the Handicapped

The Handicapped Children's Early Education Assistance Act (1968) provided for the development of model preschool and early education programs for handicapped children. In 1969, twenty-four organizations received a total of about $1 million in U.S. Office of Education grants to establish model preschool and early education projects for handicapped children. At that time, Edwin W. Martin Jr., Acting Associate Commissioner, Bureau of Education for the Handicapped noted:

> For the first time, these children will have an opportunity to begin the process of becoming responsible citizens in a society that is assuming responsibility at an increasing rate for all its children—including the handicapped. More than half of the children can have their handicapping conditions lessened—or in many cases, prevented—if they receive appropriate educational and related services at an early age. The challenge is here and the education community must respond (Breakthrough 1970).

As a result of financial assistance through federal legislation, many school systems and university programs have begun to emphasize the area of early childhood education for the handicapped. With the stress that has been placed on the importance of early experience with respect to the development of a child, and particularly a handicapped child, it seems that early education for handicapped children can and will provide programs that will change the future lives of a great many children. Education of the preschool handicapped child must place a focus on structure and must have specific objectives which will lead toward cognitive development of the children. It has become common knowledge during the past few years that one of the primary difficulties of many young handicapped children is that they have not learned how to learn. Thus, it is the task of the preschool program to provide structured environments and activities for this group of children if the objective of increased functioning is to be met. In the majority of situations a structured approach will emphasize language development and preparation for later learning. Many examples could be cited, however the study of Karnes,

Hodgins, and Teska (1968) may serve to indicate that handicapped children who were taught language development through a structured approach had greater gains in language functioning and cognitive development than handicapped children who were involved in a more traditional approach of preschool programs.

Realizing that a structured approach, a language development approach, a cognitive development approach or a combination of all of these approaches is essential to preschool programs for handicapped children, perhaps our emphasis should begin to turn toward a pressing need beyond preschool programs. How will school programs, during the elementary school years, need to be structured in order to maintain the significant gains in development of handicapped children? Improving the functioning of the preschool handicapped child is, of course, a very significant achievement; however, the development of programs beyond the preschool level which will maintain improvements and enhance further development of the children is a goal which educators must point towards immediately.

Questions which should be considered in the total field of education in relation to this problem include such areas as: To what extent must the educational program during the early elementary school years be changed in order to further enhance the development of handicapped children? How can teachers in the field or in training receive pertinent information relative to the program that the preschool handicapped child has had and the effects of this program? If a highly structured approach were provided similar to that of Bereiter and Englemann (1965), will the structure need to be continued during the early elementary years and, if so, to what extent? If a preschool program has helped a handicapped child increase his skills in the area of language development, how can the need for further development be communicated in this area; and how can the first grade teacher be assisted in the selection of appropriate approaches and materials to enhance this development? Based upon past experiences which have been encountered in attempting to reintegrate handicapped children into regular education, what problems, if any, will we meet when handicapped children who have "graduated" from preschool programs attempt to reenter the regular education program? It seems that in-service training of school administrators and regular teachers is essential if the concern for the preschool handicapped child is going to be felt throughout the school community. The prevention of "wash out" effects of the efforts of preschool programs for handicapped children seems to also be a matter with which there should be considerable concern.

In summary, the concern of the authors is that the effects of providing preschool programs for handicapped children should have significant effects on the development of appropriate changes in the existing instructional programs of elementary schools. If the early childhood education programs throughout the country are going to be successful over a period of years then the personnel of these programs must become concerned with being influential in bringing about changes within programs to which the handicapped child will be assigned during his elementary school years.

OVERVIEW

Special education has progressed through many changes in recent years. New changes will continue to develop as more information is obtained regarding effective program modifications for exceptional children. The job of developing and improving special education programs should never become stagnant or static. There are many challenges with which all special educators will be confronted and the new special educator must become a vital part of this process. Changes in philosophical approaches and educational programs are necessary, not for the sake of change, but for the purposes of improving services for individuals.

Predictions regarding the future of special education have been provided by many professional persons. Perhaps one of the best discussions of this topic focuses on predictions about the year 2000 A.D. and special education. In this discussion Leo Connor indicates the following:

"For special education all of this should add up to a greater struggle for mastery of its own world—but with more effective weapons, greater satisfaction, more tangible gains, better instruction, more effective evaluations, tighter teamwork, saner diagnoses, perceptive teachers, insightful supervisors, decisive administrators, revolutionizing researchers, and exhilarating professors. Literally, I mean that the seeding and tilling will be more difficult but the harvesting should be more bountiful and satisfactory." (Connor 1968)

Bibliography

Axelrod, S. "Token Reinforcement in Special Classes." *Exceptional Children* 37, no. 5 (January 1971).

Bereiter, Carl, and Engelmann, Siegfried. *Teaching Disadvantaged Children in the Preschool.* Englewood Cliffs, N.J.: Prentice-Hall, 1966.

Birnbrauer, J.S.; Burchard, John D.; and Burchard, Sara N. "Wanted: Behavior Analysts." In *Behavior Modification: The Human Effort,* ed. Robert H. Bradfield. San Rafael, Calif.: Dimensions Publishing Company, 1970.

"Breakthrough in Early Education of Handicapped Children," *American Education* 6, no. 1 (January-February 1970).

Connor, Leo E. "Reflections on the Year 2000." *Exceptional Children* 34, no. 10 (Summer 1968).

Cormany, R.B. "Returning Special Education Students to Regular Classes." *Personnel and Guidance Journal* 48, no. 8 (April 1970).

Cratty, B.J. *Movement Behavior and Motor Learning.* Philadelphia, Pa.: Lea and Febiger, 1967.

Grant T.E., and Renzulli, J.S. *Sub-Cultural Indices of Academic Potential.* Storrs, Conn.: University of Connecticut, 1971.

Karnes M.; Hodgins, A.; and Teska, J. "An Evaluation of Two Preschool Programs for Disadvantaged Children: A Traditional and a Highly Structured Experimental Preschool." *Exceptional Children* 34, no. 9 (May 1968).

Lindsley, Ogden R. "Precision Teaching in Perspective: An Interview with Ogden R. Lindsley." *Teaching Exceptional Children* 3, no. 3 (Spring, 1971).

Moss, J.W. "Resource Centers for Teachers of Handicapped Children." *Journal of Special Education* 5, no. 1 (Winter-Spring 1971).

Musgrove, D.G. Physical Education and Recreation for the Handicapped—An Interdisciplinary Approach." *Contemporary Education,* 42 no. 3 (January 1971).

Renzulli, Joseph S. "Talent Potential in Minority Group Students." *Exceptional Children* 39, no. 6 (March 1973).

Smith, Robert M. "Collecting Diagnostic Data in the Classroom." *Teaching Exceptional Children* 1, no. 4 (Summer 1969).

Torrance, E.P. *Torrance Tests of Creative Thinking: Norms-Technical Manual.* Princeton, N.J.: Personnel Press, 1966.

Ullman, Leonard P., and Krasner, Leonard ed. *Case Studies in Behavior Modification.* New York: Holt, Rinehart and Winston, Inc., 1965.

White, William F. *Tactics for Teaching the Disadvantaged.* New York: McGraw-Hill Book Co., 1971.

Yates, James R. "Model for Preparing Regular Classroom Teachers for 'Mainstreaming.' " *Exceptional Children 39,* no. 6 (March 1973).

TRENDS IN SPECIAL EDUCATION
Study Sheet #1

1. Choose one of the trends discussed in this chapter and discuss how this trend is being implemented in your state or community.

2. Discuss the ways in which current trends in special education will affect the role of regular classroom teachers.

Appendix

Agencies, Associations and Organizations
Relative to Exceptional Children

For information concerning specific exceptionalities; parents, teachers, and interested personnel should write to the following:

Alexander Graham Bell Association for the Deaf, Inc.
1537 35th Street, NW, Washington, D.C., 20007

American Academy for Cerebral Palsy
University Hospital School, Iowa City, Iowa 52240

American Academy of Private Practice in Speech Pathology and Audiology
P.O. Box 53217, State Capital Station, Oklahoma City, Okla. 73105

American Association for Health, Physical Education, and Recreation
1201 16th Street, NW, Washington, D.C. 20036

American Association of Psychiatric Clinics for Children
250 W. 57th Street, Room 1032, Fish Building, New York, N.Y. 10019

American Association of Workers for the Blind, Inc.
1151 K Street, NW, Suite 637, Washington, D.C. 20005

American Association on Mental Deficiency
5201 Connecticut Ave., NW, Washington, D.C. 20015

American Corrective Therapy Association, Inc.
811 Street Margaret's Road, Chillicothe, Ohio 45601

American Foundation for the Blind
15 W. 16th Street, New York, N.Y. 10011

American Heart Association, Inc.
44 E. 23rd Street, New York, N.Y. 10010

American Occupational Therapy Association, Inc.
251 Park Avenue S., New York, N.Y. 10010

American Orthopsychiatric Association, Inc.
1790 Broadway, New York, N.Y. 10019

American Physical Therapy Association
1740 Broadway, New York, N.Y. 10019

American Printing House for the Blind
1839 Frankfort Avenue, Louisville, Ky. 40206

American Psychological Association
1200 17th St., NW, Washington, D.C. 20036

American Rehabilitation Counseling Association of the American Personnel and
    Guidance Association
1607 New Hampshire Ave., NW, Washington, D.C. 20009

American Schizophrenia Foundation
Box 160, Ann Arbor, Mich. 48107

The American Speech and Hearing Association
9030 Old Georgetown Rd., Washington, D.C. 20014

Association for Children with Learning Disabilities
2200 Brownsville Rd., Pittsburgh, Pa. 15210

Association for Education of the Visually Handicapped
711 14th St., NW, Washington, D.C. 20005

The Association of Rehabilitation Centers, Inc.
7979 Old Georgetown Rd., Washington, D.C. 20014

The Council for Exceptional Children
1411 S. Jefferson Davis Highway, Arlington, Va. 22202

Council of Organizations Serving the Deaf
4201 Connecticut Ave., NW, Suite 210, Washington, D.C. 20008

Epilepsy Foundation of America
1828 L St., NW, Washington, D.C. 20036

Goodwill Industries of America, Inc.
9200 Wisconsin Ave., Washington, D.C. 20014

International League of Societies for the Mentally Handicapped
12, Rue Forestiere, Brussels-5, Belgium

International Society for Rehabilitation of the Disabled
219 E. 44th St., New York, N.Y. 10017

Joseph P. Kennedy, Jr. Foundation
719 13th St., NW, Suite 510, Washington, D.C. 20005

Muscular Dystrophy Association of America, Inc.
1790 Broadway, New York, N.Y. 10019

The National Association for Gifted Children
8080 Springvalley Dr., Cincinnati, Ohio 45236

The National Association for Mental Health, Inc.
Suite 1300, 10 Columbus Circle, New York, N.Y. 10019

National Association for Music Therapy, Inc.
Box 610, Lawrence, Kans. 66055

National Association for Retarded Children
2709 Ave. E. East, P.O. Box 6109, Arlington, Tex. 76011

National Association of Hearing and Speech Agencies
919 18th St., NW, Washington, D.C. 20006

National Association of Sheltered Workshops and Homebound Programs
1522 K St., NW, Washington, D.C. 20005

National Association of the Deaf
2025 Eye St., NW, Suite 321, Washington, D.C. 20006

National Association of Social Workers
2 Park Ave., New York, N.Y. 10016

National Committee for Multi-Handicapped Children
239 14th St., Niagara Falls, N.Y. 14303

National Council for the Gifted
700 Prospect Ave., West Orange, N.J. 07052

National Council on Crime and Delinquency
44 E. 23rd St., New York, N.Y. 10010

The National Easter Seal Society for Crippled Children and Adults
2023 West Ogden Ave., Chicago, Ill. 60612

National Epilepsy League, Inc.
116 S. Michigan Ave., Chicago, Ill. 60603

The National Foundation—March of Dimes
800 2nd Ave., New York, N.Y. 10017

National Rehabilitation Association
1522 K St., NW, Washington, D.C. 20005

National Therapeutic Recreation Society
1700 Pennsylvania Ave., NW, Washington, D.C. 20006

The President's Committee on Employment of the Handicapped
U.S. Department of Labor, Washington, D.C. 20210

President's Committee on Mental Retardation
Washington, D.C. 20201

Southern Regional Education Board, Special Education Division
130 6th St., NW, Atlanta, Ga. 30313

United Cerebral Palsy Associations, Inc.
66 E. 34th St., New York, N.Y. 10016

U.S. Public Health Service, Health Services and Mental Health Administration,
National Institute of Mental Health
5454 Wisconsin Ave., Chevy Chase, Md. 20015

U.S. Public Health Service, National Institutes of Health
HEW South Bldg., Rm. 5312, Washington, D.C. 20201

Social and Rehabilitation Service, Assistance Payments Administration
330 Independence Ave., SW, Washington, D.C. 20201

Social and Rehabilitation Service, Children's Bureau
330 C St., SW, Washington, D.C. 20201

Social and Rehabilitation Service, Office of Research, Demonstrations, and
  Training
HEW North Bldg., Rm. 3315, Washington, D.C. 20201

Social and Rehabilitation Service, Rehabilitation Services Administration
330 Independence Ave., SW, Rm. 3139 D, Washington, D.C. 20201

Western Interstate Commission for Higher Education, Special Education and
  Rehabilitation Program
30th St., University East Campus, Boulder, Colo. 80382

Author Index

Aberson, Albert R., 5, 7
Adelman, Howard S., 214, 215
Affleck, James Q., 15, 22
Allen, Amy A., 44
Anderson, Janet W., 53
Anderson, Robert M., 53, 280
Andrews, Theodore, E., 17, 22
Axelrod, Saul, 259, 329

Bakan, Rita, 69, 72, 73, 75
Balow, Bruce, 6, 9
Barker, Larry R., 297, 298
Barnett, M.R., 170
Bateman, Barbara, 185
Benoit, E., 29, 30
Benson, Wilbur, 263, 264, 265, 266
Bereiter, Carl, 339
Betwee, Marcus, C., 228
Bice, H.V., 123
Birnbrauer, J.S., 329
Blatt, Burton, 21, 22
Bloom, B., 97, 337
Bogman, S.K., 171
Bower, Eli M., 242, 243, 257
Braddock, David L., 5, 7
Brow, Kateri D., 15, 22
Bruch, Catherine, 103, 104
Bryan, Trudy, 8, 9
Buell, Charles, 142
Buhler, C.F., 228
Bullock, Lyndal, 250, 251, 312,
Burchard, John D., 329
Burchard, Sara N., 329
Burke, F., 266, 267
Butterfield, Earl C., 45

Calovini, Gloria, 11, 12, 13, 22
Caplan, Gerald, 231
Chapman, A.H., 240, 241, 242
Chiappone, A.D., 38
Clements, Sam D., 189, 208
Cogan, Victor, 16, 17, 23
Cohen, Julius, 44

Colton, Kathryn C., 123
Concannon, Lester, 105
Conners, Keith C., 262, 265
Connor, Leo, 340
Cooke, Robert E., 65
Cooper, Eugene B., 162
Cormany, R.B., 303, 334, 336
Curry, E.T., 151, 156
Cratty, B.J., 333
Cravioto, J., 69, 70
Crawford, John E., 268
Cross, Jacque L., 44
Cruickshank, William, 11, 12, 23, 115, 126,
    128, 138, 145, 148, 170, 172, 182, 190,
    206, 213, 214, 215, 216, 262
Cumming, John, 230
Cutler, Richard L., 243

Dalton, M.M., 139
Davis, Hallowell, 147, 150
Doll, E.A., 29
Douglas, Joseph, 103
Dunn, Lloyd M., 123, 124, 137, 138, 140,
    145
Dupont, Henry, 230

Engelmann, Siegfried, 339
Ensminger, E.E., 311
Ewing, A.G., 168

Farber, Bernard, 49, 50, 52
Fargo, George, 252
Fine, M.J., 303, 304
Frohreich, Lloyd, 312
Furst, Caryn M., 71, 74

Gallagher, James J., 6, 16, 21
Gensley, Julian, 94, 102
Gensley, Juliana Townsend, 98
Gibby, Robert, 37
Glavin, John P., 260

Subject Index